WINGED DAGGER

ROY FARRAN

WINGED DAGGER

Adventures on Special Service

CASSELL&CO

None of the characters in this book are fictitious, but some,
for obvious reasons, are not wearing their own names.

Cassell Military Paperbacks

Cassell & Co
Wellington House, 125 Strand
London WC2R 0BB

Copyright © Roy Farran 1948

First published by Collins 1948
This Cassell Military Paperbacks edition 1998
Reprinted 1999, 2002

British Library Cataloguing-in-Publication Data
A catalogue record for this book is available from the
British Library

ISBN 0-304-35084-2

Printed and bound in Great Britain by
Cox & Wyman Ltd., Reading, Berks.

CONTENTS

Book I
THE MIDDLE EAST, 1940-1943

Book II
THE SPECIAL AIR SERVICE

Book III

OPERATION IN ITALY, 1945

Book I

THE MIDDLE EAST, 1940-43

CHAPTER ONE

ARRIVAL IN THE MIDDLE EAST

I SUPPOSE the curtain really went up on Port Said Harbour in
September, 1940. When Churchill made his great strategic
gamble of sending our last Armoured Brigade to the Middle East
after Dunkirk, we sailed from Liverpool in the *Duchess of Bedford*
with two other tank battalions. In September we were sitting
on the deck of a troopship at the mouth of the canal. There at
last we had anchored in the inner harbour, gazing at the red
roofs and dun yellow walls of the town, hot and shimmering
in the heat of Egypt. After weeks of confinement in this sweating,
overcrowded prison afloat, we longed to explore the mysteries of
a strange, foreign town. Avidly we traversed our binoculars
across its busy scene.

The harbour was covered with tiny motor launches, skimming
aimlessly to and fro between the convoy like water spiders on a
pond. Green Egyptian flags fluttered behind their trim white
sterns, and officials in red fezes sat pompously in their waists,
portfolios under arms, carelessly tapping ankles with leather-
covered canes. For these were important men—ambassadors of a
king—and in those black portfolios they held the keys of an
empire. What was more, they did not intend to surrender them
without some fine show of dignity. How many forms they would
make these pink-faced Englishmen complete! What delays they
would enforce! After all, were they not a free people and liberty
was not to be so lightly surrendered?

Somebody, an old soldier, had been East before. With great
pride he pointed out the things to see, not because they were
worth seeing, but because it was important that next time we
also should be able to demonstrate our knowledge to the new
boys. "You see that over there? That is the Canal Coy. Building.
Those funny buckets they pull up on a pole are signals to ships.
You see that fine hotel with the red roof—bloody awful pub
called the Casino. That statue over there is Ferdinand de Lesseps
—some sort of frog who built the canal."

We gazed at a green iron statue way out at the harbour

mouth. Most of us were apathetic; some conjured up visions of a brave adventurer carving a waterway through a desert, driving hundreds of ragged coolies to change the face of the world for ever; and others thought of the films and Simone Simon in tight red knickerbockers. It stood on a grand corniche, grimly outlined against the blue sky and the sea beneath. But then, suddenly, there was something more worth while to see. Life, moving, pulsating, new, mysterious life, that was what we were all searching for. Three pairs of glasses focused on a wild, berobed horseman, galloping along the beach behind the statue. With his legs flapping madly against the belly of his steed, he was racing along the edge of the sea, the white foam as his background, all alive, frantic and exciting. This was what we had expected—the romance of the East.

Then somebody spotted a slim dark girl in a red summer frock, walking along the quay with a white terrier on a lead. "What do you think of her, eh? Not bad, what? Nice legs. Maybe, difficult to tell from here. They all get fat round about the age of thirty, you know. Who said I was interested in her at the age of thirty?"

At ten o'clock our wishes were granted and we filed down the gangway to the quay. Staggering under the weight of their kitbags and unkempt in ill-fitting khaki drill, the regiment shuffled along until it was formed up by squadrons facing the sea. Then there was a long wait in the hot sun. We sat on the grass in front of the Canal Company Buildings and argued with ragged hawkers, who pestered us with bottles of lemonade. They were merry rogues, eyes twinkling from behind their rags, tongues ready with a sly retort, who did not intend to be deflected from their happy game of squeezing money from a crowd of pink Englishmen, more innocent than the smallest child in the bazaar. But we were firm. Had not the old stagers told us never to take water from a native, never to eat unwashed salad and to keep our topees on at all times? Admittedly, it was tempting. The sun was very hot and we could see pieces of ice floating round the bottles as they clanked against the side of the bucket. "Jones, there is a man drinking that filthy fizz in the rear rank. Stop him immediately, before the whole squadron dies of dysentrey."

The Canal Company Building was guarded by tall Sudanese

dressed in naval uniform inherited from Trafalgar Days. Their straw hats and tight blue trousers looked ridiculous against the Oriental background of domes, minarets, and palm trees. I felt sure that they wasted no time in changing into more comfortable galabiehs as soon as their duties were finished. Every so often they would scurry across the lawn to haul up a black ball to the top of the signal-mast. I suppose they knew what they were about, but to us it looked like a side-show off the ring at Bertram Mills Circus.

The troops cheered as our transport, the *Duchess of Bedford*, steamed away from the quay into the middle of the canal. Overcrowded though we had been, we felt no small regard for this ship, which had borne us safely across troubled seas from Liverpool via Cape Town to Egypt. Now, her job completed, she was bound for home.

The order came for most of the regiment to march down to the railway station. We, of the rear party, were to remain behind with the baggage. With their kitbags balanced over their shoulders, brushing against outsized topee brims, the dense files of sweating soldiers tramped off through the dock gates, followed by a swarm of hawkers harassing their flanks.

At three o'clock a lighter came to ferry us across the harbour. Our job was to unload the tanks from the three cargo ships berthed on the far side of the canal. In accordance with common army practice in the early years of the war, no arrangements had been made for the reception of our hundred odd men. The transit camp was full so that there seemed no alternative to sleeping on the docks. A kind merchant captain came to the rescue, however, and we were billeted for the next three days in the hold of his ship. Hammocks were slung for the men and the six officers crowded into one tiny cabin.

Our longing to explore the town was squashed when all ranks were confined to the dock area. A port always looks enticing from the seaward side, and there is nothing so frustrating as being separated from its mysteries by an expanse of water impossible to cross.

Unloading began immediately and went on throughout the night by the light of arc lamps. The first vehicles to be unloaded were the Matildas of the 7th Battalion of the Royal Tank Regiment, and it was estimated that work would not begin on our transport until the next day. Thankfully we bedded down in our restricted quarters for some long overdue rest. The excitement of seeing the lights along the banks of the canal had kept us up late the night before. Outside, the winches screeched and creaked as they lowered the heavy tanks with a crash on the quay. Noisy attempts to start a long idle engine would begin, until at last the tank rattled away over the boards. This din went on throughout the night to the accompaniment of shouts and sing-song chanting from the Arab stevedores. At about one o'clock the sirens went and the arc lamps were extinguished. No bombs were dropped and, after about an hour, work began again.

We slept heavily until the guard roused us at first light the next morning. Work began after a breakfast of tinned herring and tea—the best the ship could provide. Parties were despatched to the hold to supervise the hitching-up of the cranes, and drivers stood ready on the quay to take away the tanks as they were unloaded. The first one swung down at about ten o'clock. The batteries were flat and the petrol tanks empty, so that after valuable minutes had been wasted in tinkering with the engine, troops and coolies put their shoulders to the back to push it off the quay. Chanting together, these Arab ragamuffins cheerfully performed feats of strength for which their bodies were never designed. "Salla alei, illi illi! Salla alei, illi illi!" On the operative word "illi," they teamed together to shift a seven-ton tank about three yards.

As soon as a space was cleared, the derrick swung round again to pluck another vehicle from the hold. A tank was lifted high into the air—paused—and then dropped slowly into the waiting hands of the dockers.

I watched, speculating on the chances of the cable snapping, in which case I reckoned the tank would smash through the wooden boards, crushing about three Arabs in its path. The belly of a tank looks strange from underneath. It reminded me of the underside of a shark I once saw as a boy in Port Sudan Harbour.

I felt a need for a cigarette, and not finding any in my pockets, I looked around for a friend. Then I noticed a smooth little brown face with shining eyes, smiling sweetly up at me. I made the mistake of smiling back. Immediately this bonny little Arab boy was galvanised into the most energetic seller of fly-swats I have ever met. Of course the Major would want a fly-swat or at least a cane, said he, gazing with awe at my single shining pip. The louder my protests became, the more encouraged he seemed to be. And then, in all my innocence, I had an inspiration. If I gave him backsheesh, would he get me some cigarettes? I fumbled in my pocket for a ten-shilling note. He packed his fly-swats under his arm, seized the money in his left hand, and saluted smartly with his right. With a grin, he promised to return in five minutes and then scurried off helter-skelter through the dock gates. We have never met since.

Unloading went on all day and throughout the following night. The tanks were driven on to flats standing on the railway line in the docks. At eleven o'clock the next morning the train chugged slowly out of the station, Cairo-bound, with the crews sitting on the open trucks beside their vehicles.

At midday I was told to take command of a convoy of twenty three-ton lorries and to proceed by road to Cairo. Imagine the pride of a subaltern in his first command on a foreign strand. I fussed around the drivers like a school teacher about to take his pupils for a nature walk. I showed them each the route on the map and proudly taught them the Arabic for "Where is Cairo?" which I had learned from Hugo on the ship. As we were passing the petrol pump, the last vehicle came in for filling. I told the senior N.C.O. to go on with the rest, while I waited for a few minutes to follow up with this last charge. Oh yes, it was a pretty decision, for was there not only one road and, with me behind, all my chickens would be in hand so to speak. Nobody had ever told me that a convoy should always be commanded from the front.

Unfortunately there was a certain amount of delay at the petrol pump, owing to our arrival having coincided with the Egyptian lunch-hour. Stern orders over the telephone soon produced a complaining Egyptian with the key of the pump, but it was fifteen minutes later before we started down the road to Ismaliah after the others.

We drove fast down the road after them—over a wooden bridge guarded by Egyptian soldiers in red fezes and along the canal towards Ismaliah. There were ibis in the fields, flapping their wings as they poked their long beaks in the mud. How impressed we all were with this first taste of the Orient; with the white-robed fellaheen clattering up the road on donkeys; with the long strings of camels, swinging their rumps away as the trucks went past; with graceful felucca sails, their forty-foot masts reaching up to the sun; with square mud hovels clustered beneath the palm trees; and with the waters of the Nile meeting the sand of the desert in one silver sea stretching like a sheet of polished tin from one horizon to the other.

Time went by with no sign of my convoy in front. We reached the village of El Kantara, where a ferry spans the canal to the Palestine Railway Station. I was becoming very worried. It looked as though I had failed in my first responsible job as a regimental officer. Giving in to my anxiety, I turned back towards Port Said, dejected, downcast almost as much as if we had lost the war.

It was four o'clock by the time we again reached the wooden bridge on the outskirts of Port Said. I asked an Egyptian police-man if he had seen anything of a long convoy of lorries. He seemed to understand and pointed down a sandy track on the side of the river. My eyes came to rest upon a notice-board in English by the bridge. Slowly I digested its message and cursed myself for a fool.

"3-ton limit. Lorries over 3 tons detour to the right."

My lorries were heavily laden! They had not been allowed to cross.

I drove down the sandy track towards a railway bridge, hope rising slowly in my heart. We rounded a hill and there, in a dip below, was a scene to wrench all the optimism from my breast. All twenty vehicles were pointing in different directions, immobile in the soft sand. At least ten of them were up to their axles. One after another their drivers had run head first into a drift and then, panicking as their wheels began to spin, had tried to turn out. It was an awful mess—enough to daunt the most hardened soldier. However, there were still two hours before dark.

A vehicle was sent back to the docks for a Recovery Lorry and a runner was dispatched to an Artillery camp nearby. This admission of my incompetence nearly broke my heart. The rest of us dug, shoved and pulled at the bogged lorries. Two Scammells came over from the Artillery, but they too got stuck in soft sand before their aid could become effective.

Eventually the Light Aid Detachments Recovery Vehicle arrived and steady pulls on the winches did the trick. After each

18

man had had a pint mug of thick sweet tea, we recommenced our journey.

It was dark and we were not allowed to use our headlights for security reasons. I had fears that an inexperienced driver might put his truck in the canal, which ran parallel to the road. We reached Ismaliah without mishap and there we had a meal for a small fee in the Church of Scotland Soldiers' Home. A military policeman on a motor cycle led us on to the Cairo Road.

Stopping occasionally to put my "Feyn Cairo" phrase to odd Egyptians, we drove on for about four hours, along deserted roads lined with trees, through mud villages lighted by a few gipsy fires, past canals and over bridges to Cairo.

A sentry welcomed us at the gate of Almazar Camp and directed us through the lines of tents to the transport park. After the lorries had been parked, and my men had been fed and quartered, I made my way to a lonely bell-tent, which was to be my home for the next four weeks. I unrolled my bedroll, wriggled inside and was soon deep in slumber.

CHAPTER TWO

CAIRO, 1940

WHEN THE REGIMENT went up to the desert, I did not at first accompany them. Instead, with one or two other newly-joined subalterns, I remained with a rear party in the base at Abbassiah. There we had very little work to do, since most of the men were on courses in the depot. Like most of the young officers in Cairo at the beginning of the war, with the threat of battle over our shoulders, we overspent our incomes with a reckless, gay abandon in the cabarets and fleshpots of Cairo.

There was something about Cairo that drew us like a magnet from our tents in the desert near Almazar. Sometimes we tried to stay in the mess, but soon after dinner we would gaze at the bright lights behind the palm trees, hear the faint strains of Arab music borne upon the evening breeze and scent the hot smell of jasmine or jackala trees. It was irresistible. Sometimes gaily and sometimes sadly, we would ring up for a taxi and be whisked off for another night of merry-making.

There were many places of amusement, for Cairo was a gay city in those days. After a drink at the Continental, where one could meet, at some time or another, every officer in the Middle East, we would dine on the Roof Garden, where one could see a floor show, or St. James, where a film could be seen from the dining-room.

After a wonderful dinner of curried prawns or roast pigeons with far too much to drink, we would move on to one of the many cabarets. As cavalry subalterns, we were supposed to be rich and gay, which may have accounted for our popularity above all comers. It was not long before we knew almost every artiste by name. We would be led to the best table by the dance floor, where we would sing and dance and carouse with the girls until the small hours of the morning. Most of these artistes could only be kept in good humour by bottles of weak champagne, but there were others whose bubbling gaiety never ceased and who did great service in lightening our lot in those careless, reckless days at the beginning of the war. Officially, we were allowed four days' leave in the Delta in every three months, and it was rare for any one to return to the desert with a single penny of his three months' pay. It was also rare for officers to be completely sober for the whole of their four days in Cairo. We knew that perhaps death and certainly boredom lay before us, and we meant to make the most of our brief taste of worldly pleasure.

Few of these girls were beautiful and some were definitely vicious, but the majority were happy carefree people, who made the most of the boom war had brought to their business. Some of them married well to British officers and were whisked away to more sober surroundings. I sometimes wonder if they were happy. The others, I suppose, are still trekking round from one cabaret to another between Istanbul and Egypt, gradually getting older and looking back with regret on the happy times they had during the war.

There were many celebrities. In particular I remember two gay little American acrobats, who performed at the Kit Kat. The smaller one, whose name I think was Jo, was a pretty little blonde with a turned-up nose, who was very kind about not asking for too many drinks from her friends. She would toss back her corn-coloured hair with a gurgling laugh and chuck you under the chin until you thought that you were the luckiest man in the world. She was always surrounded by a ring of admirers and you could be sure that it would be a merry evening if she was at the table. Three months later, when we were sitting near Agheila after the first Wavell Campaign, we received an old, tattered copy of the *Egyptian Mail*. The authorities had discovered that her parents were Italian and had deported her from the country. No longer could poor little Jo complain that the war had trapped her in Egypt.

As I sit back in my chair, I can see them all passing in a long parade, smiling and bowing as they recognise me, their heavily painted lips whispering "champagne" and breathing over me a faint scent of jasmine. First of all is Miss Fatima, clad in a scanty costume of pale blue, star-spangled silk, thin enough to show the graceful lines of her milk-chocolate legs. She could wobble her tummy better than any one in Cairo and she was very kind about helping you to buy the best perfumes for people at home. I forget whether she graduated to the films or was the girl who was imprisoned when two German parachutists were found in her room. I would say that Fatima was a nice, good-natured sort of girl. And then comes Camillia, her big bosom heaving under a black lace gown, singing "J'attendrai" into a microphone. She has a beauty spot on her full round cheek and a red rose peeps from her shining, long black hair. Confidentially, she winks her eyelashes as she passes and frames the word "Paree" with her thick red lips. Next, laughing gaily, come the three Greek girls, who all married Allied officers. Their arms are linked behind their backs and, in front of my chair, they swing in a polished tango. They are beautiful, tall and slender. The haughty finish of their movements seems to say "you should know that our act is too good for this sort of thing." And then, hopping along in tights with a piece of white fur stitched to her bottom, is Kiki, dressed as a rabbit. She is slightly too plump for such a revealing costume and there is a tendency for her to overbalance round the bends, but she is a giggling successful artiste, who earns lots of champagne with her empty, light-hearted prattle. Lulu stalks by in a tight red gown, one slender leg peeping provocatively from a slit at her side. Every few paces she throws back her head so that her long black tresses brush her ankles and her breasts look as though they are about to make a dash for freedom.

One after another they trip by in a rustle of brightly coloured silk, some bouncing up and down, and others slowly twisting their bodies as they pass my chair, all anxious to please. There are Arab dancers and singers, Greeks, French, Hungarians and Poles, all believing in their hearts that their rightful place is Paris or Hollywood. Last of all comes Madame Badia, a magnificent old woman, who is the queen of the cabaret. She has graduated from being a popular dancing girl to the ownership of cabarets throughout the Middle East. She is ageless—always the toast of the party. Clad in a plain white dress and beating time with a silver wand, she croons "ya habibi" softly in my ear. Perhaps her face is no longer beautiful, but her voice has all the romance and mystery of a thousand Arabian nights. She makes me think of Shou-Shou.

I first met Shou-Shou in the Badia Massabni near English Bridge. It was an old cabaret consisting of a tent made from tattered carpets, thrown over a ramshackle wooden structure in a garden by the river. The clientele was almost entirely Egyptian and, in consequence, the programme included no European turns. The Egyptians are not too fond of dancing and there was a long floor show. Since we were keen to see something new and which savoured of the country, we shunned the more modern bright spots in the town and preferred to spend our evenings in this more humble place, little frequented at that time by other British officers. Night after night we went there, at first I thought because we liked the strange Eastern atmosphere, the red-capped Egyptians smoking rubber-piped sheeshahs, and the mixed heavy scent of coffee, tobacco and jasmine. One night I realised that the real reason was Shou-Shou. She was late appearing and I found myself anxious, worried that she might be sick.

There had been a team of child acrobats, building themselves into a pyramid on a table. When the applause subsided there was a long hiatus. The chattering, smoke and noise at the tables rose to its normal pitch and I began to fear that she was not going to appear. The cigarette vendors began to wander over the floor, the girls resumed their forced dutiful giggling, and the orchestra showed signs of pre-occupation with the maintenance of their instruments. I thought of sending for Madame Badia to inquire about her health. Then, suddenly, my fears were allayed. The lights grew dim. Silence was demanded by a rumble of the drums and the flute picked out a plaintive Bedouin melody. As the harpsichord joined in the lilting, rhythmic air, she glided on to the floor with her hips swinging as she placed one dainty foot in front of the other. A rose-coloured beam of light from a lantern overhead picked out her lovely figure as it swayed and twisted to the music.

A thin transparent costume of pale blue, flimsy silk covered her breasts and her long graceful legs. She had pinned back her hair in a tight knot, which seemed to put her soft-brown, oval face in a black shining frame. Over her shoulders she had draped a wisp of the same delicate material and in her teeth she held a rose.

Her skin had a pale brown texture of some beautiful fragile fruit. She was young, maybe seventeen, but her figure had already ripened to maturity in the manner of the East. Her face was like the unmutilated Sphinx on an Egyptian pound note, but there was nothing inscrutable about it. Her deep sloe eyes were wide apart and constantly shaded by a veil of thick black eyelashes; her lips were full and sensuous; and in the magic of her thin, slender hands she held us all enthralled.

Then she halted momentarily in front of my table. Putting her long palms together, she snapped her forefinger against the soft flesh of her left hand like the report of a pistol. A shudder convulsed her body and slowly, sensuously, she began to sway. Ripple after ripple of emotion travelled down her body from her heaving shoulders to her ankles. She seemed lost in a dream of ecstasy, oblivious to the smoke and eager faces around her. Gradually the rhythm reasserted itself, and she writhed the lower part of her body to the tum-tum of the drum. The crowd, relieved from its pent-up excitement, clapped its hands in time with the music. Laughing, she threw the rose at an open-mouthed farmer and cast the scarf from her shoulders. As the tempo of the music quickened, she moved her hips at a speed almost too fast for the eye to follow. The silk below her waist fluttered as though struck by a strong wind as she slowly shuffled her feet round the floor. All the movement was below her waist now and, fascinated, we could not take our eyes from the passionate spell she was weaving. Then again she stopped, facing the tables. She threw back her head and laughed—a wicked, contemptuous laugh as much as to say, "I have you in my power because I know what you are really like." She shook her shoulders so that her soft breasts trembled beneath the silk and, throwing back her head, she laughed again. Fools, all fools, all men are fools! Covering her face with both hands so that her arms formed a graceful bow, she began to sway slowly again to the music, now softer, more insidious. The voices hushed and the clapping ceased, as every pair of eyes was riveted upon her navel. I managed to snatch myself away from the attraction of that tortuous, slowly moving area of soft brown flesh to look around at their transfixed faces. It reminded me of the python, who hypnotised the Bunda monkeys in Kipling's Jungle Stories. Their hungry eyes followed every movement as they leaned forward towards her over the tables. Drinks, pipes, cigarettes and other girls were forgotten. This was the magic of the Arabian nights, the sport of the sultans. In their minds they imagined that she was already theirs.

The lights brightened and again she clicked her fingers. She held her hands aloft and, at the sharp crack of her forefingers, she bent her knees to throw the lower part of her torso forward in one quick, sensuous gesture. The orchestra became louder with a faster, gay rhythm, and she moved round the floor, swaying and smiling at the admiring throng. Everyone clapped in time to the music, shouting "tayeb" and "masard." Smiling her

24

understanding, she evaded the grip of an Egyptian whose enthusiasm had got beyond control and sped through a door at the back of the bar.

When she had changed into a more modest green gown she came over to sit at my table. Smiling sweetly, she put her hand in mine and I bought her a garland of jasmine. The scent was intoxicating as she leaned towards me. I longed to touch her soft brown shoulders. My Arabic was limited, but I was learning fast under her tuition. I said "you were beautiful, you were lovely." She smiled and pinched my cheek. Turning swiftly in her chair, she called to another girl in an excited, shrill treble, "He said I was beautiful in Arabic. Inti latif. He is a darling and furthermore a gentleman." Twisting round to face me again, she allowed her hair to brush my cheek. "Buy me one bottle cedra." It was impossible to refuse. I clapped my hands and a waiter rushed up with a bottle of champagne in a bucket. Whispering excitedly and drawing her chair closer to mine, so that the jasmine assailed my nostrils, she gulped down the champagne at a most alarming rate. I offended her by saying that as a taxicab runs on petrol, she ran on champagne. Only another bottle would mollify her. Bewitched, I clapped my hands again.

So it went on, night after night, with all my savings being spent on bottles of cedra, champagne, dolls and jasmine, but it always ended when the cabaret closed at one o'clock. Sometimes when I danced with her it was good to hold her tight, although her attempts to mix the sinuous writhings of the Oriental dance with Western music were not exactly successful. At ten minutes to one her mother appeared to take her home. She was a little wizened old woman in a black veil and it did not seem possible that she could be Shou-Shou's mother. I shuddered to think what her father might be.

At last she agreed to allow me to take her home. I had told her that soon I would be leaving for the desert and, in her grief, she wept on my shoulder. We mounted a taxicab outside the cabaret. I kissed her soft hot lips and she wriggled her body close to mine. I was slightly drunk. "Where do you live, my dear?" When she said Saida Zenab, I was a little shaken since I knew it to be one of the filthiest quarters in the "Out-of-bounds" Area. However, having got so far, I was not to be dissuaded by a small consideration like that. I told the taximan to drive on and to hell with the consequences.

25

Between kissing Shou-Shou in the back of the cab, I occasionally glanced out of the window. My spirits were sinking as the effects of the alcohol wore off. We were passing through dark narrow streets, just wide enough to take the taxi, and the whole place smelled of dried urine. Once I caught a glimpse of a horrible leering face behind a grilled window. At last, after we had gone through a maze of cobbled alleyways, Shou-Shou said we had reached her home. Firmly she kissed me good night on the step of the taxicab, making me promise to see her again at the cabaret the next night. I reluctantly let her go.

We tried to turn the taxicab round in the narrow street, but only succeeded in jamming it between the two walls. A crowd of Arabs began to gather, appearing like ghosts from the shadows. They hissed ominously as they gathered round and shook their fists at me through the windows. I could see that the driver was frightened and I could feel a certain panic rising in my own breast. With a deft twist of the wheel he managed to swing the cab back into its original position. He began to slide across his seat as though to dismount—a movement which filled me with no little horror and a certain amount of anger. Two Arabs had jumped on the running-board. I brought my stick down on the top of the cabby's tarbush and ordered him to drive on. After looking first at the Arabs and then at me, he slipped back into the driving seat. The taxi went forward with a jerk, throwing the Arabs off into the street. They ran after us for a short way, shouting and throwing stones, but we were clean away. The only trouble was that we were lost. After driving for what seemed like hours through narrow, unlit streets, we came out on the Pyramids Road, miles from home. The taxi fare amounted to some two pounds plus a large tip for the driver.

I did not see Shou-Shou again until the middle of 1942, just before the Battle of El Alamein. She had moved to a new, tinselled cabaret called the Opera Casino, which Madame Badia had opened in the centre of Cairo. She had grown fat on so much champagne and had been relegated to Number Three on the list of dancers. Her stomach had begun to protrude and she had lost her powers of fascination for the audience. The place was full of drunken soldiers, the lights were too bright and the tables had a vulgar polish. Somehow the romantic spell of that tattered old tent on English Bridge, with the starry sky showing through the tears in the roof, had been broken. Shou-Shou was like any other cheap

26

cabaret girl. No longer was she queen of the harem. When she saw me, she rushed over to throw her arms round my neck. Overjoyed, excited, she dragged me off to a table by the dance floor. But she was too quick with her demands for drink. This time there was no magic and I thought of my bank balance before her. Disappointed, she moved on to try her luck with the Australians at the next table.

When there was no work for us to do and when we were not sleeping off our excesses of the night before, we sometimes went into Cairo to see the sights. One afternoon I went with two other members of my regiment to see the Mousky, Cairo's famous bazaar. Refusing the services of the dragomen who haunted the steps of the Continental, we strode off down the street into the shopping area. The town rapidly becomes more primitive as one gets away from Opera Square, and we were soon amongst the barrows, the donkey-carts, the open stalls and the teeming crowds of the Sukh. There were many horribly deformed beggars, covered with flies, on the streets, totally ignored by the jostling crowd of ragged coolies, tall white-robed fellaheen, proud Bedouin from the Desert and stalking Sudanese from Upper Egypt. Little heavily veiled women in black dresses dodged inconspicuously between the legs of the busy, shouting multitude. Merchants grabbed us by the arm to coax us into their shops to inspect their wares. They offered us cups of coffee, dangled silver bracelets before our eyes and shouted, "No need to buy—just look." We strode on with our eyes fixed to the front, afraid to turn aside for fear that we might be inveigled into buying something we did not want.

As we were walking along the noisy thoroughfare, a kind-looking old gentleman, who had been walking along in front, turned to say "Good afternoon." He gave us this greeting with a charming smile and we graciously answered, surprised to hear English so well spoken. He was a nice old man of about sixty, dressed in a clean white galabieh and carrying a walking-stick. His eyes had a benevolent twinkle and were wrinkled at the corners. He slowed down his pace until we had drawn alongside.

"I suppose you children are seeing the sights?"

I said yes, rather gruffly, since I was suspicious of his motives. With another disarming smile, which dispelled all our fears, he said: "I am a teacher at the Mohomed Ali School. I teach history

27

and geography. My classes do not begin until four o'clock, and if you would like to see the Blue Mosque, I will be passing that way."

We were enchanted and readily agreed. As we walked along, he entertained us with amusing anecdotes about his pupils and the school. We removed our shoes at the gates of the mosque and tiptoed inside. The magnificent columns and blue mosaic walls filled us with awe. There was a large paved courtyard, rubbed smooth by millions of stockinged feet, and in the middle was a bubbling ornamental fountain. A veranda ran round the courtyard, supported by beautiful, slender columns, thousands of years old. A flock of white pigeons flew across to the minaret.

"My children, would you like a charm to keep away the bullets in battle?"

Although as a good Roman Catholic I could have no faith in its powers, it would be fun to have as a souvenir. We gratefully said that we would.

"Then, my children, you must give me fifty piastres each to give to the High Priest. While he is blessing the charms, perhaps you would like to see the minaret."

With a little less enthusiasm we gave him the money. He led us to an iron door at the foot of the minaret, but it was necessary to produce a further twenty piastres each before a porter would give us the key. We ascended old worn stone steps to the top of the tower. From it we could see the whole of Cairo's tumbled-down Eastern Quarter laid out like a model town. Nearby a woman was milking a goat on a roof. I felt like David about to poach from Uriah the Hittite. However, the tower was swaying in the wind, so as to mar our delight with a feeling of insecurity. We went rapidly down the stairs.

I was just in time to see the old man scribbling on a piece of paper. He thrust it into his galabieh with a quick, guilty movement when he saw me approaching across the courtyard. All smiles by the time we reached him, he led us with honeyed words out of the mosque. I asked him for the charm.

"I must hurry now or I will be late for school. I hope you have enjoyed your afternoon. Before I give you this charm, which has been blessed by the High Priest, you must promise never to look at it. If you do, the spell will be broken. Put it near to your hearts and it will keep away the danger in battle."

Giving us all a piece of paper, he hurried away into the

crowd. We walked back down the bazaar, laughing at the novelty of the thing. When I said that I was going to look at mine, spell or no speell, the others were strongly against it. Nevertheless the temptation was too great. I took it from the pocket of my bush shirt and, with the others looking over my shoulder, I unfolded it. Awe-stricken, we gazed at the unintelligible Arabic letters. I sought the aid of a passing Arab. He read the note and handed it back to me with a curious look on his face. It was an old laundry bill.

It was difficult for a young officer to get a gun in the Army Shoot which was out at Tel-el-Kebir, and when we saw the neat rows of all kinds of duck laid out in the mess kitchen, we were very jealous of our seniors. With justified pride they would give us a lecture on the various species, pointing out the markings of teal, shovellers, wigeon, pin-tails, mallard and pochard, so that when we graduated to the honour of a part in the shoot, we also would be able to discourse with intelligence on the subject. Our envy increased to the point where we succumbed to the sales talk of an old shikari who used to hang about outside the front door of the mess.

"Mister Major sir, I know a very good lake where the duck are so thick in the sky it is like night. This lake is near the lake of the King, who feeds his duck very well. To-morrow, sir, I have heard some friends of the King will be shooting. There will be many duck. I am shikari to the 11th Hussars, the 3rd Hussars, the Scots Guards, the Coldstream Guards, the Royals, the 4th Hussars and all the best regiments, sir. I have been shikari for thirty years, even when Lord Kitchener was here, and I am a very good man. I am the best shikari in Egypt, Mister Major sir."

Of course it was really the touch of calling me Mister Major which did it. I prided myself on having such an air of authority that he had mistaken my single pip for a crown. Three of us agreed to pick up the shikari at four o'clock the next morning. The idea of getting up at such an unearthly hour was not exactly relished by any of us, but since it was obviously the way these things were done, we reluctantly made arrangements with the guard to give us an early call.

At half-past three a rough hand shook me. Rubbing my eyes and regretting that I had ever been foolish enough to agree to an outing which promised such acute discomfort, I dressed myself in an old suit. Half asleep, I wandered down to the garage and, after many unsuccessful attempts, succeeded in starting the car. The others failed to arrive at the rendezvous. I railed against them bitterly, accusing them of lack of guts, softness and letting me down. Secretly I was furious that they had had the sense to stay in bed while I had been bruising my knuckles in trying to start the car in the half light of a cold morning.

I picked up the shikari and drove on alone, cursing under my breath. On the Pyramids Road we passed many donkey carts on their way to the market in Cairo. They carried no lights, which made driving in the dark quite dangerous. What was more, they were so unused to seeing a car at that hour of the morning that they had seen fit to occupy the centre of the road. Perilously we made our way towards the country.

Just before Giza, we turned off to the right down a hard mud track. After bumping along for about four miles, the shikari told me to halt.

"From here, Mister Major sir, you must take a donkey."

"What do you mean—take a donkey?"

"I mean you must ride on a donkey, sir,"

"What, that thing?"

He pointed out a miserable animal in the last stages of debilitation. Its ribs protruded like the strings on a harp and there were running saddle-sores on its rumps. With growing misgivings, I opened my legs and walked on to it from the rear. But in spite of its sorry appearance, this donkey still retained some shreds of pride. Why should it be made to work before it was even light? All the Trades Union rules of donkeys were against it. Showing a grim determination not to be exploited any further, the poor beggarly beast staged a stand-up strike. Leaning backwards, it dug its forelegs into the mud and refused to budge. The best shikari in the world screamed threats of dire punishment and belaboured its hind-quarters with a stick. What it objected to most of all was being tugged by the mouth. At last, when it had withstood all the tortures ever administered in the history of donkeys, the old Arab dropped his hands and looked at me with a forlorn expression of despair. The donkey began to amble forward, having achieved its point. Who said donkeys are stupid?

Our ridiculous cavalcade wound slowly through the marshes —the donkey and I in front, followed by the shikari and three ragged beaters. We came to a small lake, about the size of a large puddle.

"Here, Mister Major sir, you take a boat."

The boat consisted of a water-logged raft made from dried maize leaves and bamboo stems tied together with string. It was propelled by one of the beaters, who waded in the water up to his knees. There was a tendency for him to upturn this rather flimsy craft, which made it difficult to maintain one's balance. I dropped a box of cartridges into the water.

After a journey only rivalled by the Puritan Christian in the *Pilgrim's Progress*, I found myself in a hide. It consisted of bamboo stakes lashed together and interlaced with green maize leaves. Only the most inexperienced duck in the world would have been taken in by it. I filled my pockets with cartridges and squatted on my haunches to wait for the birds, the shikari by my side.

I had shivered in the cold for about half an hour when a sound of popping came from the west. The shikari whispered:

"That, Mister Major sir, is shooting on the King's Lake. Watch very carefully—maybe you will get a shot."

Two teal came over very high, but I judged them to be out of range. The old Arab seemed to be furious that I had not fired. He made me feel ashamed that I was a novice and I resolved to fire at the next bird, regardless of my chances of bringing it down.

Suddenly there was a whir of wings and a shoveller came very low over my head. I put up my gun and followed it with my barrel until I was leaning backwards at an angle of forty-five degrees. I pulled the trigger as I felt myself falling over. The explosion was still ringing in my ears when I rescued the shikari from beneath me. Dusting his crumpled galabieh I apologised, but he seemed quite pleased.

"Mister Major sir, that was a very fine shot, very fine! You have shot a very big duck."

"Have I really?"

Nobody could have been more astonished than I, but it was the first and last duck I shot that day. I sat in the butt for about an hour, growing more miserable and thinking about my breakfast, but no more duck appeared. There were quite a lot of coot about and the old shikari was very keen for me to shoot them. He was anxious that I should have at least a little sport and it appeared that his family loved coot, seldom eating anything else. It was too easy. The beaters put them up on the far side of the lake, and they would lumber over towards me like heavy transport planes, squawking their disapproval. I shot seven before I tired of the sport and my shikari was delighted.

After what can only be described as a miserable morning, I eventually got back to camp to find that my friends were still happily asleep in bed. The whole trip cost me an official fee of five pounds for the shikari and an unofficial levy of two boxes of cartridges, stolen by the beaters.

CHAPTER THREE

THE FIRST WAVELL CAMPAIGN

ROUND ABOUT the beginning of October, 1940, we found ourselves in a troop train in Cairo Main Station, bound for the Western Desert. Red-coated porters were fighting for the honour of carrying our baggage; hawkers were thrusting their persistent heads in the carriage windows with offers of chocolate, cigarettes and lewd magazines; R.T.O.s were disturbing the comfortable few to make room for latecomers; and above it all were the whistles and shouts of the railway officials.

I shared a compartment with four other officers. We packed our valises between the seats so that we could stretch out our legs during the forty-eight hour journey. Somebody produced a pack of cards and we began to play.

The troops cheered as the train jerked out of the station. Some of them began to sing "Roll out the Barrel" at the back. A crowd of ragged Arab children kept up the race until the speed became too much for them. Shouting up at the carriage windows as their tiny legs moved faster and faster in a vain attempt to keep level, they begged for biscuits, cigarettes and backsheesh. The soldiers threw out packets of biscuits and cigarettes with good-natured shafts of Cockney wit. All along the track, Egyptians returned the waves of the troops, and handkerchiefs could be seen fluttering from the windows.

Many were going up to the desert for the first time. Some were returning from leave. None could guess what the future might hold, although the old hands knew that they were returning to a monotonous life in the sand and the flies. There would be no cinemas, no girls, half a pint of beer a week and a staple diet of bully and biscuits. But they were happy. Subconsciously they took pride in doing their bit.

The train halted frequently—sometimes in railway stations, but more often on a deserted stretch of line. The troops would leap from their carriages and attempt to brew tea. Little fires would appear all down the line on each side of the train. Battered braziers made from punctured petrol tins were produced like magic from their kit, and soldiers would double back from the

33

engine with billy-cans splashing full of water. If the train started before the water boiled, the fires would be extinguished and the troops would curse as they leapt back into the wagons, still holding the full brew-cans in their hands.

At every station a crowd of children gathered, yelling for backsheesh. Their faces were sweet and winning, unlike the ugly features of the adults. If the train failed to stop, they hurled stones at the carriages. Once a ragged urchin lifted up his shirt to flaunt his naked body at the troops. Delighted at their derisive jeers, he danced up and down with joy.

By the next day we had reached the empty wastes of the desert. No longer were there children—only endless sandy ridges and the sky. On the right we caught an occasional glimpse of the sea. Rich and blue, it was breaking in long lines of white foam on the shore. The view was interrupted by groups of white dunes. Salty, glistening in the sun, they were like huge mounds of sugar. Flat, treacherous salt marshes lay between them, pink-hued like a highly-polished floor.

Past Daba Station—two huts and a roll of wire—the ridges gave way to a flat tableland. The sand was strewn with stones and dotted by small tufts of camel scrub. Here and there a larger bush gave off a faint smell of sage. We could see trucks moving up on the desert road, parallel with the railway.

Near Fuka an escarpment began to appear as a black shadow on the horizon to the south. As we approached the end of our journey at Garawla, the railway ran closer to this escarpment and we could see that it was a sheer cliff, breaking two levels of flat desert like a step. Where the face was broken by wadis, dusty paths wound up to the top.

Garawla Station consisted of two tents and a siding. Two stations short of Mersa Matruh, it was at that time the railhead for the 7th Armoured Division. We lifted out our kit and sat on the sand beside the track, uncertain of our next move. We put our backs to the cold bitter wind and turned up our collars against flying particles of sand. We felt lost and forlorn in a strange new world. A few drops of rain increased our misery. Lonely, unwanted, we tried to get some information from the corporal in charge of the station.

"There *may* be a truck in about an hour. He *might* give you a lift to the Service Corps. Then you *might* get up to Brigade with the rations. No, I haven't got any tea and I haven't got any food.

What do you think I am? The Naafi? You can have these biscuits if you like."

With that he spat on the ground, turned on his heel and walked away down the line. He was unkempt and matted with sand like all the other soldiers we saw. His unbuttoned greatcoat flapped in the wind. Our confidence was pricked. There had been no sound of respect in his voice, but what could we do? For the rest of the morning we sat huddled in the rain, munching biscuits and trying to light cigarettes.

A truck, with the red desert rat of the 7th Armoured Division painted on the rear, drew up to the station in a cloud of dust. Shouting, we ran towards it. We begged the driver for a lift to the Service Corps Camp and he said that he would be only too pleased, but we might have to wait for a couple of hours, since he had to load up with petrol cans and there was nobody else to help him. Reluctantly we took off our greatcoats and formed a chain to hand the petrol cans up into the back of the truck. It seemed undignified labour for an officer, conscious as we were of our single pips. But there were already many points about this desert life which were rudely shocking our conceptions of army methods.

Perched on the top of a pile of tins with our kit stacked around us, we began our first journey into the desert. The lorry bounced and bumped over the camel scrub, tossing us about like corks until our buttocks felt like bruised steak. Sometimes we managed to save ourselves by grabbing the framework overhead, but more often we were thrown on top of each other in a confusion of flailing arms, petrol cans and valises. The wheels threw up a cloud of dust, which made us look as though we had plastered our faces with bright yellow face powder.

We were quite relieved when we reached a collection of widely-dispersed lorries and tents, which was the Service Corps leaguer. A fat jovial Major wearing a peaked cap, which looked as though it had been run over by a tank, conducted us to their mess tent. He was very kind and, before long, we were sitting on upturned boxes round a large packing-case, eating fried bully fritters and tinned potatoes. Although the salty water had caused the tea to be covered by a skin of grey-white brine, it was welcome and satisfying. The Major told us that the supply column would not be leaving until five o'clock the next morning. Until then we could sleep in the leaguer. I made the mistake of asking where.

With pained surprise he pointed outside the tent: "Why, anywhere you like out there. My servant will wake you in the morning."

After dinner we sat in the mess tent, drinking whisky and salt water out of battered enamel mugs. The tent was lighted by an ill-disciplined hurricane lamp, which alternatively smoked and went absent without leave. Outside, the wind had grown stronger, bringing more rain and, wrenching at the guy ropes and flapping the canvas, it threatened to blow the whole structure to Khartoum. Some of the more sensible Service Corps officers had hidden their ears in thick woollen Balaclavas, for it was bitterly cold. They told us that sometimes they had ice on their water in the morning. I shuddered. I could not remember whether the freezing-point of salt water was higher or lower than normal, so I decided to try to forget my misery in sleep.

When I got outside the mess tent, I found difficulty in getting my bearings. The night was very dark and there were no familiar landmarks. I had unrolled my valise against the wheel of a truck not far away, but there was only the light of the stars and the wind made concentration difficult. I lumbered off in what I thought was the right direction, but was brought to my knees by one of the ropes of the tent. A sympathetic voice called from inside, telling me to stay where I was. An understanding Service Corps subaltern appeared and guided me to the truck.

"You know, I always go home on a compass bearing. Lots of people get lost and stay out all night. Once our Colonel, slightly blotto, wandered about all night and found himself three miles from the leaguer in the morning. It's terrible how dark it gets."

I found that my valise was resting in a puddle of water. I was too tired to care. Fully dressed, I wriggled inside and was soon fast asleep.

Next morning, as dawn was breaking, we left in a large convoy of some two hundred trucks. The desert was fresh and sweet after the rain. Birds were singing and we could smell the fresh earth as the wheels broke its surface. There was no dust and the wind had dropped. As the sun rose in a red ball towards Cairo, all the world seemed virgin, clean and good. A soldier was whistling in the back of the truck. I felt fitter than I had ever been since we had left England. Outside, the trucks were moving in irregular formation like men-o'-war at sea. I saw a hare start up from under a bush and zigzag away between the trucks to safety.

Standing on the tailboard and looking over the canvas cover, I saw that we were heading for a group of black squares, which seemed to be suspended in the air above the skyline, floating in a mirage. They seemed too tall for trucks and too regular for houses. The heat shimmered up between us to make it seem that we were looking at them through crude glass. As we approached, they gradually joined with the earth and resolved themselves into a leaguer of three-tonner trucks—the Brigade supply point.

I made my way, after many inquiries, to the location of our Regimental Transport Echelon. The first person I met was an old friend. Doozico King, the Regimental Postman, was the oldest member of the unit and the stories about him were legend. He had first joined the regiment in Egypt in the First World War and had served with it in Turkey. He was called "Doozico" after a particularly strong brand of arak, much drunk by the troops at that time. It was said that he read all incoming and outgoing mail, which was borne out by a story about his having told a certain officer that a parcel contained a new hat for which he had sent home three weeks before. It was also rumoured that Doozico had been known to sell a three-halfpenny stamp for threepence. In Turkey he had won the Regimental Mule Race by putting a tin tack in his reins.

Greeting me with a broad grin, he said, "Well nah, how nice to see you, sir! I've been expecting you all week. You'll be going to ' B ' Squadron, who are with the 2nd Tanks nah. Have a nice trip up? How's Cairo? I bet there's much more booze since the old Third left, sir, eh? Heard about Mr. Hartigan, sir? He's up with ' A ' Squadron, patrolling up in the front. He shot up the whole Iti army with a pistol from the top of his tank the other day. Trust the old Third."

Sitting in the front of a fifteen-hundredweight truck, I accompanied the Squadron Quartermaster-Sergeant up to the Squadron Area. Since we were equipped with light tanks, we had been attached to the 2nd Battalion of the Royal Tank Regiment as a reconnaissance squadron to their heavier cruisers. It was the only cruiser tank battalion in the desert at that time and as such contained all the punch of the 7th Armoured Division.

The British Forces had withdrawn in front of Marshal Graziani's push and were now encamped in the desert south of

37

Mersa Matruh. The 7th Armoured Division was very thin on the ground and Matruh Fortress was only held by a small garrison. Behind us the newly arrived 4th Indian Division was training in desert warfare. One armoured regiment equipped with obsolete light tanks was patrolling towards the Italian positions in the forward area.

The Italians had advanced along the coast road as far as Sidi Barrani, where they had built a semi-circular arc of perimeter camps stretching to the south as far as Sofafi. The strongest of these camps were at Rabia, Nbeiwa and Tummar in the extreme south. They had also established an outpost position at Maktila, on the coast road half-way between Sidi Barrani and Mersa Matruh. For some reason they had baulked at an attack on the Mersah Matruh defences. Most experts now agree that their superior numbers might have carried them much farther into Egypt had they chosen to advance. Their timidity can perhaps be explained by the usual Italian tendency to exaggerate the numbers of the enemy. Perhaps they were also taken in by a thin, hopelessly inadequate minefield we had laid at Charing Cross, south of Matruh and astride the track to Siwa.

The squadron was leaguered on the east side of the Siwa Track under the shadow of the escarpment. The tanks were widely dispersed against the danger of air attack and the soft vehicles of the transport echelon were encamped some three miles farther east. The troops had made tents for themselves by digging holes in the sand and covering them with small bivouac sheets. Each crew cooked its own food beside its vehicle. The staple diet was bully beef and biscuits with occasional tins of herring, sausages and fruit. It was amazing how skilful the troops had become at varying the form in which they cooked their monotonous rations. Bully beef was served cold, stewed and fried. Biscuits were crushed to make flour for fritters and even porridge. When they returned from leave in the Delta, they brought additional luxuries such as onions and tinned soups. A meal was always washed down with thick, sweet tea. Tea was brewed three or four times a day, and if the supplies had ever failed, the morale of the army would have been reduced more than by a major defeat.

The officers' mess consisted of a square wooden hut in the middle of the leaguer of which we were justly proud. Planks and an old tarpaulin had been stolen from the Egyptian railways in Mersa Matruh. The officers had constructed it themselves and we believed it to be the best squadron mess in the division. We were also very proud of an old gramophone with one record—"Tristesse" on one side and "J'attendrai" on the other.

Towards the beginning of November the weather becomes bitterly cold. The thousands of flies disappear and an icy wind penetrates even the thickest clothing. Sometimes there is heavy rain at this time of the year, but in the winter of 1940 there was very little. We spent our time in training and in reading novels sent out in parcels from home. These parcels also contained warm clothing, which was very welcome. The brave little notes inside, such as "Best wishes, boys, from Mrs. Smith of Newcastle-on-Tyne," tied us with an invisible link of affection to the people who were enduring bombing raids in our tiny islands, many miles away on the other side of the world.

My first job was to guide in the transport echelon with the rations for the battalion. I set off, driving myself in the squadron eight-hundredweight pick-up. I was told later that the squadron leader stood in the door of the mess, closing his eyes every time I bumped over a tuft of camel scrub, terrified that I would break a spring. It was some time before I learned to avoid the bumps by means of quick twists of the steering-wheel. I arrived safely at the supply point, but it was late in the afternoon before we started off for the regiment.

Although I had done a navigation course in Cairo, it was not so easy in practice to find one's way in the desert. I was very conscious of my responsibility and leapt out often to take a new bearing with my compass. Every twenty minutes or so I would walk a few yards in front of the truck and take a bearing on the skyline. Having found some object such as a bush on the horizon, I would tell the driver to steer towards it until the time came for me to check again. As a rough guide, I took the variation of the compass when held in my lap in the truck.

When the trip showed that we had covered the correct distance, I began to worry about there being no sign of the regimental leaguer. Trusting my instincts, which is a fatal thing to do in desert navigation, I suspected that we had gone too far to the north. I therefore decided to drive on a bearing for another mile to the south. Still there was no sign of the collection of black silhouettes I expected to see on the skyline. It was now getting dark and I was panic stricken. If I did not find the regiment before dark, perhaps I would not find them at all. Desperately I took another bearing to the west. We drove on for another three miles and I could see that the S.Q.M.S. was getting agitated as he sat in the front of the three-tonner behind me. Perhaps it would be best to consult him, even though I hated to admit that I was lost. He recommended trying another thrust to the north. After another five miles, it had become quite dark and I had given up all attempts to navigate. Instead, I wandered aimlessly about in the hope that I might see the lights of the leaguer. The long column of trucks trailed behind me and I could guess the contempt with which the drivers would regard my inefficiency.

The only way to navigate is to have complete faith in your instruments. Almost as bad as trusting to your instincts is to attempt to drive towards a light in the hope that you might find someone who knows his exact position. The light might prove to be twenty miles away.

At about eleven o'clock, when we had driven fifty miles farther than we should have done, a green Verey light was fired approximately a mile away to the east. I had abandoned all hope of finding the regiment before the morning, but I seized upon this last chance of meeting someone who knew where he was. As we motored towards it, another light was fired in the same direction. In a few minutes we found ourselves inside the squadron leaguer area.

"Where the bloody hell have you been?"

"I am afraid I got lost."

"You got lost, did you? You've been motoring round the leaguer for the last four hours. Why the hell didn't you flash a torch?"

"I didn't know where I was."

"Oh, I see, you didn't know where you were. Do you realise that the whole regiment has gone without its evening meal? Do you realise that the Colonel wants to have you executed?"

The contempt he put in his voice was quite sufficient punishment. I slunk off to bed. For several days I was afraid to open my mouth in the mess.

On December 7th the Tank Corps Colonel summoned us to an officers' conference. He sat on a petrol tin, with everyone in a half-circle on the ground around him. He was a fat, heavily-jowled man and I can vividly remember how ugly were his white, fleshy knees as he sat facing us, dressed in badly-cut shorts and waving a blue horse-hair fly-whisk. I expected to hear a lecture on the inefficiency of junior officers, but was relieved to hear him begin the address with an account of the general war situation. Then he began his orders.

The Western Desert Force would carry out a reconnaissance in force with the object of testing the strength of the Italian defences around Sidi Barrani. At dawn on 9th December the Indians supported by Matilda tanks would assault the perimeter camp of Nbeiwa. Having taken Nbeiwa, they would roll up the string of camps to the north starting with the Tummars. At the same time the 7th Armoured Division would penetrate the gap between Rabia and Nbeiwa and would fan out in the rear, destroying dumps and troop concentrations. The garrison from Mersa Matruh would attack Maktila. The operation was designed to last at least forty-eight hours and at the most four days.

He then went into the details of our own part in the attack as the reserve regiment to the 4th Armoured Brigade. I began to dream. These were the orders for our first battle. Would I be killed? Would I do well? Was I a coward? A hundred questions sped through my brain. In conclusion, the Colonel read an order of the day from General Wavell. I know it had a great effect on us, as with all orders of the day which don't talk about having the glint of battle in your eye, but I cannot remember the exact wording.

And then there was a great commotion as tanks were filled with petrol, loaded up with rations, and teed up for the big advance. Guns were cleaned and the ammunition was straightened in the Vickers belts. Map-boards were marked with coloured chinagraph and I spent the whole day making quite certain that there were no arithmetical errors in my calculation of the bearing. The troops have great sang-froid in these things. They did not seem in the least bit excited. I heard the same old mouth organs playing "My brother Silvest's got forty thousand hairs upon his chest" as I went to bed.

At five minutes to four the next afternoon we were ready on the start-line at Bir Abu Khanayis. The other two squadrons were in open order behind us. It had been a fine day and the sun was just going down behind the escarpment in front. We sat on the lids of our tanks, looking now and then at our watches. Suddenly an enormous column appeared in a cloud of dust behind us. In a disorganised mass of guns, carriers and trucks, it drove straight through our formation towards the west. It looked like a gold rush on the Klondike. I could see that the Squadron Leader was furious, because if we started now as we had been ordered, we would lose our formation in this huge, confused column. I was secretly relieved, because at least they would show me the way to the battle.

After a short delay the order came over the wireless to advance. Fifty tanks rolling forward over the desert, each with a cloud of dust behind, is a fine display of strength. I looked behind with pride and wondered how the Italians could possibly hope to stop us. As far as the eye could see there were vehicles. Just before dark I caught a glimpse of the Indian troop carriers and the heavy Matildas away on the right. Through glasses I could see grim-looking Sikhs, with turbans wound round their beards as a protection against the dust, sitting rigidly in the trucks.

The pace slowed down when night fell, because it was necessary for me to stop frequently to check the bearing on a star. I found the track up the escarpment without difficulty for the column in front had made a wide dusty road across the desert. My driver put the tank into a slit trench in the dark, which jerked me forward to bang my nose on the front flap. I think the Light Tank Mark VIB must be the most uncomfortable vehicle ever invented. It is like travelling along on the inside of a sharp-cornered rocking-horse and it is impossible to move anywhere without skinning your elbows.

We halted at about four o'clock to fill up with petrol. No fires were allowed, but a certain old soldier in the squadron contrived to give me a mug of tea. I think he must have brewed it on a stove inside his tank. The Italians were firing balloon flares over towards Barrani, which showed that they were nervous, until at dawn we rolled forward to the attack.

Since we were in reserve to the Brigade, it was my job to maintain a distance of fourteen hundred yards from the last vehicles of Brigade Headquarters. This was easy. It meant that it was unnecessary to navigate carefully, provided that I kept my eyes on two ambulances in front.

Happily I sat on the flaps of my tank, feeling that it was really me who was commanding the regiment. It was a bright, crisp morning and only the sound of guns to the right reminded me that we were really going into a battle.

Somewhere north of Point 108 I came up from a short stretch

of dead ground to find that there were two sets of identical ambulances on different bearings in front. My confidence evaporated in a moment. Here was a dilemma. I could not decide which vehicles to follow. Worse, I did not know where we were on the map. I decided to take a chance and follow the right-hand column.

We had not gone more than two miles when strange fountains of sand began to spurt up between the tanks. A whistle and a small explosion told me that it was gunfire. A shell burst nearby and little pieces of metal rattled against the side of the tank. Hastily I groped about inside the turret for my tin hat. Before I put it on, I had the sense to look back at the squadron leader. Unperturbed, he was still sitting on the top of his tank. I sheepishly returned my steel helmet to its hook. Suddenly I found myself laughing. The Italians were such bad shots that they were not doing any damage at all. Not a single tank had been seriously hit. An angry voice came through the headphones, which quickly removed the smile from my face.

"Hallo, Cuty Able, Cuty calling—You, I say again, you have led us into the wrong battle. They were the guns from Nbeiwa. Move on a bearing of figures 310 degrees. Is this understood? Cuty to Cuty Able over."

When we had finally sorted ourselves out, we pushed out patrols on to hills round about to give reports on the movements of the enemy. On a ridge above Sanyet el Kur, a series of black dots showed that it was the position of an Italian column. Our artillery was having a duel with some guns below this ridge. One of our twenty-five pounders received a direct hit, setting on fire a quad full of ammunition. In fact, there were bangs all around us, but it was difficult to tell what exactly was happening.

At midday a message came through to the effect that the Indians had succeeded in taking Nbeiwa. It appeared that the Italians had no answer to our heavy Matilda tanks. We were thrilled to see a collection of strange green lorries over towards Brigade Headquarters. They were our first prizes and the battle was going well.

In the afternoon we moved farther north to cover the Italian line of retreat from the Tummar Camps. When he had posted the squadron in a hull-down position on a ridge, the Squadron Leader told me to guide him to Battalion Headquarters for a conference. It was astonishing how he continued to place faith

43

in my powers of navigation. Navigating in a Light Tank Mark VIB is bound to be a haphazard affair, since the cruel way in which it bounces about its crew makes it nearly impossible to hold a compass on an even tilt. If the sun is clouded over, the accurate sun compass cannot be used, and therefore the only sound way to navigate is by actually getting out of your tank to take a bearing once every twenty minutes. This method is not very practical in the middle of a battle. With an outward show of confidence, I set off in the right direction (provided that we were where I thought we were), the Squadron Leader following along behind in his tank. We had gone about six miles according to my trip, when I noticed a collection of large tanks in a wadi in front. Their crews were sitting smoking cigarettes on the hulls, all looking in the opposite direction. We were within two hundred yards of them when, simultaneously with my driver, I realised that they were Italian M11's mounting a thirty-seven millimetre gun, which could make short work of our flimsy light tanks. Horrified, we swung round to return in the direction from which we had come. I noticed that the Squadron Leader had already turned, without waiting to ask questions. We escaped without being noticed by the enemy and, after wandering about for several hours, we succeeded in finding the Colonel. He was so angry at our late arrival for the conference that he chose to disregard our reports of enemy tanks some-where to the south. Actually they surrendered to the gunners during the night, after having knocked out some of our supply transport.

For the rest of the day we sat in a position of observation behind the Tummars. The Italians sent over several circuses of Savoia bombers and C.R.42's, which dropped their bombs in sticks from a great height. They were usually chased off by gallant little Gladiators before they had done any damage, no bomb ever falling closer than two hundred yards away from our leaguer. Just before dark a lone Italian bi-plane came very low over our squadron area. Every kind of gun was blazed off at it, including two-pounder tracers from the cruisers behind, but it merely wiggled its wings in a contemptuous fashion and flew on out of sight.

As the sun was going down and the guns of the tanks were blackly outlined against the twilight of the desert evening, casting long shadows on the ground, the Squadron Leader told me to return to Battalion Headquarters to bring in the petrol and cooks' lorries. I arrived to find the whole echelon bogged down in soft sand. By skilful use of sand channels, pushing and towing with friendly cruisers, we succeeded in rescuing them by about nine o'clock. Night had fallen and navigation had become a thousand times more difficult than during the day. To my consternation, we had not gone more than two miles before the petrol lorry again sank up to its axle in loose sand. I knew that the squadron was waiting for its evening meal and any further delay would do nothing to increase my popularity with the men. The leaguer could not be more than a mile away on a straight bearing and it was inconceivable that the cooks' lorry would not be able to find it if it proceeded on alone. To make quite certain, I asked the Squadron Leader to fire green Verey lights as an additional guide. Making my instructions absolutely clear to the driver, I told him to drive towards a certain star for one mile and no more. It was over an hour later when we succeeded in getting the petrol lorry once more on the move. The Squadron Leader was in a state of speechless anger when we arrived. The cooks' lorry had not turned up. In fact it wandered about the desert until the morning, delivering our rations at about ten o'clock the next day. My popularity was at the lowest level ever, for the squadron had not only missed its evening meal, but had also gone without its breakfast.

I was in a position overlooking the Indian attack on the Tummars on the 10th December. Sitting on my turret, scanning the horizon through my glasses, I could see Italian dive-bombers getting amongst our transport. The trucks seemed too close together, although the distance might have given me a wrong impression. Wicked little single-engined bombers were diving low between the bursts of ack-ack to drop their cargo slap-bang amongst the lorries. Two trucks were on fire, sending up thick columns of black smoke into the sky, and I could see bearded Sikhs fighting to extinguish the flames. An 11th Hussar armoured car came up to my hill to join me. The commander was an old friend called Cunningham, who eventually became both General Auchinleck's and General Alexander's aide-de-camp. He was just in time for a mug of tea and, as we shared it, he showed me a neat hole in the hull of his car, through which an Italian anti-tank rifle bullet had penetrated to kill his gunner the day before. Apparently he had tried to take the perimeter camp at Mahomed el Gerrari by charging the main gate, but had been repulsed, although it was captured shortly after. The prestige of the 11th Hussars was such as to make it seem an honour for one of their cars to share my position. They were the kings of the desert at that time.

Early in the afternoon the squadron was ordered to move north to take part in an attack on Sidi Barrani from the west. Although there was no sun, I navigated over the long march of twelve miles without a single fault, a feat of which I was very proud, although I do not think that the others appreciated the difficulties. The start-line was a hill on the coast road, some five miles west of Sidi Barrani village. We were to advance in three waves of tanks between the coast and the sea—our light tanks in front followed by two squadrons of heavier cruisers. This was the *coup de grâce*, which was to finish the battle already won by the Indians and the Matildas to the south.

It was evening when we began to advance. Our pennants fluttered against the setting sun as the little tanks rolled forward on a wide front towards the enemy. The ground was pock-marked by a maze of trenches, but the Italians had no stomach for the fight. We cut into their four miles of intricate defences as hot wires cut through cheese. Here and there an anti-tank gun fired a few rounds for the sake of honour before surrendering, but the reports on the wireless told a colourful tale of success. Tiny figures in green uniform waved pathetic white towels from their weapon-pits and the prisoners began to come in in droves. An excited troop leader reported that he had captured two thousand on the coast. I came to a strong Breda position on a hill. Two bursts of Vickers produced a horde of shouting, pleading and gesticulating prisoners, hands aloft, waving white handkerchiefs. Firing a few rounds at their heels with a pistol, I set them off towards Battalion Headquarters at the double. One Breda gunner in the centre fired his weapon to the last, killing the Squadron Leader of the second wave of cruisers. He was eventually silenced by a Sergeant Roper, who ran his light tank over the position. Then, suddenly, as it was getting dark, the white walls of the village appeared in front. We hesitated a moment before entering in order to get our tanks in line for the final thrust. As we sat there, alertly watching in all directions for signs of resistance, a wave of infantry came running from the direction of the town. We could see the evening sun glistening

46

on their bayonets as the little black figures doubled towards us. We fired several bursts at them, fortunately without inflicting any casualties, before we realised that they were the Cameron Highlanders, who had entered the village from the east. The battle of Sidi Barrani was over.

We had captured approximately forty thousand prisoners and our own casualties were negligible. As we rolled back through their positions to the start-line, we shepherded in hundreds of disillusioned Italians. Swarthy, undersized little fellows as they were, scurrying along with their hands tightly clutching bottles of chianti and battered cardboard suitcases, they did not understand that their pleas for mercy were incongruous and unnecessary. We had nothing but pity for these wretched little men. At the same time, it was impossible not to be amused by the thought that these were the tools with which Mussolini hoped to carve a new Roman Empire. Perhaps they were brave enough when they were marching down the Via Roma behind the band, flaunting their gay uniforms to all the pretty girls, but now that they had met the harsh realities of battle they did not think that war was such an amusing game. It was unfortunate for them that our administrative arrangements had not been designed to cope with such an enormous number of prisoners.

I was put in charge of a troop of three tanks with instructions to guard the prisoners until the Service Corps could arrive with lorries to take them to the rear. It was quite unnecessary to guard them, but this was our first experience of war and I took my duties seriously. The troops ushered them into a tight, dense crowd, shouting in mixed Arabic, English and Italian, prodding them with sticks until they were seated on the sand like an obedient herd of cattle. The tanks were posted on the edges of the circle, their guns trained on this pathetic mass of wailing humanity. It was bitterly cold and I could see them shivering as the wind whistled through the inferior material of their greatcoats. They were shouting to each other across the crowd, calling names, trying to find their friends. Some of them begged for water, but we had none to spare. I sent two members of my crew to see if they could find some blankets in the abandoned slit trenches round about. They came back horror-stricken, having uncovered two corpses wrapped up in a roll of blankets. The prisoners' sorrowful lowing went on throughout the night. "Bruno! Antonio! Acqua! Mamma mia!" One Italian ap-

proached my tank with an offer of a swig of chianti. I accepted
and he said:

"O.K., Bud. I'm an honest-to-goodness American citizen.
Pittsburg, yeah. I'm no goddammed wop. Yeah, and I fought
right alongside the British in 1918. Yeah, and if I could get
my hands on that goddamned bastard Mussolini, I'd kill him
right now. Duce, Duce! Who the hell does he think he is with
this goddamned Duce?"

At dawn the next morning the pursuit began. Very few
Italians had succeeded in escaping the net, but now our offensive
had developed from a simple attack on Sidi Barrani to an invasion
of Libya. General Wavell had sized up the quality of the opposition and had launched us on a campaign which was to conquer
Cyrenaica in two months, although originally only designed to
last four days.

We drove due south on a long first leg until we were below
the escarpment at Rabia and Sofafi, approximately back to the
position from which we had launched the first attack on 9th
December. I had at last mastered this business of navigation and
we reached the rendezvous without difficulty. When the whole
of the 4th Armoured Brigade had collected, it began to advance
steadily westward towards the frontier.

The tracks of the tanks made marks on the virgin desert, never
broken by a vehicle before, like great zip fasteners closing behind
us. Everything seemed clean and sweet. It occurred to us that
this was the place to fight a war. Here there were no women
and children, no homes to destroy, no herds of cattle or streams
of refugees, but only the sand, the scrub and the sky. Once we
saw two gazelle, startled by the tanks, running away to safety
in the south, with their white tails bobbing up and down like
the flags of the Italians the day before. There were some stretches
of bad going, where the tanks bucked over loose stones and tough
lumps of camel scrub, but sometimes we put on a burst of speed
over a patch of open gravel.

In the afternoon we were halted by an Italian delaying position
at Sidi Suleiman. Our tanks darted round the fringe, searching
for a weak spot, and being fired at by ill-aimed artillery. A
squadron of Savoia bombers came over and dropped a stick of
bombs on the leaguer. We followed the silver eggs down with
our eyes as they were released from a great height and we watched
them burst with satisfaction over two hundred yards away. They

threw up fountains of sand like thick, brown poplar trees. There was also a dog-fight between four Gladiators and four CR.42's. Both types of plane are very manœuvreable and the sky was filled with their zooming and diving. We were disappointed that the fight should end in the Italians shooting down two Gladiators without loss to themselves.

The patrols were recalled to Squadron Headquarters towards evening. The light was bad as they were returning and one troop leader reported on the wireless that he was being followed by three Italian tanks. To our relief and the troop leader's discomfiture, they proved to be the tanks of another patrol returning from the same direction. Observation under desert conditions is not exactly easy. During the day the great distances and the heat tend to blur one's vision. Inexperienced troop leaders have been known to report bushes or a herd of camels as enemy tanks. One young officer, when pressed for a more accurate description of a column he had reported, protested vigorously that it was impossible to give more detail since they were upside down in a mirage. I can remember a whole squadron stalking one of our own armoured cars for two hours.

The Brigade began to advance again after dark, leaving Sidi Suleiman to the troops behind us. We moved in close column with the tanks nose to tail for fear that they would get separated in the dark. The crews had now been for three nights without sleep and were getting very tired. Driving in close column with the dust blowing in your face and concentrating on the vehicle in front to avoid bumping into it at a sudden halt, is enough to tax the senses of the freshest crews. We were not allowed to show lights and by midnight I was finding it difficult to keep my eyes open. The Brigade had posted sentries to warn us away from a field of thermos bombs dropped by Italian bombers the day before and we swung round it in a large arc.

In reserve at the tail of the column we could see the dense mass of guns, lorries and tanks in front, winding round like a slow goods train on a curve. At about two o'clock the Brigade passed through a narrow gap in the wire which marked the Libyan-Egyptian frontier. It was a great moment. Although we were still moving across the same type of country in the same cloud of dust, we all felt that somehow we had crossed the threshold of a foreign country—a country which promised new, exciting

49

adventure. The troop leader in front had a bottle of rum and began to sing something about an umbrella man. I joined in and was rebuked by the Squadron Leader. Then I found myself falling asleep. My eyes would close, slowly my head would fall forward and suddenly I would realise what I was doing and pull myself together with a jerk. This happened several times until at last the column halted, I suppose for the Navigating Officer to take a bearing. I told my driver to watch the vehicle in front for any signs of movement, while I went to sleep for ten minutes. He could take a turn next time. Twenty minutes elapsed before I woke up to the horrifying discovery that although there were seven tanks behind, there were none in front. My driver had succumbed to his tired senses and the column had moved on while we were asleep.

I ran back to rouse the soundly sleeping crews of the other seven tanks. The only possible course was to follow the tracks of the other vehicles. I walked along in front of my tank, peering at the ground, while the others followed behind at a snail's pace. Sometimes the tracks became plainer, so that I could direct the driver by sitting on the wing at the front. Usually I had to walk. Altogether we must have covered about ten miles before dawn revealed the squadron leaguered in a dip ahead. Ashamed of having nearly caused a disaster by falling asleep, I told the Squadron Leader that we had been delayed by my tank having a petrol stoppage. Perhaps he believed me. I doubt it.

Now we were swinging north to cut the highway between Bardia and Tobruk. We crossed a metalled road near an aerodrome at Sidi Azeiz and advanced up a broad track towards the coast. My squadron was leading when we reached the edge of the escarpment. From it we could see the coast road, vehicles still driving along it, and the foam-flecked line of the Mediterranean. I felt like stout Cortez gazing on the Pacific, or Napoleon looking on the Plains of Lombardy, for the road lay open to us as much as if it were in the palm of our hands. Two troops of light tanks climbed down the escarpment to cut it, while the remainder stayed in their dominating position on the top of the cliff. The troops had great fun during the day, shooting up trucks which had no idea that the British forces were so close. A certain amount of mental anguish was caused to us all during the night, when one of our subalterns accidentally opened fire on a convoy of four ambulances. They had refused to halt and their red crosses were not easily distinguished in the dark. The squadron area was filled with the moans of the wounded.

But the Italians did not intend to let us have it all our own way. A circus of C.R.42's dive-bombed and machine-gunned the tanks about once every half-hour, buzzing about in the sky like a swarm of angry bees. Their bullets failed to penetrate our armour, although they made the metal inside fly off in tiny flakes, causing painful burns to the crews. In an effort to disrupt their aim, we drove around in a figure of eight. It was more annoying than dangerous, since we had nothing with which we could hit back. They seemed to disregard our small-arms fire and there were no anti-aircraft batteries with us at that time.

We maintained our position astride the road for three days, totally cutting off Bardia from either escape or reinforcement. During this period the Italian aircraft did not abate their attacks in the least. It was all the more infuriating that our right-hand troop could see them taking off from an aerodrome at the foot of the escarpment. Repeatedly the troop leader begged for permission to attack, but was refused on the grounds that it was outside our area. On the third day, after a particularly bitter raid in which two of our soft vehicles were destroyed, this officer took the law into his own hands. His wireless set suddenly went off the air. About an hour later a faint signal came through as he returned towards the squadron area:

"Hallo, Cuty, Cuty 4 calling—Have attacked and destroyed seven aircraft, aerodrome installations and a dump of bombs. Own casualties nil. Am now returning to base—Cuty 4 to Cuty over."

The success of his attack saved him from a reprimand. Instead, he earned the praise of the Colonel. Such is life.

In the afternoon we were relieved by another armoured regiment and told that we would now go into reserve for a well-earned rest. Thankfully we motored back along the same broad track, past the signs of many units which had arrived in our wake, to the aerodrome at Sidi Azeiz. We were lucky to miss an uncharted minefield on the edge of the airstrip, which caught two vehicles of the 7th Hussars later in the day. A signal came over the air from the Colonel, ordering the squadron to proceed to the area Sidi Omar.

It appeared that the fort of Sidi Omar, which stood on the frontier, had been overlooked in the advance, and instead of going into reserve to rest, the battalion would take part in an immediate attack on the Italian positions. The plan was for three armoured squadrons to assault the fort under the cover of an artillery barrage. The heavy cruisers of the 2nd Tanks would come in from the north, while at the same time the light tanks of the 7th Hussars and the 3rd Hussars would attack from the south and south-west respectively. At ten minutes to four the guns of the Royal Horse Artillery put down a number of shells, scoring direct hits on the main building. It was a large mud fort, patterned on P. C. Wren lines, but it was soon obscured by a dense cloud of mixed sand and smoke. As the gunners were firing, we jinked up towards the Italian positions. The enemy field guns were firing hard, lobbing high-explosive shells between the tanks, but none was hit. At first I closed my lids, but after a cautious look at the Squadron Leader had revealed that his were still open, I shamefacedly poked my head out of the top once more. At the stroke of four o'clock we all darted forward, as fast as the tanks would go, towards the Italian trenches. It was a glorious charge in good old cavalry style, with the pennants flying in the wind, the commanders cheering and waving their hats, and the Vickers chattering away like rattles at a fair. Our excitement carried us straight through the defences in one headlong rush. Although their artillerymen fought on until they died at their guns, it was too much for the remainder. The inevitable white flags appeared and the usual hordes of prisoners, although some were so scared that they had to be routed out of their dugouts. One cruiser charged right on to bury its nose in the wall of the fort, totally wrecking its front bogies. Another fired a two-pounder shell through the fort from the north to hit my Squadron Leader's petrol tank as he advanced from the south. These were the only two vehicle casualties of the battle.

I was so carried away by the excitement of it all that I unintentionally hurt the feelings of the 7th Hussar Squadron Leader. In those first desert campaigns we were away from base for so long that our dress became raggedly unorthodox, to say the least of it. It is not surprising that we put fear into the hearts of the Italians. Arriving suddenly from the wilds of the desert, usually from an unexpected direction, we were like a horde of pirates with our long matted hair, torn corduroy trousers, coloured kerchiefs and woollen caps. On this occasion, when I was screaming at terrified prisoners in an endeavour to get them into some sort of order, I addressed a ragged figure in a torn greatcoat in somewhat abusive terms. When he failed to respond, I fired two pistol shots at his feet. My consternation was complete when he revealed himself to be a British Major.

It was natural that after the battle the Squadron Leader should take my tank, since I was the most junior officer in his command. Nevertheless it rankled as a slight, as I feared that it was really a punishment for my inefficiency. However, there were some compensations. I was left with his own crippled vehicle, a well-loved tank called "Brown Jack," to guard the thousands of Italians until the arrival of the Service Corps. We had great fun together for several days. I moved them into a compound some way from the fort and deputed a fat, jovial Neapolitan to act as cook. There was plenty of food and water, and he turned out some very fine meals of spaghetti for all of us. They seemed quite happy, singing and playing piano accordions all day. There was only one unfortunate incident to mar our good relations. Three Italian aircraft came over very low one day and machine-gunned the leaguer, wounding two Italians. Another was wounded by a member of my crew with a Bren gun, when he started a rush to break away from the compound. When the aircraft came round again for a second dive, there was no question of holding them. Italian prisoners ran stricken with panic in all directions. I feared that they might turn the guns of the fort on me, for they were still intact and there was no shortage of ammunition. However, there was nothing hostile in their intentions, although we were still rounding them up when evening fell. Part of the next day was spent in receiving instruction on the Breda gun from an Italian machine-gunner.

Perhaps the most irksome thing was the way in which these unhappy, wretched men insisted on our looking at endless photographs of their families. One of my men discovered the photograph of a beautiful girl with an address in Cairo scribbled on the back, together with several other documents in the fort. I confiscated it, intending to have some fun if I ever got back to the Delta on leave. When I was eventually evacuated from Tobruk, four months later, I paid a visit to the address, only to find that the house was occupied by a fat Egyptian. He denied all knowledge of the photograph, but in such a way as to arouse my suspicion of his motives. I handed it over to the Field Security Police and believe that it led to the arrest of an enemy agent.

When at last the Service Corps had relieved me of my wards I made my way back to the squadron in a captured enemy truck. They were sitting on the outskirts of Bardia, holding the ring while the Australians prepared their attack. The officers had constructed a wonderful underground mess in accordance with the squadron tradition. They had dug a large square hole in the sand, which they had covered with a pent roof, made from wood found on Sidi Azeiz aerodrome. We would sit round the table at night, smoking "V" cigarettes (or an even worse brand called Spitfires), drinking tea and reading novels. We were a happy little group and none would have thought that in two more years I would be the only one left in the battle. Peter Young, who was a gay, laughing young regular soldier, was to die of some obscure disease in Cyprus. No one could have thought that a person so full of life, with his happy swagger and his pipe rooted firmly between his teeth, was so soon to leave us. And there was Tom Chadwick, with whom he planned to share a cottage after the war, who was said to be one of England's most promising young artists and who was so soon to be killed with his brother on the battlefield at El Alamein. And John Bentley-Taylor, a gallant, phlegmatic farmer, who was to endure the ravages of a Japanese prison camp with the remainder of the squadron. If the future could have been revealed to us, as we sat round that flickering hurricane lamp in a hole near Bardia, we would never have believed it. We spent Christmas Day, 1940, in that dug-out. The Christmas dinner was bully beef and salty water, but the Colonel had authorised a special issue of rum. Our thoughts were with the people at home. The troops sang carols to the accompaniment of the mouth organ round their tents. In the evening we switched the wireless sets in the tanks to listen to the news. We were astounded to hear that all the troops in the Western Desert were getting turkey for Christmas. Some turkey!

Since I had not got a tank, the Squadron Leader gave me a roving commission to scrounge extra fare for the squadron. My first visit was to the Service Corps dump at Sollum, where I successfully looted two crates of oranges. I was astonished to see the large quantities of various rations in the dump, which somehow never seemed to get to the forward troops. I paid a visit to the fort at Sidi Omar, where I clashed with a full Colonel on the same errand. When I arrived, I was astonished to find a

THE WESTERN DESERT, 1940-1942.

large Parma cheese lying in the main gateway and I wasted no time in putting it into the back of the fitters' truck. While I was rummaging about in the fort for further treasures, I heard an irate voice shouting outside. At that particular moment I was concerned with the capture of a scrawny chicken which had miraculously survived both the bombardment and the notice of successive waves of hungry troops. The voice grew more insistent. I now connected it with the cheese, but chose to ignore it. At last I secured the capture of the chicken. The Colonel was now getting beyond control, so I decided to capitulate.

"Are you looking for a cheese, Colonel?"

"Of course I'm looking for a cheese. That cheese belongs to the Brigade mess and I'll trouble you to give it back to me immediately. Damned impudence!"

"I am sorry, Colonel. I did not realise it was yours or I would not have dreamed of taking it."

"Well, put the confounded thing in the back of my car. What's your name, anyway?"

Reluctantly I told him. Going to the back of the fitters' truck, I loudly ordered a Corporal to put the cheese in the back of the Colonel's staff car. At the same time I winked my right eye. A few minutes later the Colonel left, happily confident that the cheese was in his possession, when in reality it was still in the fitters' truck of the 3rd the King's Own Hussars.

On the way back to the leaguer near the Trigh Capuzzo, a wide track first made by the Turks which spanned the bulge of Cyrenaica, we came across four gazelle. They started up at the sound of the truck, bounding with graceful leaps towards the more deserted regions in the south. I was driving the fifteen-hundredweight truck at the time and decided to give chase. My batman stood beside me, rifle poised ready for a shot. They moved at an astonishing speed, so fast that our speedometer once registered forty miles an hour. The ground was so rough as to make it dangerous to travel at that speed. When we swung round to follow them on another tack, I had fears that the truck might capsize. Only their white buttocks gave away a camouflage which otherwise made them indistinguishable from the sand. They were such beautiful, effeminate animals that it seemed a pity to shoot them, especially since they were making such a gallant bid for safety, but fresh meat would be so welcome in the squadron that we could not afford to be soft-hearted. We had closed to within twenty yards when I told my servant to shoot. He fired five rounds before he brought one down, skidding and turning over in the dust. We had passed the spot by about thirty yards when I finally brought the truck to a halt, and it took us some minutes to find our kill in the sand. It was a large fat buck with great brown eyes and a tiny mouth still panting in its death-throes. We did not feel very brave hunters. I gutted it on the spot with a bayonet and slung it on the top of the truck. Laden with spoils which would gladden the hearts of the squadron, we motored back towards our camp.

The Australians began their attack on Bardia on January 2nd, my twentieth birthday. We did not take part in the battle, but sat on the top of the escarpment watching the fun. The rumble of the barrage was louder than anything we had known at Barrani and to it was added the thunder of guns from a naval monitor off the coast. There was some bitter fighting before the New Zealand Engineers bridged the anti-tank ditch, but after that the Australians rolled steadily forward behind the tanks. It was the same story over again. The Italians had still got no answer to the thick armour of the Matildas. By the second day the Australians had made deep penetrations into the defences on the south-east of Bardia, and it was obvious that the total collapse of the fortress was only a matter of time.

The 7th Armoured Division moved on during the night to complete the ring round Tobruk, the next objective. After a long approach march up the Trigh Capuzzo, we were foolish enough to place our officers' mess truck on a prominent bir or well, two miles east of the perimeter. We paid for this folly at ten o'clock on the following night when the Italians lobbed five shells in the middle of the leaguer, forcing a hasty move in the dark.

For the next fortnight the squadron was engaged in a rather peculiar and somewhat pointless military process known as "tapping in." It consisted of our sending our troops as close as possible to the Italian defences to tantalise them into firing at us. We would then plot the position of the gun-flash with a compass. It was not as dangerous as it sounds, owing to the hopeless inaccuracy of the Italian fire. Another favourite sport was baiting the "monkeys-on-a-pole." These were tall observation towers which the enemy had constructed all round the outer defences. A drain ran from our position in the Bir el Abiar sector to the edge of the perimeter wire. We would crawl down it and pot at these observation fellows with a rifle, trying to bring them down from their lofty perches. The Italians soon became wise to our game and hoisted dummies up to the tops of some of the poles. Dummies were very much in evidence at this time. When Tobruk was eventually taken, it was discovered that the enemy had shown a fine sense of humour by placing a dummy gun opposite one of our dummy tanks.

About a week before the big attack, we moved over to the other side of the El Adem Road to relieve the 6th Tanks. Our vehicles had had a gruelling time since the first attacks at Sidi Barrani and our casualties had been heavy from breakdowns. Several battalions were sent back to the Delta to refit and their vehicles were used to bring us up to strength again. I was very proud to receive a new tank.

It was a pleasant leaguer area in clean sand at the foot of the escarpment. The vegetation was quite thick, and blue flowers, green sage and camel scrub grew around the wheels of the trucks. There were even two man-sized bushes within sight, a rare phenomenon in that part of the desert. Each day a large coastal gun known to us all as Bardia Bill would fire heavy shells over our heads to land with a thump on El Adem airfield. There would be a small explosion from the centre of the fortress and then, some moments later, a shell would swish through the air over our heads. Its speed was so slow that sometimes we could follow the projectile through the air with our eyes.

As we sat on our tanks through the long days, gazing through binoculars at the enemy defences, we felt that we were men doing a man's job. We soon got to know the best routes by which to sneak up close to the perimeter without being observed. The cleverest way was to move your tank very slowly, avoiding a tell-tale dust cloud behind, in the hope that the Italians would mistake your black silhouette for a derelict vehicle. Every little movement of the enemy was reported back over the wireless. Occasionally they caught us napping by firing a shell close to the tanks. If a fountain of sand appeared on both sides of us, we knew that the enemy had bracketed our position and it was time to move.

I was on patrol outside the Pilastrino sector when the Australians began their second big attack. They cut through the south-east corner, where the anti-tank ditch was not deep owing to the hard surface of the ground, and encountered little opposition as they thrust deeper into the fortress area. One squadron of Matildas moved north-west and I moved parallel with them outside the wire. It was an impressive sight. The great tanks lumbered forward, spitting death from their guns, while hordes of Australians swaggered along behind, the sun glistening on their bayonets as they moved along with the same steady, loping gait. Sometimes a pill-box would show signs of fight, causing the leading files to take cover while a tank shot forward to pump two-pounder tracers into the enemy, but in a few moments they would be advancing again and a tiny knot of Italians bearing white flags would pass through them to the rear. I managed to get in one or two bursts at obstinate trenches with my Vickers from outside the wire. One of my tanks blew a large hole in its belly on an N5 Box mine. The driver was seriously wounded, with both legs smashed to pulp and his eyes blinded by acid from the batteries. We filled him up with morphia for he was in great pain, although he maintained the same cheerful spirit to the end. The doctor did not arrive until after dark and he was forced to operate on the spot without a proper anæsthetic and by the light of a candle. The poor fellow died before the morning. He was conscious to the last, knowing well that his legs had gone although he could not see them. Before he died, after cursing Hitler and the enemy, he told us to write to his next-of-kin. He died as he had lived—a happy, cheeky soldier full of impish wit.

As at Bardia, when it became obvious that victory at Tobruk was a foregone conclusion, the 7th Armoured Division continued its drive to the west, anxious to deliver the death-blow to the remnants of the Italian army. From here onwards there were no accurate maps. We advanced westward along the Trigh Enver Bey (first made by the Turks in 1911) towards the next fortress at Mekili, on the south-east corner of the Jebel Akhdar, an area of fertile, mountainous country between Derna and Benghazi. The going was good and the tanks made fair speed, rolling along like ships at sea with their aerials bent back against the wind, coloured pennants fluttering in the breeze. We stopped for ten minutes in every hour to knock new pins into the tracks and, more often than not, to fortify ourselves with a brew of tea. When evening fell, we were still making good progress through a barren country of flat desert with occasional sugar-loaf dunes. The track became faint, making it necessary to concentrate hard to follow its trace in the pale moonlight. I judged from our captured Italian map that we had to go for another thirteen miles along the track before we swung off towards the rendezvous on a bearing to the north. There was a lot of chatter over the wireless from units which had lost their way in the dark.

Suddenly there was a tremendous commotion from directly in front. Tracer shells criss-crossed over the sky and bullets whistled through the flags on the aerials overhead. We had no idea what it was all about for we had not been expecting trouble. The Squadron Leader decided to withdraw five miles down the track and to wait for daylight to clarify the situation. As we turned our backs on the disturbance, star-shells began to light up the desert all around. When dawn came, we found ourselves almost under the walls of the Italian fort of Mekili. The inaccurate map had nearly led us into taking it by an unpremeditated assault in the dark.

We pushed our patrols towards the enemy defences and the main part of the squadron leaguered in a "ghot" (the Arab name for the shallow depressions in the sand in which camel scrub and blue flowers grew in thick profusion), until we had solved the problem of our exact location. Plaintive messages came over the wireless sets all morning from units which had lost themselves during the night and now had no idea in which direction to turn. Red and green Verey lights were going up all round us, the inevitable sign of confusion in an army. I was posted on a hill above the "ghot" to keep look-out towards the west.

It was a fine day and I was enjoying myself in the sun, reading snatches from an anthology called *Knapsack*. A silver fox ran across my front and I hollered loud as I watched it through my glasses. It was a lean, wispy looking animal with a splendid silver brush. And then my attention was attracted to a line of fourteen large tanks coming line abreast towards us. I took them to be a squadron of the cruiser battalion which had lost its way in the dark, until I suddenly noticed that they were not flying the normal recognition pennants. I still could not believe that they were hostile, for the Italians had never dared to make a counter-attack since the beginning of the campaign. I hesitated. Their suspension looked strangely unfamiliar. And then I gave the alarm. There was no sense in taking chances and that battle line looked ominously hostile. The Squadron Leader took one look at them from beside my tank and then, running down the slope, he shouted the order to withdraw to the south, having no doubt in his mind that they were indeed Italian M 13's. By the time the squadron had begun to move, one sergeant not bothering to replace a fan he had dismantled, the enemy had closed to a range of about three hundred yards. Our light machine guns could not hope to penetrate their thick armour, yet their thirty-seven millimetre guns would make short work of a light tank.

I moved in the rear of the squadron with one other officer to give what covering fire we could to facilitate the retreat. The enemy were firing now as their tanks lumbered forward in a long black line. I was reminded of a school of sharks chasing small fish in a calm sea. We had a slight superiority over them in regard to speed, which enabled us to halt to fire a few defiant bursts from odd ridges without losing too much of our lead. And then we came to an escarpment, which took so much time to negotiate that we forfeited all our advantage. As I was speeding away over the flat ground at the bottom, the fourteen black monsters opened fire from the top of the cliff. The first shell came into the bottom of the tank by some miraculous ricochet; a few moments later another penetrated under the gun mantle, which was facing the rear, and passed between the gunner and me to burst in the petrol tank behind the driver. Flames shot up in front of my face as I gave the order to abandon tank, and as we were hurling ourselves out of the hatch, another shell passed through the wireless set. We began to run; three fat little figures pelting across the sand with tracer bullets cutting up the earth at their feet. My driver's leather jerkin was on fire and he threw it off as he ran. I was panic-stricken and I could not think what to do. I felt that I could not run much farther, and the only cover was a slight fold in the ground some two hundred yards ahead. I thought of waving my handkerchief. Then our prayers were answered when another tank from the squadron swung round to pick us up from under the very nose of the enemy. Moving straight across the front of the enemy line, he paused for a moment to allow us to climb on to the hull. We kissed the sides of that tank as we sped away to safety through a hail of fire. The only hurt we received was from small stones thrown up by shells which narrowly missed the tank. The Italians were stupid enough to halt, gloating over their kill, while they looted the wreck of my tank. While they were engaged in this, they were taken by surprise by a squadron of cruisers which had come up to the rescue from the rear. Seven

Italian tanks were destroyed before the remainder made their escape behind the defences of Mekili. They had paid for their brief taste of success with a hard knock which dissuaded them from launching another counter-attack for the rest of the campaign.

For the next three days we sat astride the track between Mekili and Derna, attacking odd trucks which attempted to run the gauntlet. I had received another tank to replace "Beau Sabreur," the one I had lost the day before. I particularly remember how two Italian motor cyclists successfully escaped through the machine-gun fire of four tanks, miraculously avoiding tracer bullets which seemed to be hitting the ground all around them. On the third day the Italians abandoned Mekili and withdrew into the hilly country of the Jebel Akhdar. We tried to follow them for a day, but the going was too difficult for our tired, worn-out tanks. At the time, although there may have been some reason for it, we regarded this as the only mistake in the direction of the campaign. It should have been possible to have prevented the escape of the Italians by more effectively sealing the ring round the fort. In the end the decision was justified by the Italian army being trapped in the desert south of Benghazi, after it had lost time and been sadly depleted in vehicle strength by its gruelling drive through the Jebel, although I doubt if this was foreseen at the time.

After our short abortive thrust into the Jebel, we withdrew to a pleasant leaguer area on the flat sand north of the Sheiba Track and south of the mountains. We sat there for a week, maintaining our vehicles while there were rumours of the sappers building a road through the hills to Benghazi. For the first time for weeks, we washed and changed our clothes. For most of the campaign the normal ration of water was half a gallon per man each day. Here, however, there was plenty good water in wells at the foot of the Jebel and we were able to have a considerable extra ration for washing. Splashing about in the sun, we revelled in the pleasure of a bath in an old tarpaulin, after having had to sponge ourselves down with two inches of water in the bottom of a mug for two months. The sun was quite hot and the crews walked about stripped to the waist most of the day. Lines were run between the tanks to hang out the washing and it was a common sight to see a sunburnt trooper dressed in a woollen Balaclava and a pair of khaki shorts, squatting on his haunches over socks boiling in a petrol can, stirring them with a stick with one hand, while he played a mouth organ with the other. One could often see an officer or a man sitting on an upturned petrol tin having his hair cut. Some of the men started a fashion for having their heads shaved, leaving odd tufts of hair in various patterns on their scalps. By this time we had become experts in desert lore. We knew all the little tricks for distilling or filtering dirty water, for getting a quick brew of tea on the move by tying a can full of water to the hot exhaust pipe of the tank, and for getting a good night's sleep by turning the vehicles to protect us from the wind. We had an endless repertoire of desert yarns. The favourite was the story of the first 11th Hussar officer to be captured by the Italians, who threw a great banquet in his honour at Fort Capuzzo. He entered the hall dressed in his normal ragged desert attire and looked down the table lined with immaculate, bemedalled, little Italians. "Is there anybody here who speaks English?" he said. A fat General, proud of his linguistic talent, said that he did. "Well, in that case, you can go to hell for a start!" Another popular tale concerned an officer in the 7th Hussars who told his Colonel when asked why he had produced only two of three prisoners, that the other one was so small that he threw him back.

It was while we were enjoying this pleasant respite from the battle that the first German aeroplanes appeared in the desert. On two occasions a flight of twin-engined Me 110's came in at a low height to strafe the leaguers round Mekili. We remarked upon the difference between the German low-level attacks and the Italian haphazard high-level bombing. There was nothing timid about the German approach, and, although we did not recognise it at the time, these aircraft were the heralds of a new deadly menace in the desert—the Deutsche Afrika Korps which was rudely to shake us out of all the notions we had acquired in this "gentleman's war."

On the 6th February we received sudden orders to move westwards at top speed. It appeared that the armoured cars had seen large Italian columns moving south from Benghazi, presumably in an attempt to evacuate Cyrenaica. All records were broken for cross-desert marches. Over terrible going, which jarred every bone in our bodies, we flogged the battered old tanks into a last supreme effort. Moving almost non-stop across virgin desert, the 4th Armoured Brigade covered a hundred and fifty miles in thirty-six hours. By midday on 7th February the armoured cars had taken Msus without much opposition. In the afternoon, we began to notice odd patches of green grass from the tops of the tanks. After three months in the sand and the camel scrub, these few green blades were like a long draught of clear, cool water to a thirsty man. Soon the grass became thicker and we came across Bedouins with large flocks of sheep. We felt that a phase of our lives was over. We stopped for a few moments by a tall water-pump driven by sails, where we revelled in the luxury of unlimited water.

During the late evening, as we cut the road, our khaki drill was reduced to wet clinging rags by a heavy rainstorm. Four cruiser tanks held the block on the road and during the night we heard the sound of heavy firing.

At about three o'clock in the morning we were ordered to move up to their position to escort back a number of prisoners, including a complete heavy anti-aircraft regiment, to Brigade Headquarters. We had a certain amount of difficulty in finding them in the dark, even with the help of a guide, but we got to them at about four o'clock. The cruisers had had a glorious shoot at some Italian transport and the area was littered with burnt-out lorries and guns. The position was being shelled by some Italian artillery, which frightened the prisoners so much that we had difficulty in forming them up in the captured lorries for the move back. Then began one of the most miserable night marches I can remember. The rain was pouring into the turrets of the tanks, driving hard into our faces so that it was sheer misery to have to concentrate on the bearing. Every few miles one of the Italian trucks would stall or stick in soft sand and would have to be towed out by one of the tanks. I lost my way near Brigade Headquarters and spent the rest of the night gazing into the rain for green Verey lights, which were supposed to be being fired by the Brigade Major. Included in the column was an Italian pilot in a civilian car. He had a supply of excellent chianti, but most of all we cast jealous eyes on his fur coat and fur-lined jackboots. When somebody succumbed to the temptation and quietly relieved him of the coat, he appealed to the Squadron Leader, who ordered the offender to return it. Sheepishly, reluctantly, it was handed back, although I would have been prepared to have staked a lot of money that he would lose it again before the day was out.

We delivered the prisoners after dawn, but it was eleven o'clock in the morning before we returned to the area of the road. By then the Battle of Beda Fomm was well under way. At about the time of the first skirmishes around Tobruk, the Italians had landed a brand-new armoured division equipped with their famous M 13 medium tank, which was more than a match for our Light Tanks Mark VIB. We had had the first brush with them near Mekili, when our cruisers had proved that they could be beaten, but now the whole division was being thrown in *en masse* in an attempt to break through to Tripoli. Jim Richardson, a Squadron Leader of the 2nd Tanks, takes all the honours for the battle. Putting his eight cruiser tanks around a pimple-shaped mound on which stood the mosque of Beda Fomm, he broke up wave after wave of Italian tanks. The M 13's were coming in along the line of the road in batches of thirty tanks, but each time their attack met disaster when they encountered the cruisers around the mosque. Their crews were brave enough, but their tactics were almost too crude to be sane. It must be admitted that there were certain grave deficiencies in the design of their tanks, but that alone does not account for their conspicuous failure. Although their guns had to be elevated by hand while ours had a shoulder piece to facilitate rapid fire, and although they only had one wireless set to every thirty tanks, they had such a tremendous advantage in numbers that if they had shown just a little more sense they would have won the day. But it seemed that the Italian commanders could only think of launching one suicidal frontal attack after another down the line of the road. Behind the battle area a dense mass of Italian equipment was jammed nose to tail along the road as far as Soloch.

The battle went on all day, until the pimple by the mosque was littered with burning tanks. We hovered around the edge of the tank battle in our lighter vehicles, reporting movements and firing odd bursts at the column of transport on the road. Once we went up to the pimple to take over some prisoners from Jim Richardson during a lull in the battle. He was smiling, strong and confident from the turret of his cruiser, and he told us not to waste time in picking out the best pairs of binoculars, but to hurry the prisoners back to the rear before another attack developed. As we were ushering them along like cowboys on a round-up, a malicious Breda gun spotted the black mass of frightened humanity and opened fire. As each shell came over,

65

their heads went down like ears of corn in a breeze until at last we were out of range. Around the cruiser position Italian tanks were burning, their ammunition exploding into the air like fireworks and their wounded crews lying in pitiful little knots beside them.

I was told to patrol to the east of the road in the afternoon. I moved up gingerly towards the Italian column, hoping that they would not observe my silhouette in the middle of a herd of camels. Suddenly three shells crumped around the tank, wounding a camel in the neck. I withdrew rapidly out of range, followed, to my horror, by thirty big black Italian tanks, which were attempting to move down the east side of the road for the first time. My wireless set was out of action, so that the only way to warn the Colonel of this new menace was to drive into Battalion Headquarters myself. He was terribly worried by my unwelcome news, since every cruiser was already committed in the battle round the pimple. I moved back to watch the flanks of the Italian thrust. For some reason they came on very cautiously, pausing often on the tops of ridges to fire one or two shells at me, although I was sensible enough to keep out of range. Before they reached a dangerous distance from Battalion Headquarters, they were halted by the sort of miracle which sometimes happens in war. Six cruisers of the 1st Tanks arrived from Derna, where they had been supporting the Australians, and wasted no time before they went into action. Their commander stopped for a moment by my tank to ask where the battle was. I told him that it was a thousand yards ahead and that if he advanced another two hundred yards he would find out all about it. Without a moment's hesitation he plunged his tanks into the battle, cutting into the Italian M 13's like a hot knife into butter. Four enemy tanks were set on fire before the remainder scuttled back to the other side of the road. It reminded me somehow of the story of Blücher at Waterloo.

When night fell we withdrew from the road to lick our wounds. The Italians were still in great strength and everyone was pessimistic about our chances on the morrow. The 2nd Tanks had fought a brilliant action, knocking out over a hundred enemy tanks, but there seemed no end to the enemy's resources and we were very thin on the ground. It had been an heroic stand, but the odds were too great. Twice during the night I paddled over in my stockinged feet through the puddles to ask the Squadron

Leader if he had heard the rattle of tracks coming towards us from the road. Together we sat there in the drizzle, listening.

In the morning we girded up our loins for the fight and moved back towards the road, determined to keep the initiative to the end. There was an amazing silence over the battlefield and not a sign of movement. The only Italians were the dead bodies round the hulks on the pimple. We moved slowly across the road, suspecting a trap. Suddenly an Italian armoured car darted across the front of the right-hand squadron. Every gun in the regiment blazed at it until it was reduced to a burning, tangled mass of metal. When the guns had finished firing we moved on again in the same uncanny silence. And then, in the dunes by the coast, we found the answer to the mystery. For ten miles as far as the eye could see, there was a mass of abandoned lorries and tanks. The enemy had panicked in the night after his vehicles had got stuck in soft sand during an attempt to wriggle past us down the coast. Leaving their lorries, their guns and their tanks, almost all undamaged, they had bolted down to the beaches. It was a glorious victory. The Italian Army of Cyrenaica was completely smashed. Not a handful escaped to Tripoli.

For the next three days we rounded up the prisoners and towed in captured transport. It was a beautiful end to a hard campaign. The lorries were crammed with all sorts of loot which the Italians had hoped to get to Tripoli, and the tanks were so full of bottles of wine, boxes of chocolate and tins of fruit that we could not traverse the turrets. There were china plates and silver cutlery in the officers' mess; we all wore clean Italian shirts; every officer in the regiment had a civilian car and every soldier had a motor cycle; the fitters found tools they had only dreamed of; the doctors had medical equipment which would not have disgraced the best London hospital; our wrists were adorned with brand-new watches; round our necks dangled Zeiss binoculars; on our belts were dainty little Beretta automatics and in our kits were the finest cameras in the world; captured flags fluttered gaily from our wireless aerials; and for the first time in three months we tasted fresh eggs and vegetables. We were so drunk with success that we thought it the end of the war and frivolously talked of policing Libya until the Germans surrendered.

A popular rumour amongst the men was that the Italians

had women delivered to the front in a red truck called the "Passion Wagon." It was even said that the 11th Hussars had captured one such wagon near Capuzzo. On the day after the battle I was approaching a group of deserted lorries when my gunner caught a glimpse of a skirt disappearing into the back of a red truck. "Cor, sir, the Passion Wagon!" Our hearts were thumping with excitement as we drove up. A dark-eyed Italian signorina with a baby in her arms peered with terror from behind the tailboard. Going on her knees, she begged us for mercy. With a fine show of gallantry, I kissed her hand and told her that there was no need to be afraid of the British, who were gentlemen. She would be granted safe conduct through the lines. It appeared that she was the wife of a Benghazi jeweller who had been fleeing with the army to Tripoli. It was no small problem to be responsible for the welfare of a woman in the sort of conditions we lived under in the desert. Amused at their embarrassment and rubbing our hands at the opportunity to have a dig at the staff, we passed her on to Brigade Headquarters.

While the rest of the squadron was engaged in towing in the captured transport, my troop was detailed to bury the Italian bodies around the pimple. It was perhaps the most unpleasant job I have been given in the whole war. The corpses had been exposed to the sun for five days and the stench was appalling. My men were magnificent and concealed their revulsion with fine Cockney wit. Most of the bodies were charred beyond recognition and we were compelled to shovel them out of their shattered tanks with picks and spades. Under an Italian Colonel's body we found an attache-case crammed full with lira notes. The men were suspicious and unbelieving when the Squadron Leader confiscated them in accordance with the latest Army Regulation. They could not be made to realise that it would be wrong to allow them to keep the money, which they thought that they had earned by the right of conquest. One tank was so horrifying that we left it to the last. Known to the troops as Madam Tussauds, it was an M 13 which had not caught fire when hit by a two-pounder shell. Instead, the shell had whistled round inside the hull to decapitate the four members of the crew, who were still sitting, headless, in their action stations. I climbed inside to open the hatch, but it was too much. I was sick in the sand. I decided to tow it into a safe place, where we could blow it up by setting fire to the ammunition with diesel oil. We hitched it up with a tow-rope to another tank and, taking up the strain, began to pull. Madame Tussauds gave a cough, a splutter and began to move forwards under its own steam. A curl of blue smoke came from the exhaust. Gathering speed, it snapped the tow-rope and passed the other tank. We gazed open-mouthed, unbelieving, terrified, as it rolled down the hill to the wadi driven by four headless men, whose brains were spattered round the wall inside. I crossed myself. It stopped in the exact spot in which I had intended to blow it up. We began to believe in the supernatural, although I suppose the logical explanation was that the engine was still switched on and one of the dead men had his foot on the accelerator. The men were horrified and it was several minutes before we could bring ourselves to sneak up to it again. Somebody said, "Sorry, Toni, me boy, you are a game bastard, but you stink so much, we can't give you a proper funeral," as we poured in the diesel oil and the tension was broken. As I set light to the trail of petrol, I prayed for forgiveness.

CHAPTER FOUR

THE FIRST WITHDRAWAL IN CYRENAICA

AFTER THE Battle of Beda Fomm, almost all the troops which had taken part in the first advance went back to Cairo to refit. We were left behind as part of the so-called 2nd Armoured Division, which consisted mainly of fresh troops from England. Although this formation went under the courtesy title of a division, in reality it consisted of no more than a weak brigade. There were two regiments equipped with worn-out light tanks of which we were one, one regiment of Italian M 13's salvaged from the battlefield and one regiment of old cruisers recently arrived from England. In those days there were no tank transporters and the cruiser regiment had long out-driven its official track mileage, mostly in an unopposed approach march from Tobruk. We were told after the battle of Beda Fomm that our own light tanks could not be expected to go for much more than another five hundred miles, which did not allow us much latitude in the event of a battle. In point of fact, all these tanks did more than the experts ever expected, and we had far exceeded our official mileages in patrolling before the enemy attacked. The situation therefore amounted to Cyrenaica being held by a skeleton force while the greater part of the Middle East Forces were engaged in fighting in Greece, Malta and East Africa.

Round about the middle of February we moved down to the area by El Agheila on the Tripoli frontier. Here the firm going of the Cyrenaica Plain was linked to Tripolitania by a narrow neck of land between the sea in the north and the soft sand of the desert proper in the south. This bottleneck was spanned by two salt marshes—one between El Agheila Fort and Mersa Brega, and the other along the line of the frontier. Behind these two salt marshes on the Benghazi side was a line of hills to the west of Agedabia, which might be said to be in the shoulders rather than the neck of the bottle. The sand sea was separated from this strip of hard going by a deep rift valley called the Wadi Faregh.

It was hard to understand our tactics at that time. We had lost all contact with the enemy, but the Brigadier insisted upon our doing quite pointless patrols up and down the Tripoli frontier, using up our valuable reserve of track mileage. The main part of the Brigade was leaguered in the hills by Agedabia, so that the tanks were required to cover about sixty miles a day to get to and from their patrol positions. One would have thought that we would have done better to have moved up to the line of the second salt marsh, which was at least in the narrow part of the bottleneck and would have reduced our need for movement to a minimum. I have always attributed a large share of the blame for the disasters of this campaign to the multiplicity of the staffs. There were no less than a Corps Headquarters, a Divisional Headquarters and a Brigade Headquarters all controlling the lives of four tired regiments. Apart from the fact that none of these headquarters had any experience of desert warfare, there was that fatal desire of new boys to do something, however stupid. In order to keep their maps covered with gay pins, they marched us up and down like so many Liberty Horses at a circus, although when they eventually got us involved in serious fighting they could not agree on what to do. What is more, it was found that their plans for the line of retreat were so inadequate as to be almost non-existent. There were only two dumps across the desert behind us—one at Msus and the other at Mekili—which were too wide apart and contained but a bare fraction of our needs. Such was the set-up when we moved down from Beda Fomm to the frontier.

It was only natural that we should resent the interference of the new boys, who were contemptuously dubbed "palefaces" or "inglesi," so that much of my criticism can be put down to desert snobbery. If the truth were told, we never stood a chance of success.

For about a fortnight the squadron patrolled along the salt marshes and down to the Wadi Faregh, making going maps and contacting the local Bedouin camps. Most of the wells in the foothills were full after the heavy rain and there was no shortage of water. It was a pleasant life, sitting on the top of one's tank in the hot sun, reading a book or writing a letter home. During the whole of this period we did not once see an enemy vehicle, although the entire regiment spent several hours stalking a King's Dragoon Guard armoured car during a reconnaissance in force over the frontier. In fact the first rumours of German troops in Tripoli did not reach us until the middle of March, which goes a large way towards proving that the headquarters were unaware of the great menace which was developing, since at that time information did not take long to percolate down to the lowest levels.

At the beginning of the last week in March our light tanks had at last begun to give up the unequal struggle against the bumps and the camel scrub. We were therefore moved up to the old battlefield at Beda Fomm to re-equip with salvaged Italian tanks, as the 6th Tanks had already done. In some ways we were proud to have these big tanks with their 37-millimetre guns, but on the other hand it was impossible not to think of the charred bodies, the gaping cracks in the armour and the sweet smell of death we had known amongst the same vehicles two months before. The diesel oil stench was something we had always associated with Italians, and however much we painted the insides of the tanks, we could not remove the awful bloodstains round the turrets. The battlefield itself had a sinister smell of death and it was not unusual to come across the foot of some long-dead corpse poking up from its thin covering of sand. The only instructional handbooks were written in Italian, so that we had to find out most of the things about these vehicles by experiment. They were difficult tanks to drive, since the lubrication system was so bad that the gears were unbelievably stiff. There was also a grave weakness in their tendency to overheat when driven across rough going. The turrets, which were taken from a half-damaged tank to make up another, were not always a good fit, which made it hard work to traverse them.

German aircraft began to appear in large numbers at about this time. They often shot up transport on the coast road, parachute mines were dropped in Benghazi and leaguers near the frontier were frequently strafed. I believe that our own Air Force only consisted of one squadron of Hurricanes at Agedabia so that there was very little opposition to the German raids.

Although the German attack had been in progress by then for forty-eight hours, the first intimation we received was from a convoy of Service Corps trucks speeding helter-skelter down the road towards Benghazi. Surprised at the frantic speed of his vehicle, we managed to halt one driver, who told us through excited panting breath that the Germans had broken through on a wide front, that the British Army was in full retreat and that if we did not want to get captured we had better get moving.

After an unsuccessful attempt to contact Brigade Headquarters, the 6th Tanks Colonel decided to move to Antelat, which was on the line of retreat to the east. As the sun was setting, we rolled forward in our battleship-grey captured tanks, all determined to put a stop to the German game.

The scene at Antelat was an indescribable mess of disorganisation. Trucks, carriers and tanks were jammed together in a confused huddle with many small detachments separated from their parent units. An air of panic, even of terror and of lost confidence, ran through the whole army, which had apparently been surprised by a strong German attack along the coast on the 29th March. The units had been widely dispersed as a precaution against air attack and had been in no position to resist the enemy drive. We heard pitiful tales of the failure of our much-vaunted cruiser tanks in an action against German Mark III's, when four cruisers had been lost without damage to the enemy. The Tower Hamlet Rifles had fought a gallant little action against the German infantry on the coast, and claimed to have killed a large number of Germans, although they had been compelled to withdraw after forty-eight hours in the face of a strong enemy tank attack. In consequence they were perhaps more disorganised than the rest of the Brigade, which was saying a lot, and odd penny packets of carriers came into our leaguer during the night.

We were perhaps the most compact organised unit left in the force and as such were ordered to leaguer to the south of Antelat with a view to covering the withdrawal the next day. The tale of the next seven days is perhaps one of the most inglorious in the history of the British Army. Mr. Churchill made a speech on the wireless, which caused hot resentment amongst the troops, when he as much as accused the 2nd Armoured Division of rank cowardice. It was unjust, since we were so outnumbered that a stand-up fight would have resulted in our annihilation and if any one is to blame for the frittering away of our strength in an inexpert withdrawal, it is the staff. The courage of the troops never faltered, and if it had, the tale of the siege of Tobruk might have been very different.

When the Brigade began their headlong retreat on the 1st April, the 6th Tanks and ourselves remained in hull-down positions south of Antelat prepared to fight to the end against the Germans. We had not been there for more than an hour when Brigade Headquarters ordered us to move north behind the Brigade, although there was still no contact with the enemy. It

73

appeared that the staff had abandoned the original plan of withdrawing through our dumps on the line Antelat-Msus-Mekili for a new scheme of covering the retreat of the Australians in the north by moving up to El Abiar near Benghazi. Even the most junior subaltern knew that this was unwise, for an armoured regiment cannot fight without its supplies and our nearest dump was at Msus.

It is painful to attempt to describe the muddle in which the column withdrew to the north. Armoured cars, guns, trucks and tanks were mixed up without regard to their units; jumbled, jolting forward at a speed which indicated that the panic of the higher command had communicated itself to the troops. A good pointer to the state of mind of the Brigade was one particular scare when it was reported that German armoured cars had mixed themselves in with the vehicles of the column—a report which could only have held water in a totally demoralised and disorganised force. It eventually transpired that these so-called enemy armoured cars were a patrol of the King's Dragoon Guards coming in from the rear.

We came to a halt in the evening near a defile through the escarpment at Es-Scheledeima, a high ridge which ran north to south parallel with the coast road to Benghazi. Through the glasses we could see vehicles moving up the main road towards the port, which must by then have been in German hands. We were now involved in an awful pause of indecision. There were frequent conferences at Brigade Headquarters, until at last the Colonel of the 6th Tanks called an Officers' Conference, at which he shocked us all by his grave tidings. He told us that the original plan of the Brigade had been to proceed to El Abiar to cover the flank of the Australians, but that they had now realised that we were nearly out of petrol, to say nothing of water. The R.A.F. had reported that German tanks had entered the dump at Msus, setting fire to all the stores. We were therefore in the unenviable position of being an armoured brigade in the middle of the desert, with nobody on our flanks, cut off from our supplies. Visions of several years in a prison camp flitted across our minds. He told us that he had decided to proceed to Msus in defiance of orders from Brigade, in the hope that something might be salvaged from the dump, and he hoped that all officers would agree with his decision. Needless to say we agreed that it was the only course to take, even if it involved a risk of our having to capitulate through thirst, because it was quite plain that a move to El Abiar would mean the loss of our tanks. What a miserable anti-climax it was to the glory of our first advance across Cyrenaica, and I am afraid that we put all the blame for our disaster on the shoulders of the new boys from England. If only the Germans had not been merciful enough to spare us from bombing at that time, I fear that we might never have escaped from the trap.

The whole Brigade finally moved through the defile along the track to Msus, jammed together in a tight knot between the cliffs. Behind us our trail was marked by a line of fires, where trucks and tanks had been abandoned and sabotaged. Almost back as far as Antelat we could see the spirals of black smoke which marked the retreat of a defeated army. If a truck broke down, even for a small thing like a puncture, the drivers were afraid to lose the main column by halting to repair it. Instead, they put a match to the petrol tank and leapt on to a passing vehicle. Our Italian tanks were proving unequal to the strain of prolonged trans-desert travel and gears were jamming, cylinder blocks were cracking from over-heating and steering was breaking down, so that the track was littered with the corpses of armoured fighting vehicles.

The dump at Msus was intact, disproving the alarmist reports from the R.A.F., but the disorganisation of the Brigade precluded proper replenishment. The R.A.S.C. personnel had long since withdrawn, so that the first units to arrive obtained the best of the stores, including all the tinned milk, an important thing to an army which marched on tea. The supply services had made a terrible omission when they constructed the dump in that there were no supplies of diesel oil. All our Italian tanks and the fifty per cent of our transport which consisted of captured vehicles ran on diesel oil. This was tantamount to writing off half the Brigade.

The Brigadier took the only course by ordering a large number of the tanks to be sabotaged, so that their fuel could be used to replenish the remainder.

We leaguered east of Msus while this terrible work of destruction was taking place, my squadron having been chosen as one of those to be disbanded. Then at last the Germans took a hand in the matter for the first time since we had withdrawn from Agedabia. The sky was suddenly filled with wicked, diving Stukas, which screamed down on the leaguers like mosquitoes on an uncovered body. We bolted away from the vehicles or crawled under the tanks, lying with our faces to the ground as the bombs crumped around. Several trucks were destroyed in the leaguer, sending up the same old clouds of black smoke.

At the moment when the squadron received its first casualties in the campaign, except for those who had been lost in the haste of the withdrawal, our famous doctor, Tom Summerville, whom we had all thought to be on leave in Cairo, arrived in a captured Italian ambulance with the Regimental White Horse painted on the side. Tom was a wonderful old man who had refused countless offers of command of a base hospital because he preferred to stay with the regiment, and was the best possible fillip to our morale. Later he was reported missing at Derna when a shell was seen to hit his ambulance, but when we eventually escaped from Tobruk we found him waiting for us in Cairo, having evaded the Germans by driving through their lines in a fifteen-hundredweight truck. He finally died of starvation in Crete, when he refused to leave the wounded on the beaches at Sphakia, walking out of the back door of the dressing-station when the German doctors came in the front.

When we had burned our tanks, we were told to attempt to drive through to Cairo in the few vehicles remaining to us. I accompanied the Squadron Leader with at least ten other men in a fifteen-hundredweight. First we paid a visit to the 3rd Hussars to say good-bye to the Colonel, from whose command we had been detached when we first took over our Italian tanks.

He was sitting in the top of his Light Tank Mark VIB surrounded by the remnants of the regiment. Dour little man that he was, with his peaked cap tilted over his eyes, he did not intend to let us share in his depression. The sun was blazing hot and I flopped down on my back in the shadow of his tank while the Squadron Leader discussed the situation. The heat and the strain of the march had been most exhausting, especially since we had had no water ration for two days. An impudent little coloured bird hopped on to my chest, but I was too tired to be surprised. A hand stretched down from the turret of the tank, holding a water-bottle. "Here, boy, have a drink of this." Unthinkingly, I took two greedy gulps before I realised what the Colonel had done. There was no more water to be had and yet he, who must have been as thirsty as I was, had given me his last reserve. Such little things lead men to die for one another.

Before we left we learned that the Brigade was immobilised by another lapse of indecision on the part of Brigade Headquarters. Instead of moving on the line to the next dump at Mekili, where Divisional Headquarters was already situated, they were obsessed with the idea of moving north to El Abiar once more. Later the miserable remnants of the 2nd Armoured Division fled northwards through the Jebel to the coast road, which they followed to Tobruk, leaving the Divisional Headquarters to be captured at Mekili.

We ourselves drove on through the night into the cool uplands of the Jebel Akhdar. We followed narrow paths, winding round the sides of steep cliffs, until we hit the road near Tecnis. On the way, when our mouths were parched and dry from thirst, we found an abandoned water-cart, full of delicious cold water. It was like a gift from heaven.

After a short halt near Tecnis we drove down the main road through hills covered with rhododendron bushes, past white-walled Italian cottages and through herds of sheep to Derna. When we reached the bottom of the pass, which winds down some five hundred feet from the mountains to the flat coastal plain, we at last halted for some rest, thinking ourselves safe. We cooked a meagre breakfast and bathed in the surf, all relieved to think that we had escaped the clutches of the enemy.

At about eight o'clock, loud explosions from Derna town indicated that the Engineers were demolishing stores, a thought which started new fears racing through our minds.

The men were packing the kit on to the truck for a rapid move on to Tobruk, when we noticed an endless column of trucks coming nose to croup down the pass. When we reached the road from the beach, we met the leading vehicles. It was the last of the Brigade, which had overtaken us in the speed of its withdrawal and, like us, it was retreating at full speed towards Tobruk. Trucks, guns, armoured cars and a few tanks were mixed up carelessly in the disorganised column. We felt ourselves infected by the general air of *sauve qui peut* as we fitted ourselves into one of the few gaps in the convoy.

As we were passing through Derna town, a great explosion shook the sides of the truck and we noticed a cloud of white-brown smoke half-way up the pass, where the road wound out of the town towards Tobruk. The column halted for some unknown reason, trucks and armoured cars wedged in a solid traffic jam

77

in the narrow streets. One or two drunken soldiers came staggering with crates of whisky from the direction of the N.A.A.F.I.,
calling to their comrades the wonderful news that unlimited
drink was there for the taking. These were the gallant boys whom
the newspapers at home would laud for their glorious determination, for their crusade against the evil German, and for the dogged
spirit with which they withstood disaster. And strangely enough
it was true. Old-fashioned soldiers might have shot them out of
hand for looting, but the few officers there seemed to understand
that these brave spirits were at least showing that the enemy
had no terrors for them. In a few days they would be the ones
who would bolster up the round-eyed, pale-faced youths, now
gazing apprehensively at the top of the pass or searching the sky
for aeroplanes, their knuckles showing white against the steering-
wheels. For, after all, free beer was free beer even if the army
had been defeated, and it would be a pity to leave it to the
Germans.

A disturbing rumour was spreading down the column to the
effect that the loud explosion had been the sappers blowing the
pass in front of us. I believe some Generals at the tail of the jam
decided to find a way round the block via Giovanni Berta, twelve
miles behind us on the road. They were all captured by a German
patrol before they had gone very far. The vehicles in front had
no alternative but to stay with the rest of the column, jammed as
they were, radiator to tailboard. Then a more encouraging
report was passed from vehicle to vehicle down from the front.
The hole in the road, which had been intended to delay the
Germans for days, was not very deep, and the men up front were
repairing it with rubble and tar barrels.

After about an hour the column began to move again. A
large Italian lorry caused a certain amount of delay when it
refused to climb the steep slope, but somebody eventually tumbled
it over the cliff to lie as a warning to incautious drivers at the
bottom of the ravine.

Before we reached the top, our fears were again roused by the
sound of shells and machine-gun fire. A small force of German
armoured cars, a field-gun and a few infantry had cut the road
by the aerodrome. The column did not halt, some trucks pulling
off into the shelter of the wadis at the top of the cliff and others
running the gauntlet through the German fire.

We ourselves drove our swaying, overcrowded fifteen-hundredweight at top speed through the danger zone, until we reached the quiet open road on the other side. We learned afterwards that the Germans were eventually driven off in a gallant, desperate little action by odd fighting units which emerged in turn at the top of the pass. A few tanks and an Australian anti-tank gun took most of the credit for getting the column through. Only by a narrow margin did we avoid a reversal of the Battle of Beda Fomm.

Near Gazala, half-way to Tobruk, we drove through the positions of the Northumberland Fusiliers, who had been moved up from the rear. It did us good to see the quiet, efficient confidence of a fresh unit.

We were stopped by the Military Police on the outskirts of Tobruk and ordered to proceed to a certain wadi near the coast, where the Brigade was re-forming. The defences of Tobruk were in much the same state as when we had captured them from the Italians. Tobruk has no natural strength, although it has been misnamed a fortress, and I had little confidence in our ability to hold it. However, I had not reckoned with that stubborn trait of the British, which refuses after a time to allow any one to push them about. It is usually a patient, docile race, even in defeat, but there comes a time when that obstinate streak appears, and, digging in its feet, it refuses to budge for any one. I have heard people say that the Australians are only good in attack, but those critics can never have understood what happened at Tobruk and can never have seen a too true, fair dinkum, bloody-minded Australian in a prison camp. For this reason, neither true conservatism nor true socialism will ever work in Britain. Similarly, we will never have and never have had a highly disciplined army. On the other hand, there were certain military factors which contributed to our first successful defence of Tobruk and which were not present when the South Africans surrendered in 1942. The Germans were surprised by the speed of our head-long withdrawal, since they had only planned for a limited advance to Agedabia when they first attacked at El Agheila. They were never able to concentrate their whole effort on Tobruk, since they were always embarrassed by an extremely active little British force on the Egyptian frontier. Futhermore, they were given a false impression of the strength of the defences when their first two attacks foundered on unsuspected minefields.

We were still gathering in the wadi, a dispirited collection of disarmed tank crews, when we received news of the first attack against the Australians astride the main road to Derna. Our elation knew no bounds and our morale began to rise up again from the depths when we heard that the Australians in the forward positions had allowed enemy tanks to pass on, and had appeared from their slit trenches to slaughter the German infantry behind. There was visible evidence of our success in the hundreds of German prisoners collecting in a cage above our wadi.

The remnants of the Brigade were then moved up to the Pilastrino Sector to hold the line as infantry. There were a few rifles, a few Bren guns and one or two Boyes anti-tank rifles, but most of us were only equipped with pistols like all tank crews.

We lived in some ammunition galleries under the same observation towers we had teased three months before in the days of the Italian occupation. There were rats and rubbish and the musty smell of Italians in the tunnels, but at least they were safe from the endless Stuka raids. German aeroplanes came over about once every half-hour, dropping most of their bombs on the shipping in the harbour, but always diving to squirt their guns at the outer defences on their way home. There were few casualties and morale was high, although the men were not at ease in their unaccustomed role. They were tank crews and felt like fish out of water as bogus infantry, for ever chafing to be back with armour.

The second attack came on the 7th April. After the way had been paved by a series of fierce Stuka raids, a number of German tanks penetrated the perimeter in the Bir el Adem sector. They were beaten off by the few cruisers we had in the garrison in a bitter little action in which the score was about even. For three hours I lay with a drawn pistol alongside a Boyes rifle expecting the enemy tanks to appear at any moment. We were not even properly sheltered in a weapon pit, having no spades, but we were determined to fight to the end, although nobody could say that we were not relieved when they sheered off on another tack towards the east.

On the same evening we were told that a ship had got into the harbour from Alexandria, loaded with enough tanks to re-equip half the regiment. The others would be evacuated on the same vessel to refit in the Delta. There was no little excitement when the lots were drawn as to who were to stay behind in besieged

Tobruk. It was a waste of time to conceal how much we all hoped to be in the evacuation party. Again that odd perverseness in the British character was demonstrated by the fact that we did. It was no secret that the chances of Tobruk resisting a prolonged siege were slender. We had been used to the clean virgin desert, moving like nomads to a fresh area every few days. Here we were forced to live in the filth of an old battlefield; there were the constant duststorms caused by the passage of three armies; the old tins, broken wine bottles, bits of uniform and the foul smell of stale excreta; the water tasted like weak brine and our rations were worse than at any time in the previous two campaigns; and most of all we were effected mentally by the humiliation of being incarcerated in an Italian fortress we had helped to capture only three months before. Against this was the temptation of a few days' peace in the luxury of Egypt. It is not to be wondered that we gazed with eager eyes on the hat which would reveal our fate. And when the lucky ones drew a ticket, they immediately offered to change places with those who had been less fortunate. My hands trembled as I unfolded my own scrap of paper. When I read on it the single word "DELTA," I silently thanked God for his kindness.

We marched down to the harbour area the next morning, after saying good-bye to our comrades, some of whom we were never to see again. We hid ourselves in some caves near the Derna-El Adem crossroads, until the time came for us to board the ship under the cover of darkness. The remnants of an Indian Cavalry Brigade, which had escaped from the net at Mekili, were leaguered on a salt marsh on the opposite side of the road. The air raids were ceaseless. Once I was caught in the open on the salt marsh when sixteen Stukas came screaming down on the harbour. Two bombs landed fifty yards away as I lay on my face in the mud. Great hunks of clay showered down around me and then, as if slightly delayed, the front part of an Indian's foot plopped on to the marsh in front of my eyes. I noticed in a quick frightened glance at the sky that they were climbing again in preparation for another dive. I ran across the road to an ancient Italian air-raid shelter, already crammed full with men. Staggering down the road were two Indians with great gaping wounds in their bodies. I pushed them in front of me into the shelter. Then in the dark people began shouting for someone to pass up a field dressing. There was not enough room to let the poor fellows lie down, but we did what we could in that confined space to stem the flow of blood, pushing and fumbling with shell dressings in the darkness. And outside the anti-aircraft guns were firing like demons, never stopping even when bombs crashed down near their emplacements. A bomb fell on the hill above and the whole shelter was shaken by the thunder of the explosion.

During one of the brief respites, we saw a squadron of Stukas attack a hospital ship in the outer harbour. She was a white-painted liner with a big red cross on her side, and there was no mistaking her errand. Not content with straddling her with several bombs so that she was constrained to beach herself in the shallows off the southern shore, they dived twice again to rake her decks with fire, callously indifferent to her helplessness.

Our own ship, the *Barpeta*, was struck in the forward hold, killing fifteen Mauritian labourers. She was set on fire, but by the evening they had got it sufficiently under control to allow us to embark. As we were being ferried out in lighters, the red flag went up for another air raid, which scattered all the men on the docks. Fortunately, the bombs splashed harmlessly into the harbour. When at last we were all aboard, the anchor was weighed and the ship pulled out to sea, still afire forward. Although we had fears of enemy air attack, we were not molested, and two days later we were disembarking in Alexandria Harbour.

CHAPTER FIVE

CRETE

I WAS on leave in Alexandria when I first heard that a squadron of the regiment was bound for Crete. One squadron had already left for the wire at Sollum, so that including the two squadrons left behind in Tobruk, the whole regiment would be fully committed, amply justifying the remark that the sun never sets on the 3rd Hussars.

I cannot remember much of my leave in Alexandria except that it was very pleasant. We were entertained by a charming Swiss family called Seidl, who took us sailing in their yacht in the harbour. Their house in Camp Cæsar became like a second home to us and we spent many happy hours with them, basking on the beach or sipping long cool drinks in the Yacht Club.

One particular incident on that leave remains very clear in my mind, mainly because it became so useful later. One night I was walking up the stairs in the Cecil Hotel, when I heard a scream and the sound of a body falling very hard. I rushed up to find a little wizened French chambermaid nursing a large cut on her forehead, having fallen down the flight of stairs from the top landing. She protested that she was all right, but the paleness of her face belied her words. I picked her up and carried her to her room. The hotel seemed quite deserted and no amount of telephoning or shouting could produce any effective service. Alarmed by what transpired later to be only a superficial wound, I ran out into the street and asked an Egyptian the way to the nearest chemist or doctor. I mounted a carriage, which took me to a first aid post, where I obtained a quantity of lint and bandages. When I got back to the hotel the little old woman was still lying there, moaning faintly more in self-pity than in pain. I bathed the wound and applied a dressing, telling her to be sure to send for a doctor the next day. She was quite sweet in her thanks, telling me that I was a cavalier and *très gentil*, that only an Englishman could be such a gentleman and to be sure to take care of myself in the war.

I did not give the incident another thought until one night I was trying to cash an English cheque in Shepheard's Hotel in Cairo, always a most difficult process. There was a little squeak of delight from behind the cashier's shoulder, which turned to reveal my little chambermaid. She was the wife of the cashier, and ever after there was no difficulty in cashing cheques.

When I heard that the squadron was off to the wars once more, I lost no time in getting back to barracks.

We were fitted out with the same old type of light tanks with which we had been equipped in the desert—battered ancient hulks, which had been hastily patched up in Waadian Workshops. There were no proper fittings to the cooling system for the guns and the wireless sets arrived so late that there was no time to fit them before we embarked.

While the others left on the rail-flats with the tanks, I took up the transport by road to Alexandria. The desert road from Cairo to Alexandria traverses uninteresting, monotonous desert on the outskirts of the delta, until it runs across the pink salt marsh between Amariya and the port. The drivers were tired after their farewell celebrations of the previous night and several trucks ran off the road into the sand, when their drivers became so bored with the endless wastes that they could no longer keep open their eyes.

The major part of the regiment was transported to Crete in a Dutch troopship called the *Neu Zeeland*, but I was given command of thirty men aboard a freighter called the *Dalesman*. This cargo ship, which belonged to the T. & J. Harrison Line, was loaded up with our tanks and trucks, some three-tonners even being lashed to the decks for lack of stowage room.

The Captain was a fine old Irishman, whose name I think was Horner, and he treated us like princes during our stay on his ship. There was a certain amount of quite understandable jealousy from the others, who were crammed like sardines under the decks of the trooper and who envied our freedom from such irksome parades as lifeboat drills.

It was an uneventful voyage until the convoy rounded the straits between Crete and the Rhodes Group. Just before dark we were attacked by two Italian torpedo bombers, which were driven off by pom-poms from the escorting destroyers. As they slunk away, skimming the tops of the waves, I remembered that Churchill had likened Mussolini to the leader of a jackal pack.

Soon after night had fallen, the rattle of machine-gun fire

brought us tumbling out on to the deck. Another torpedo bomber had got in amongst the flock, but even as we watched, our Hotchkiss gunner filled it full of tracer bullets until it burst into flames, crashing like a meteor into the sea. In all the times I have seen machine guns fired at aircraft, this was the only occasion on which a machine was actually brought down in flames.

And then morning found us anchored in Suda Bay; around us was a crimson glow from the sun rising behind the olive-drab mountains; away over the calm blue water were the white houses of the port and behind them the avenues, the villas and the poplar trees of Canea, capital of Crete; and except for the wreck of the cruiser *York*, in the middle of the harbour, there was no sign of war.

Suddenly the sky was filled with our old screaming enemies, whistling down from the skies like buzzards to the kill. A squadron of Stukas had come in at a great height from the direction of the mainland, catching the anti-aircraft gunners unawares. Deadly bombs fell all round us, shaking the old ship at her anchor, and we sought sanctuary beneath the table in the saloon. We realised that we had been hit when a loud explosion threw us against the cabin wall. Crawling on our hands and knees, we made our way out on to the deck. A bomb had fallen on one of the three-tonners on the after-hatch to pass straight through to the bottom of the ship.

She was filling fast and had already heeled over a little. I lined up the troopers on the deck, mainly to quieten their panic, but it was unnecessary, for they, like me, had looked over the side to gain confidence from the fact that they could see the bottom. Not so the merchant sailors, who, disregarding the orders of their officers, made shift to launch a lifeboat. To the satisfaction of the soldiers and to the dismay of the sailors, their boat proved to be unseaworthy, and filled with water so quickly that they were forced to swarm up ropes back on to the ship, amidst the jeers of the troops.

By the time a pinnace had come out from the shore to take us off, the *Dalesman* had settled firmly on the bed on which she was to rest for many years.

The pinnace landed us on the docks where the *Neu Zeeland* was anchored, and there we rejoined the squadron, then in the process of disembarking. Altogether it took us about a week to collect enough stores to justify our moving inland from Suda Bay. We leaguered on the side of a hill overlooking the harbour, in the cool shade of the olive trees. It was like paradise to men who had spent long months in the desert. There were sheep to be bought, handsome smiling European peasants, and above all, the beauty of the green trees. Nearby a village sold coarse red wine to the troops. There were pretty girls in light summer frocks, and even if they were reluctant to respond to the advances of the troops, they were some vague reminder of those who waited at home.

The tanks were the main difficulty. Twelve in the upper hold were salvageable, but all the others and all the transport except the trucks on the deck were under the water. Worst of all, the wireless sets were a total loss. The harbour was being constantly bombed and we found great difficulty in persuading the Navy to give us steam to work the winches. After much thumping on the table in the office in Suda, we persuaded them to bring a tug alongside to give us steam. Stripped to the waist, we performed the unaccustomed role of dockers to unload the tanks into a lighter on the other side of the wreck. It was a terrifying job, working in the bowels of a ship to our knees in water, at a time when the harbour was being heavily bombed. Every bomb, however far away, sent concussion waves through the sea to crash against the hull.

When at last we were ready for the move on the 18th May, the Stukas began to increase the violence of their raids.

A naval friend took the Squadron Leader and me for a joy-ride in a motor torpedo boat in the harbour. We had barely cast off from the shore, when vicious Stukas tumbled down from the clouds in a power-dive on to the shipping in the harbour. Three bombs straddled us, one landing on each side and one about fifty yards astern. The sailor grabbed the wheel, my Squadron Leader fired the Twin Vickers and I hid in the bottom of the boat. The last bomb wounded one of the crew, who was standing on the deck forward, knocking ugly little holes behind both his knees. I was told to help him, and, wriggling along beside the cabin, I tried to bind him up with trembling hands. Only when at last we reached the safety of the shore did they tell me that we had been sitting on two torpedoes. I swore never to go to sea again.

As we pulled out of our olive grove towards our battle stations in the west, the enemy aircraft blew up an oil-tanker in Suda Bay, sending pieces of wood showering all over the island. The light from the burning wreck helped us along the narrow goat-tracks to the road.

We had had some intimation of an imminent German attack when a pilot was captured on the island, but even so the weight of the initial assault took us by surprise.

We were sitting round a deal table under an olive tree having breakfast at seven o'clock on the morning of the 20th May, when suddenly the sky was filled with enemy aircraft. They came low over the tops of the trees, spraying the olive groves with bullets and dropping bombs haphazardly over our positions. There seemed so many aircraft that they blotted out the sun. In addition to the whistle of the bombs, the racket of the machine guns and the screaming of their engines, some had attached sinister wailing sirens to their wings. As the bullets tore through the leaves from one direction, we scrambled over each other to seek shelter behind the tree-trunk.

After several awful minutes, between the doctor and under another troop leader, somebody cried, "The bastards are landing!" We looked up and there were puffs of green, red and yellow parachutes, forming great clouds in the sky. Hysterically the Squadron Leader shouted, "Tank crews." We floundered across from one tree-trunk to another, pausing for breath in the occasional slit trench, until we reached the tanks. The wrong crews got in the wrong vehicles, but I found myself in my own tank with a gunner in the driving seat. Looking back through the trees, I saw that my troop sergeant, Skedgewell, was also mounted. I shouted to him as I moved off, but he could not have heard because he did not follow. Perhaps I should have waited for instructions, but there seemed little chance of order reasserting itself amongst that racket for some time and I was anxious to get to grips with the enemy.

I went up the road to Galatos towards where I had seen them landing. The village streets were full of Greeks in khaki uniform, who were pleading for ammunition. I gave them a belt of Vickers, but afterwards discovered that it was no good for the calibre of their rifles. We passed several New Zealand positions, where the troops stood up and gave us the "thumbs-up" sign with a grin. Just to look at their confident, smiling faces was good for the spirit. They had been beaten out of Greece by over-whelming odds, they were ill-equipped and underfed, but it takes more than that to daunt the finest fighting troops in the world.

And then we found ourselves held up by a knife-edged road block, barring us from the Plain of Aghye. As I was looking round, wondering whether I should get out of my tank to remove it, a Schmeisser fired at me from the cover of the olive trees. I looked around through the visor for a target, but could not see a living soul. And then another machine gun spattered bullets against the turret from the other side of the road. Indiscriminately we raked the trees with fire, pouring long bursts into the

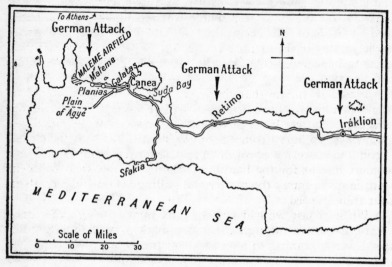

CRETE.

black shadows. At the height of the confusion, when I was still puzzled by fire from an unseen enemy, there occurred one of the tragedies of war which make it a bitter, evil business having nothing to do with God. I saw what appeared to be a German in a long grey overcoat coming up the road towards us. It was difficult to see through the visor and I had never seen a German at close range before, but it looked like the real thing to me. I ordered the gunner to fire. Bullets spattered around the figure on the road, but still it came on. Suddenly I shouted to the gunner to cease fire. I felt, as I could not feel now that I am hardened by years of war: it was a woman, a civilian, and I had shot her. She came on and we could hear her screaming now. The Germans had stopped firing and there was nothing but her screams. She was an old peasant woman in a long grey dress, her grey hair done in a bun behind her neck, and she was holding out her hands for mercy as she screamed. Her shoulder had been shattered by a bullet, splashing her dress and her wrinkled face with blood. What had I done? I tried to stop her, but she went on up the road towards the village, staggering, screaming.

The Germans, as if satisfied that the entertainment was now over, renewed their fire from the olive groves. I felt that it was futile to stay where we were, since we could still see no sign of the enemy and he could obviously see us. I ordered the driver to turn round, but he was so excited by all that had happened that he pulled the tiller too hard, wrenching off a track.

It was fortunate that the lower part of the tank should be concealed by two high banks, so that we were able to repair the track under cover from their fire. But every time we raised our heads a sharp burst from a Schmeisser rattled against the turret. I think we must have broken all records for repairing a track. We almost fought for the hammer, scrambling over each other in our desire to hurry the matter and pulling off our fingernails in our frantic speed.

When at last we had got the tank into running order once more, we drove through the village back towards our leaguer, for I was beginning to have some qualms about my having left without orders. On the other side of Galatos we were stopped by a Greek, who waved to us with a handkerchief from a ditch. As the tank bucked to a halt, he put one finger to his lips and pointed with the other hand to a figure lying prone in the ditch on the other side of the road. I nearly fell back into the turret when I saw that it was a German parachutist in all the famous regalia—steel helmet, leather pouches, camouflage jacket and all. I levelled my heavy forty-five Smith-Wesson at his head and said, "Come on, surrender, you Jerry bastard." He did not move even a fraction, lying stiffly on his face. I fired a round and he flinched as though I had hit him, but I was not to be foxed, because I had seen the dust kicked up by my bullet at least four yards away. I tried with four more rounds, each with the same result. At last, in desperation, I told the gunner to turn the Vickers on him. He did not flinch any more. A few yards on down the road we came across two other Germans, who were similarly dealt with. Five more parachutists came out of the olive trees with their hands up, although we had not meant to fire in that direction. I was not in any mood to be taken in by any German tricks and in any case the affair with the old Greek woman had made me too miserable to care. I ordered the gunner to fire. Three dropped dead, but two others managed to limp away into the trees. I do not think that I would make a practice of shooting prisoners, but Crete was different, and in the heat of the moment I had not time to think.

I was approaching our leaguer area by the back route, when I was hailed by a pale-faced man from the top window of the New Zealand Y.M.C.A., an old farm-house on the cross-roads. The place was strangely quiet, and except for this one window the whole building was shuttered. Half-hidden behind a curtain he shouted in an excited voice:

"Look out, Tommy! The Jerries have taken the dressing-station."

I waved in reply, and told the driver to slow down, the dressing-station being barely twenty yards away on the other side of the road. It was a collection of large brown marquees under the trees, and I peered carefully for any sign of the enemy. And then we were on them. Three Germans were standing round two of our trucks, over which they had draped large swastika flags, and we bowled them into the ditch with the first burst. In between the tents, a number of Germans were standing with their weapons trained on a tight knot of medical orderlies, sitting on the ground with their hands on their heads. We fired a careful burst. The Germans scattered and I believe some of the New Zealanders managed to escape in the confusion. Motoring slowly up and down the road, we sprayed the trees as if we were on the famous box-run at Lulworth Cove. Many fell dead on the ground and the gunner continued to fire at them when he could not see any other target. I saw that one clever German had climbed a tree. The driver halted, so that the gunner could aim from a steady platform, and in a few moments we had him tumbling to the ground in a heap. Most of the others retreated into the trees, where we dared not follow for fear of an ambush. By then the guns were red-hot, being deficient of the proper cooling device, so I decided to withdraw to find some water near the 7th General

Hospital. I dismounted and went in a deserted Greek hovel near the road. A New Zealander was lying, terribly wounded, on a palliasse in the corner of the room. He croaked at me:

"Water, joker, give us some water. The bastards shot up the tents in the hospital. Nothing's too bad for those bastards. Do what you can, chum. Give us some water, there's a sport!"

I found a full bucket with a ladle in the kitchen. He drank it down in big gulps, but there was nothing more we could do for him. I splashed water on the outsides of the barrels to cool the guns, and they were so hot that they filled the turret with steam. There was an anxious moment when two Me 110's flew over low to machine-gun the hospital, but they did not spot us. I never really understood the German callousness towards the Red Cross at this period of the war, for generally speaking they were most meticulous in their observance of the rules.

When I finally got back to the squadron area, I did not receive the reprimand I had expected, but instead was told to hold the road I had just left. Most of the squadron were engaged against the parachutists who had withdrawn from the dressing-station, and had sustained several minor casualties from anti-tank rifles. For the rest of the morning, I sat astride the road to Galatos. We were machine-gunned once, but there were no other signs of the Germans, although the sound of fierce battle came from all over the island.

In the afternoon I was ordered up to co-operate with the New Zealanders in an attack on the Galatos Cemetery, an important point which had been seized by the Germans in their first rush. I was not very popular when my arrival attracted the attention of a swarm of hovering Messerschmitts, but when they had moved on without doing serious damage, I found good shelter for the tanks under some trees. I walked down to the headquarters of the New Zealand 19th Battalion to report to their Colonel for orders. I had some difficulty in finding him, firstly because we were interrupted by an air raid, and secondly because he was out in the forward defence lines potting at a sniper. I ran along to him with my head ducked, bullets whistling all round, until I noticed that dodging did not quite seem to be the fashion in this part of the world. With a tremendous effort I tried to appear brave and walked up to him. He muttered, "Just a moment," out of the corner of his mouth, and only turned when he had brought the sniper tumbling from a neighbouring tree. He handed the rifle to his adjutant and said:

"Well, that's that. That joker has been causing trouble all morning. Now, I suppose you command the tanks?"

"Yes, sir."

"Well, we've had a fair number of casualties this morning and must get Jerry out of his positions near the cemetery, if we are going to stay here. Some of my chaps are pretty crook."

"Yes, sir. We would like to get a crack at them . . ." (you barefaced liar).

"Come with me. You must keep your head down because Jerry's got this cornfield pretty well covered."

We crawled along on our bellies through the thick corn, until we overlooked a fairly open plain, only broken by a cemetery sitting on a small hill in the middle. The plain was bounded by olive trees, except on our side, and we could see the flash of machine guns from behind the gravestones. Once I stuck up my bottom so much that bullets cut the corn above our heads.

After a lot of tinkering about we drove the three tanks in line ahead down the track through the cornfields to the cemetery. The idea was that at the same time the 19th Battalion should put a company through the trees on the left. Every few yards we stopped to spray the whole front with machine gun bullets. We could not see anything, but there was a chance that our tracers might do some good, and anyway they looked very pretty. Just short of the cemetery a number of mortar bombs crumped between the tanks, which was very clever shooting when you consider that we were on the move. We saw a number of Germans fold up in the graveyard, but the fire was getting so hot that I decided to swing to the right.

Coming up between the olive trees, I was astounded to see a German machine gun and a German mortar facing the opposite way, firing at the New Zealanders. We charged them before they realised the menace from the rear, and within a matter of moments the machine gun was being crushed beneath our tracks.

It was a short-lived victory, because although the New Zealanders took the cemetery, they were soon beaten out of it by overwhelming German counter-attacks. Later in the day we did another run-down, but the result was much the same. The Germans went to ground when they saw the tanks, but the cover was so good that there was little we could do against them.

In the evening I was ordered to co-operate with the New Zealanders in a night attack towards the Galatos prison, where the Germans were said to be building an aerodrome. I studied the map carefully and set off on the right line at about nine o'clock. The wire was supposed to have been cut for us, but when we arrived we found that a second tangle stretched across the track. We were already under fire by the time we reached it, so there was no turning back. I charged it head-on and got through, making a gap for the others, though the wire became so tangled up with my bogey wheels that I was to pay for it later. We went along a dark track between the trees, spraying on both sides as we went. Some fire came back and we ran across a trip wire, which set off a flare. A shower of grenades rolled off our sides, causing no damage. Finally, the track petered out before we had reached our objective.

I had only been there a few moments when some New Zealanders arrived with bristling bayonets. We waited until they had formed up, intending to at least cover their advance with a barrage of bullets. It was very cold and we sat shivering in the turrets as the New Zealanders slipped like shadows into the ditches. Before we were ready, a runner arrived from the rear to say that the attack was cancelled; we were in somebody else's area and we had no business to be there anyway. Such is the fog of war.

The next day was spent in a repetition of our manœuvres around Galatos and in the annoying frequence of attacks from the air. When night fell we were ordered to move along the coast road towards Malame, where we were to co-operate in a big counter-attack to regain the positions we had lost. The situation on the island could not have been more obscure, but it was apparent that the Germans had suffered enormous casualties in their first attacks. They had seized Malame aerodrome in the face of fierce opposition, but had failed at Heraklion and Rhetimo. Small pockets of parachutists had cut the coast road in many places and had temporarily silenced the anti-aircraft guns round Canea. All our few aircraft had been shot down. With practically no opposition, the German Air Force blackened the skies, making movement on the roads impossible and reducing Canea to a heap of rubble. The way they came over in ceaseless squadrons to bomb that helpless town was quite merciless. Perhaps the most serious threat was the thrust towards Galatos from the Plain of Aghye.

Our column of tanks motored down a deserted road through San Marino towards the west. Out at sea, we could make out the burning wrecks where the invasion fleet had been destroyed by the Navy. We stopped at Platanias village, where the New Zealanders had their Brigade Headquarters. When the Squadron Leader told me that my troop had been selected for the counter-attack, I slightly resented it, since we had been in action almost non-stop for forty-eight hours and I felt that this was almost certain suicide.

Together we mounted the steps of an old farm-house to receive the orders from the Brigadier. He was a red, open-faced man, who looked like a country farmer and it was obvious that he was suffering from acute fatigue. He asked us to wait for half an hour while he had some sleep. Disgusted, intolerant, we sat on the steps until he was ready. Then he began to explain his plan, which had the merits of simplicity if nothing else. There was no artillery apart from a few captured Italian guns, which had to be aimed by squinting down the barrel, so we were to advance without a barrage. There were no mortars because they had forgotten to pack the base-plates in Alexandria. There were no spades, so weapon-pits would have to be dug with steel helmets. My orders were to advance at a slow pace down the main road, since the ground was too rough to get off into the open country. Parallel with my middle tank, the 20th New Zealand Battalion would advance on the right and the Maori Battalion on the left. In particular, I was to beware of two Bofors guns, recently captured by the enemy, which were said to be mounted near the village and would blow large holes in my tanks. I protested that my tanks were only thinly armoured perambulators and that this was a job for Matildas, but I was sharply brought back to reality by the reminder that beggars cannot be choosers. All the Matildas had been knocked out the day before. He acceded to one request, which was that a section of Maoris should advance behind each tank, so that I could better judge the pace and to prevent Molotov Cocktails from being thrown from the ditches.

At half-past four we moved forward from the start-line, a stream outside Platanias. The fighting began almost immediately. I sprayed the front with my tracers and was lucky enough to hit an ammunition dump, which exploded like "golden rain" at the Crystal Palace. The line of figures marched steadily forward. I saw several parachutes lying in the trees and there were two dead Germans hanging on the telephone wires, blown up like green bladders. A white Verey light was fired from a cottage on the left and we gave it a whole belt of Vickers. I was astonished to notice that my section of Maoris had suffered heavy casualties in the dark. I had not even realised that we had been fired at, but the sadly depleted numbers and the bandage round the head of the sergeant were evidence enough.

Daylight found us on the outskirts of Malame village, and I think some of the New Zealanders had made the edge of the aerodrome on the right. With the light came hundreds of air-craft, straffing and diving on our advancing line. My leading tank had got a little too far ahead, in contravention of my orders and had run into trouble in the village. Coming round the corner of the street, it had run slap into two anti-tank guns in the churchyard. The first shot holed them, mortally wounding the gunner, but he bravely continued to fire until he had despatched one of the enemy guns. The tank tried to turn to get out of its impossible position, but another shell hit them in the middle. The gunner was killed, the commander, Sergeant Skedgewell, was mashed up with the seat, and Cook, the driver, received a serious wound in the foot. Which was worse, the tank was set on fire. How Cook drove it out with his damaged foot I will never under-stand, but he achieved it somehow, putting out the fire with the pyrene as he went. When it got back to me, Skedgewell was writhing in mortal agony, shouting for us to get him out. I tried to pull him from the top of the turret, but his thin, sweat-soaked khaki shirt ripped in my hands. He was obviously beyond all hope and in great pain, so I gave him some morphia (perhaps too much) and the stretcher-bearers told me later that he died in about twenty minutes. Cook managed to get his tank back to the squadron, although it was of no further use, but I believe he was drowned on one of the destroyers which evacuated wounded from Suda.

And now there was all hell let loose in the sky. A swarm of Me 109's like angry buzzing bees beset our remaining two tanks. Hot flakes of burning metal flew off the inside of the turrets into our faces. We tried to minimise their dives by halting under a tall tree, but it was of no avail. Finally, like a wounded bull trying to shake off a cloud of flies, I crashed into a bamboo field. In the long green plants we lost them, but a final disaster overtook my tank. The rough treatment had been the last straw for the bogey wheel I had damaged in the barbed wire two days before. It collapsed as though it had been made of cardboard, having also been damaged by a grenade, and there we were as immobile as the Rock of Gibraltar. There was no sign of my Corporal's tank, which had been behind us on the road.

I felt lost and afraid. My mouth was so dry that I found it difficult to speak. My terror of the aeroplanes had turned me into a frightened, quivering woman. And then Skedgewell. I knew and had known all along that the leading tank would be destroyed. Because I knew that it was bound to be knocked out, I asked the Squadron Leader if I could go in front, knowing full well that he would say that the regulations demanded that the officer should travel in the middle. On any other occasion, if I had wanted to go in front, I would not have bothered to ask. And Skedgewell had been killed. I did not care for orders when it suited me, but this time I had chosen to obey them because I knew that I would be killed if I did not. I should have been in that leading tank. Instead, there was Skedgewell dead and his pretty young wife waiting at home. I felt as if I had murdered him. And the aircraft overhead with those terrible wailing sirens were like kite hawks over a dead body.

I lost my head. I was so afraid that I could have burrowed into the ground. Instead I ran. I ran back towards the squadron, crashing through the undergrowth, tumbling into ditches, and all the time looking up at the sky at the black crosses on the aeroplanes. I came to a clearing in which some New Zealanders were guarding a small knot of German parachutists. They had made the prisoners lay out one of their swastika flags as a signal to the aircraft and assured me that they had not been machine-gunned all morning in consequence. I lay on my back in the grass, panting, thanking God for the respite. But it was not long before my faith was rudely shattered by the rasp of bullets cutting through the trees and the whine of the aircraft engines as they dived. I threw myself into a slit trench on top of a German prisoner. I could feel his body quivering against my belly.

When they had passed over, we got out, dusted ourselves and grinned at each other. The spell was broken, because this German had been even more afraid than I.

I doubled across the road, but in a moment they were diving down again. I dashed into the open door of a stable and threw myself head-first into an iron manger, while the bombs carved a big crater in the road outside. It was not until it was over that I noticed that the other mangers were all occupied by New Zealanders in a similar state. I left for the open, running between patches of cover and crawling along ditches, until I reached the squadron. In my panic I had covered three miles from my disabled tank.

The squadron were leaguered in a small grove, having covered the tanks with bracken until they looked like thick, round bushes. Over to the left, one Italian gun manned by an Australian crew was having a great game with the Germans. It would fire one or two defiant shells on to the aerodrome, now crammed with German aircraft, until a swarm of Stukas raked its position. Ten minutes later, when we had all given up hope that it still existed, it would fire another few impudent stonks. It was the Tobruk spirit over again and did us all good. No Jerry was going to discipline a fair dinkum Aussie for all the bombs in history.

The fitters accompanied me back to my tank with a bogey wheel they had taken from Sergeant Skedgewell's wreck. We found that a fire had been started in the undergrowth by a hot bullet and that the tank was now exposed in an open clearing for all to see. First we dug a deep trench into which we dived when the inevitable aircraft appeared. Sometimes there was barely time for the mechanic to turn a bolt twice before he had to dive back into the trench again. Slowly, in this intermittent fashion, the tank was made fit for the road once more.

I received orders to proceed back up the road towards Malame to cover the withdrawal of the New Zealanders from the aerodrome. It had been a gallant assay, but it failed owing to the thinness of our numbers on the ground. If the Australians had relieved the attacking battalions a little earlier to give them another hour of darkness; if there had been any reserves to hold the ground we had won; if the artillery could have covered the last rush across an aerodrome swept by bullets; and if the enemy aircraft had been a little less active, we might have won the day. As it was, we learned later that the Germans were preparing to abandon their whole attack on Crete, but, heartened by our withdrawal, they had renewed their determination to press home their attacks. Such is often the hair's-breadth between victory and defeat. Tenacity of purpose when it seems that everything has gone wrong might often win the day. It occurred to me later, during my long opportunities for reflection in a prison camp, that if the counter-attack had been made on the second day it would have stood a greater chance of success.

The situation was difficult to understand for the forward troops. All they knew was that they had defeated the Germans in a series of local actions against overwhelming odds. They were not to know that we were already being outflanked from the direction of Galatos.

I took up my position in a garden half-way between Platanias and Malame. I had been told to fall back on the Platanias position after waiting for an hour, but when the time came to go back, there was still one company of Maoris to return. I could see long lines of grey figures advancing towards me across the fields and I knew them to be Germans. An anti-tank rifle began to snipe at my turret, but he was not much of a shot. There were odd bullets whistling about everywhere and all the time I could see droves of heavily laden JU 52's coming into the aerodrome from low over the sea with fresh reinforcements for the enemy. Two donkeys were copulating in the road, regardless of bullets. How I admired their sang-froid! And then the last Maoris came along with the Germans hard on their heels, but not a shadow of fear showed on their smiling, copper faces. As they passed my tank, they winked and put up their thumbs. Some fifty yards behind the rest came two Maoris carrying a pot of stew across a rifle. There is something so engaging about this cheerful race that it is no wonder that there is no colour bar in New Zealand.

The Brigade had drawn itself up on three hills astride the road behind Platanias and we fell back with the Maoris into the village. The German pressure was so great that it was not long before they had advanced up to close contact with our positions, seizing half the village. I positioned my two tanks in the main street and every time a German put his head round the corner we gave him a short burst of Vickers. Some Maoris brewed up coffee in a nearby house and gave us each a mug. Two became so attached to my tank that they refused to leave it. We held on to our positions for the rest of the day in spite of the fact that the Germans brought up the captured anti-aircraft guns from Malame and peppered the hills behind us. The Bofors shells bounced across the ground like great balls of flame.

Towards evening a Maori came up with the exciting news that there were German aircraft landing on the beach. With the two faithful Maoris on my turret, I drove down a sandy track to the shore. I could plainly see two large troop-carriers on the sand, each with a large crowd of soldiers in the process of deplaning. I opened fire with a long burst, scattering all the men around the planes, and my gunner did not take his finger off the trigger until both aircraft were in flames.

The order came to retreat after dark. We drove our tanks past the long files of miserable New Zealanders trudging back towards Canea. I felt that I could cry. They had not been beaten and they knew it, but here they were going back again—back, always back. I wondered if this was the beginning of another Dunkirk or a repetition of Greece. Of all the troops in the British Empire there are none equal to the New Zealanders. They had fought like tigers, the Maoris had executed one bayonet charge after another and they all knew that they were more than a match for the Germans. The surprise and the shame of the retreat was written on all their faces.

For the next two days we held a road-block outside Canea against the danger of a thrust by motor-cycle troops which had been seen near the prisons at Galatos. They were an uneventful two days except for the heavy air raids which demolished a large part of our transport. One tank helped to liquidate a pocket of Germans who had infiltrated through the trees to the main road. Once we saw two British aircraft fly over at a great height—the only ones we saw in the whole battle. There was little coherent news from the front except that the division was still falling back on Canea.

At about four o'clock on the evening of the 25th May I was told to take my two tanks up to co-operate in an attempt to retake Galatos, which had been seized by the enemy during the day. It was the key to Canea, and if it were not retaken, the whole weight of the German attack would be unleashed upon the coastal plain.

As we moved along the road towards the start-line, we passed wounded New Zealanders straggling back in ones and twos, with bandages round their heads, their arms in slings and limping on sticks. I found Colonel Kippenburger at the rendezvous and he told me that his men would not be ready for about twenty minutes. I had been brooding over Skedgewell for days, I felt bitter about the turn the battle had taken and I felt sympathy for these gallant wounded New Zealanders. I asked permission to go in first alone.

It was soon apparent that the village was filled with Germans. They were in all the cottage windows, in the orchard, behind chimney stacks and in the schoolyard. I, the leading tank, sprayed one side of the street, while my corporal sprayed the other. When we reached the far side of the village, we turned round and came back in the same fashion. An anti-tank rifle pierced the turret of my corporal's tank, wounding both the commander and the gunner, but it did not put the tank out of action.

I reported to Colonel Kippenburger what I had seen and asked for two New Zealanders, who understood Vickers guns, to replace my two wounded. About three hundred volunteered. When at last the infantry were ready, night had fallen. We advanced slowly into the village under the cover of darkness.

I had got to a corner half-way through the High Street, when there was a blinding flash inside the tank and my gunner sank groaning to the bottom of the turret. He said that he had been hit. I felt a sort of burn in my thigh and thought it probable that I also had been wounded. I told the driver to turn round, but as we swung broadside to the enemy we were hit again. My driver was wounded in the shoulder and in consequence pulled the tiller too hard, putting us into the ditch. We sat there, crouched in the bottom of the turret, while the anti-tank rifle carved big chunks out of the top. I was hit twice more—in both legs and in the right arm. Stannard, my gunner, was in a bad way, having stopped one in the stomach. I pushed them both out through the driver's hatch and crawled out myself. I pulled myself along on my elbows until I was under cover of a low stone wall. There I lay in the infernal din (for the Germans were still shooting bits out of the tank), praying for the New Zealanders to arrive.

They came up the main street in a rush, but were met by a hail of machine-gun bullets on the corner. Several went down in a heap, including the Platoon Commander. I shouted, "Come on, New Zealand! Clean 'em out, New Zealand!"

The Platoon Commander was also shouting to rally them from his position in the middle of the street. I shouted across to him to ask where he had been hit and he said that he was wounded in both legs. And then someone shouted that the enemy were on the roof. I saw the Platoon Commander lift himself up on his elbows and take careful aim with his pistol. The German machine-gunner came tumbling down the slates on to the street below. It was an astonishing shot in such light and at such a range.

The New Zealanders were going in again now at the point of the bayonet and I heard a German scream like a small child in pain. Another New Zealander came up and put one foot on me as he took aim from behind the wall. I protested and he apologised: "Sorry, joker, thought you was a corpse!"

And then they had passed on. The sound of shooting and grenades became gradually fainter until we were left alone in the silence of the village. I found out that the name of the platoon commander was Sandy Thomas, a New Zealander who was to achieve great fame in the later stages of the war. Some stretcher-bearers from the 4th N.Z. Brigade Band came up and took Sandy away. He told them about me and they put me on a door. Two Cretan women now appeared from their hiding-place in a cellar and gave me a drink of water. I asked them to care for Stannard, who was still groaning as if in great pain. A straggler came through and told us that the New Zealanders had been told to withdraw from Galatos, after taking it at great cost. I cursed the inexplicable reasoning of the Higher Command, who, it seemed, had ordered such loss of life for no apparent reason.

All the world seemed quiet after the racket of the battle and I felt deserted, lost in a village which was occupied neither by Germans nor by British. I had almost lapsed into a coma of despair when I heard the rumble of tanks coming from the direction of the Germans. My heart leapt. They could only be ours since as far as we knew the Germans had no tanks. And then two of our light tanks came into the village, looking for the battle although they were already coming from the direction in which I should have thought they would have found it. Jim Crewdson, the troop leader, heard my shout and halted in the street.

They lifted us gently on to the front of the tank, covering us with blankets, and drove as slowly as they could back to the squadron leaguer. Tom Summerville, our doctor, gave us each a shot of morphia and conducted us up to the dressing-station, where we were handed over to the medical staff. They looked at our wounds, but were too busy to waste time on any one who was not very seriously wounded. I was carried off on a stretcher to an old stable which was littered with wounded.

I was lucky enough to secure a spot in the open courtyard instead of being confined in the stench of the building. There must have been no less than three hundred wounded men sprawled about on the ground. We were looked after by one doctor and a cheerful orderly, who never showed a moment's slackness in his attentions. For two days we lay there in the dung, tormented by clouds of flies. There was no question of changing our bandages and the foul odour of rotting wounds filled the air. One tattered Red Cross flag flew from the roof and the Germans strictly observed its neutrality. Once we saw two German aircraft collide in mid-air, which raised a cheer from the wounded. Perhaps the worst thing of all was the lack of facilities for disposing of our excreta. Some of the men had dysentery and dripped their fæces over their stretchers. We rolled over to urinate in an old jam tin, which was brought round by the orderly. He only stopped serving tea when shooting precluded going outside to the well for water. The doctor did magnificent work with his limited tools, but he was only able to attend to those who were fighting at that moment for life.

On my left there was a Welshman with a badly battered face, who never recovered consciousness to the end. On the other side there was a Maori, who was always cheerful although he had been badly hit, and he made frequent comic allusions to his having been wounded in the one part of the body which matters most. A runner came in on the second day to say that any walking wounded who could make the four miles to Suda would be evacuated during the night. It was extremely probable that the rest of us would be captured. Several New Zealanders staggered to their feet. My Maori friend pulled himself up on two sticks and said, "Well, if you jokers are going, I'm going too, crook or no crook." I hope he did not make it, because the destroyer was sunk the same night.

At about midday on the 28th May our stable became a point of importance in the "no-man's land" between the Welch Regiment and the Germans. At first the Welsh put a machine-gun by the door, but a German came up with a white flag to say that if they did not move it within thirty minutes he would be forced to mortar the dressing-station. After two mortar bombs had started a small fire in the corner of one of the buildings, the Welsh moved back. The fighting went on until late in the afternoon, both Welshmen and Germans coming into the stable for superficial wounds to be dressed before returning to the battle. Then the Welsh went back and there was a short lull in the firing.

Suddenly we heard shouts of "Raust Raust" from the doorway and a handful of German parachutists appeared, looking very fierce and brandishing tommy-guns. They told us to put our hands up and get against the wall, but we politely explained that much as we would like to, it was a physical impossibility. They tried to pull out a wounded Greek boy, whom they intended to shoot, but the New Zealanders protested so vigorously that they desisted. Two of them went into the alcove where our rations were kept and started rummaging in the box. The orderly pushed past them, slammed down the lid and sat on the box.

"No, you bloody don't. Those rations are for the wounded. Here, if you want to make yourself useful, go and get some water from the well and I will make you a cup of tea. Understand? Nero, Moya, aqua, water!"

He thrust a bucket into the hands of a large tough-looking blond, who looked at him in amazement. Then they began to laugh, thinking it all a great joke. They went meekly outside and brought in a bucket of water. After a few minutes they came round to all the wounded with the tea, smiling at us kindly as they told us that Britain was defeated. One very young, rosy-cheeked German could speak fair English and asked me where I had been wounded. I said that I was hit in both legs and the arm. He smiled sweetly and said that he understood that I had been wounded in the "kanee."

A German doctor appeared, who examined all our wounds, and he said that my leg was going gangrenous, which accounted for the stink, and that I would have to be flown to Greece for an immediate operation. I was picked up by four stretcher-bearers and humped over the hill to the 7th General Hospital, now operating under German supervision. I spent the night there under the tender care of a British woman, dressed in a shirt and battledress trousers, whose presence on the island is still a mystery to me. I was put in a captured R.A.F. truck the next morning and driven by a German to Malame aerodrome, where I lay on my stretcher for hours in the blazing sun. Several other wounded New Zealanders were stacked up around me on the sand.

A group of Italians, who had been captured by the Greeks in Albania and had recently been liberated from Galatos prison by the Germans, were standing about on the edge of the airfield.

They thought it great fun to taunt the wounded British and one spat in my face. A German sentry noticed the incident and proceeded to give the Italian one of the most severe beatings I have ever seen administered in the whole of my life. Such is the concord between allies.

We were finally pushed into a JU 52 transport plane, which took off towards the mainland. A tommy-gun was hanging on the wall over my head and I contemplated tackling the crew with it to force them to fly us to Syria. It was wishful thinking and I knew it, for my leg would barely allow me to crawl, let alone to take part in a mêlée. The German pilot came along with a thermos flask full of delicious fresh lemon juice. We were warming a little towards these Boches. I wondered what we would do if we were attacked by Allied aircraft, since a white handkerchief from a window would not be likely to have much effect. It was a stupid thought since Allied aeroplanes had not been exactly common in the last three months. The JU 52 came down once to look at a small boat, but apart from this maintained a steady course to Athens.

A ramshackle ambulance, driven by an Austrian with an edelweiss cap badge, drove us at break-neck speed from Phaleron aerodrome into Athens. An Australian with a severe stomach wound accompanied me, and every time we bumped over a rut he groaned in agony. I shouted at the German to go more slowly, but he merely grinned through the square aperture. We were already encountering the difference between the courtesy in the front line and the bitter callousness of those in the rear.

CHAPTER SIX

PRISON CAMP, 1941

THE PRISONER-OF-WAR hospital was a large white building on the outskirts of Athens, which had been a girls' school before the war. It was a modern structure built in the shape of a Cross of Lorraine in a wide open space near Kokinia, the Covent Garden of Greece. About half a mile away, amidst the houses of the suburbs, sick prisoners were confined in some old Greek barracks.

The hospital was run largely by captured British doctors under German supervision and the treatment was generally good in spite of the shortage of anæsthetics. The wards were crammed full with British wounded from Greece and Crete, but as they became fit enough to be convalescent they were evacuated to the prison camp.

The hospital and the camp were both under the command of the same German officer—a humourless Sudeten Czech—who insisted upon iron discipline. At first our relations were good, but after the first escape he began to reduce our privileges with a clumsy and tactless hand.

The food in the hospital was bad, but we could not blame the Germans for not having made more adequate arrangement to deal with such an unexpected number of prisoners. Our breakfast consisted of mint tea, our lunch of a slice of bread and a piece of goats' cheese, and our dinner of a cup of soup with a piece of bread. It was enough to keep alive prisoners who were lying in bed all day, but it was not sufficient for those who were able to walk about.

The New Zealanders had a number of band instruments and organised many concerts in the wards. At first the Greek Red Cross was allowed to visit us with presents, but later the Germans stopped them when they suspected that it was a means of our contacting friendly organisations outside. We were allowed to write a short letter home every ten days and after the first six weeks we began to receive replies.

On the whole the morale in the hospital was not good. Many of the occupants were bitter about the misdirection of the war, which had led them into Greece and Crete; many were glad to be safe from the Stukas and the air raids to return to their loved ones at the end of hostilities; and many were just completely demoralised by our crushing defeat. Generally speaking, the senior officers were the worst, and I think it is true to say that one is inclined to risk less as one grows older, although it is difficult to notice this tendency in the normal run of the army machine. For instance a plan was hatched for a mass break-out from the prison camp. A thousand prisoners were guarded by four sentries, and the total guard only amounted to thirty. All the Greeks round about were friendly and with the arms of the guard we might have been able to seize a destroyer in the harbour. All the naval experts were there to sail it back to Egypt and there were airmen who were prepared to have a go at the aerodrome at Tatoi. It was admittedly a desperate plan, but with New Zealand and Australian executives, it stood a fair chance of success. It was abandoned because the senior officers were afraid of reprisals and the consequent loss of life. They could not be made to realise that as prisoners we were of no further use to the war effort anyway.

We passed our days in recounting the disasters of the battle and in looking forward to the next meal. We were paid a small sum in marks each month which could be spent at a canteen run by a Greek contractor. Later, the marks were exchanged for special talismans when it was realised that we had managed to change them into the local currency.

As we became more fit, we began to discuss the chances of escape. Many talked about it, but few were prepared to put a plan into execution. In our corner of the ward a Commando officer formed an "escape group," consisting of one other Commando, myself and a New Zealander. His name was Robin Savage, a regular soldier of the Queens, and the others were Ken Maxwell, Sinclair the New Zealander and myself. Savage and Maxwell were only suffering from superficial wounds caused by the truck, in which they had been captured, overturning. Sinclair had been shot through the face and found it difficult to eat. I was the worst with the gaping wound in my thigh, although I was improving rapidly since a German doctor had cut out the gangrene.

Our plans were very imaginative and largely impracticable. We discussed the possibility of stealing a seaplane from the harbour at Phaleron, but I am glad that we were never stupid enough to try it. In the main, our meetings concentrated on the pooling of information about the state of the sentries round the hospital and the chances of escaping from the prison camp. We generally agreed that we were in no condition for a march overland to Turkey and that our only chances of getting away from Greece were by sea. There were rumours of a friendly organisation in Athens, which was prepared to help escaped prisoners, but at that time we were by no means certain of the attitude of the population as a whole. Robin Savage agreed to try to get information up to me from the prison camp (to which he would no doubt soon be transferred) through the medium of the working party which came up every day to clean the floors in the hospital.

The first definite information we received of the friendly attitude of the Greek population was when a concert party was allowed to come up from the prison camp to amuse the patients in the hospital. Pipe-Major Roy of the Black Watch played his pipes on the way up, to the delight of the Greeks in the streets, and the Germans were only able to avoid a riot by a firm show of strength.

Then began a series of escapes, which brought down reprisals on the heads of the prisoners in the hospital and camp alike. The first was a brave attempt by two New Zealanders to escape in the dirty laundry from the hospital. They wrapped themselves up, each in a bundle of sheets, and were carried down to the steps of the hospital by German soldiers, who strangely did not seem to remark upon the weight. They told us later that they lay on the steps in the hot sun for some two hours, until they were near the point of suffocation. When at last the laundry van arrived, they were thrown into the back. It was an unfortunate end to a gallant attempt that they should choose to abandon the van at the moment it was passing the gate of the Italian barracks. They were badly beaten up and returned to the hospital.

The next attempt was more successful. Jim Creagh, a New Zealander, and two others effected an escape from the prison camp by crawling between the sentries on the wire.

A few days later, towards the end of July, two Australians escaped from the hospital by an elaborate plan. The walking patients were allowed in the compound between the hospital and the wire for half an hour at four o'clock every evening. The Australians usually passed the time playing a game of chance on the toss of two pennies called "two-up." One British soldier, who had lost both legs, was an artist of considerable talent and he had curried favour with the guards by painting their portraits. On the night of the escape he occupied the attention of the sentry at the back of the hospital by drawing his caricature. Under the cover of the "two-up" game these two Australians wriggled through the wire to conceal themselves until dark in two holes we had noticed from the roof. Although they could not be seen from ground level, it was quite easy to see them from the top floor and we had to exercise great restraint not to peep through the windows to see how they were getting on.

This successful escape was the cause of considerable reprisals to the remaining prisoners, who responded with a long period of obstinate ill-discipline.

Until then the Germans had only attempted to wheedle us into making gramophone records which could be broadcast to our people at home. Many seriously wounded prisoners, whose resistance had been weakened by pain, forgot themselves enough to agree to send a short message. I am ashamed to say that I was one of them, having succumbed to the honeyed words of a German who said that he had been educated at a Quaker school near Birmingham. Fortunately, we were all warned of the true purpose of the offer by the healthier prisoners, and I think everybody withdrew their agreement before the records were made.

Now the Czech Commandant turned on every device known to prison commanders. Two spies were introduced to the hospital in the guise of R.A.M.C. orderlies, but their excuse of speaking English with an accent because they had lived a long time abroad was easily seen through. One night four Australians beat up one of these informers and locked him in the cells. The wire was strengthened and there were frequent searches. The Commandant pulled off all our bandages in his rage, seemingly convinced that some of us were not wounded at all. This was the last straw as far as we were concerned, and we resolved upon a programme of passive disobedience.

The walking wounded in the hospital and the fit prisoners in the prison camp had always made roll-call difficult by moving from one rank to the other, or answering somebody else's name. Now they refused to fall in until they were prodded by bayonets.

Rotten tomatoes and bits of paving stone were dropped from the roofs on to the heads of the sentries, who countered by firing at any one they could see from the ground. The tyres of the bicycles belonging to the guard were constantly being deflated and rude slogans were chalked on the walls. We were once treated to the spectacle of the Czech Commandant opening the silver paper on every one of a box of chocolates, convinced that we were in contact with the outside through the medium of the supplies which came into the hospital canteen.

We were ordered to salute the Czech Commandant on sight and any infringement was punished by three days in the cells. At the beginning of August I was just able to walk with the aid of a pair of crutches. I failed to salute the Commandant in the corridor one morning and he ordered the sergeant of the guard to give me a kick in the pants, which sent me sprawling in the corridor. I was so angry that I resolved to do something which would really pay him back. I had noticed some packing cases full of straw in one of the courtyards and that evening I put a match to them. It was, perhaps, a stupid trick, for it served no useful purpose except to exasperate the Commandant further.

As a punishment he forbade smoking in the wards and threatened to give any offender three days' solitary confinement on bread and water. Great notices signed on behalf of the Supreme Command of the Reich were posted on the walls, but they only had the effect of further reducing our small reserve of cigarettes. Everybody smoked. The cells were soon full to capacity and the Czech Commandant gave up the unequal struggle.

Our concerts were stopped when "Run, Adolf, run," and "Hang out the Washing on the Siegfried Line" were included in the programme.

An Australian and a New Zealander pulled off one of the most spectacular escapes of the war, when they pole-vaulted the wire in the prison camp. Although many bullets were fired at them they got clean away. Robin Savage came to visit me with the working party the same day. He was very excited, telling me that he had been able to make contact with certain Greeks outside. He would not tell me any of the details at that moment, but promised that he would get a message to me the day before he escaped. At the time he was contemplating a break from the working party half-way between the prison camp and the hospital.

During the night there was a fierce storm in which the wind blew so that you could barely hear yourself speak and the rain came down in torrents. Thirteen officers and thirteen men escaped through the wire from the prison camp. A spectator told us later that they were passing through two separate holes like a long line of rabbits. A German sentry shone a torch on one officer as he was half-way under the wire, but failed to see him. Included in the escapees were all my friends—Savage, Maxwell and Sinclair—and Pipe-Major Roy, who left with his pipes in full marching order.

I did not know whether to be furious or happy when I heard the news the next morning. I felt deserted in a way, for they had promised to give me some information before they left, and now I was all alone in the hospital.

The Czech Commandant was furious. He told us all that he would lose his job if there were any more escapes, and that he was going to make it his business to see that there were not. He placed eight machine-guns round the prison camp, strengthened the wire and doubled the guard. The wire at the hospital was also strengthened. Greek boys had been in the habit of swooping up to the wire on bicycles and throwing packets of cigarettes across, but this was now stopped by deliberate rifle-fire. Ten Greeks were shot within sight of the prison camp—as an example —when a sentry reported that someone had fired a rifle bullet at him.

After a fortnight I felt that I could walk well enough to begin to take active steps towards my escape.

CHAPTER SEVEN

ESCAPE FROM PRISON, 1941

ON THE FACE of it, it appeared that the hospital was more difficult to escape from than the prison camp. It was in an open space of ground, about a thousand yards square, and the wire consisted of a normal fence, eight feet high with close vertical and horizontal strands, connected to a roll of concertina wire by a diagonal sheeting. One sentry stood on each corner of the wire, and after dark a patrol walked round the outside. At the camp, from which there had been many more escapes, the Greek houses were only separated from the wire by the width of the road. The perimeter was longer and the ground inside the wire was quite broken.

I resolved to make my first reconnaissance in the prison camp. The large wound in my thigh was still far from healed, but I persuaded one of the English doctors to pass me as fit for the camp. The rumours of an impending move to Germany or Italy lent additional urgency to my plans. The march down was most fatiguing and I found my leg so stiff that it was difficult to walk for two days.

I was disappointed by the outlook in my new abode. The Germans had tightened up their security measures considerably since the big break, and I could see no obvious way of escaping. A lovely Greek girl with a beautiful voice used to sing "South of the Border, Down Mexico Way," from the roof of a house opposite at the same time every evening, and once we glimpsed the red hair of one of the New Zealand escapees through the window. Unless it was a Gestapo trap, this house was certainly friendly.

I had been in the camp for two days when a Scots doctor whispered that he would like to see me outside the hut during the evening exercise period. When I met him, after a cautious look round about, he said that he had a message from Maxwell. I was to get in touch with a certain New Zealand corporal in the cookhouse.

I found this friend the next morning, but he stoutly denied that he knew anything about Maxwell or anybody else. After I had argued with him for some minutes, he took me aside and whispered, "If you really want to escape, I can get a message to some people outside. You see, I go in with the ration truck every day. When the German gets out to open the gate of the dump, I can pass messages into the crowd. Are you fair dinkum on the level? O.K.! Leave it to me. Come and see me on Tuesday."

I met him again on the Tuesday and he said that if I escaped certain friends would be waiting in a ruined house five hundred yards from the wire on Thursday night. He told me to confirm that I was going on the Thursday morning.

It was a tall order since I had no idea how to elude the sentries, and my leg was not really in any condition for acrobatics. To escape is difficult enough, but to have to get away by a certain time is too much for even the most expert of escapers. On Thursday morning I reluctantly told him that I was unable to make it.

The defences at the camp were so strong that I now resolved to try my luck with the hospital, where the sentries were not quite so alert. A bout of sand-fly fever helped me to convince the German doctor that the wound in my leg was deteriorating. He was so taken in by my groans of pain every time he touched the wound, that he railed against the doctors who had been stupid enough to discharge me. I was carried back to the hospital on a stretcher by four Germans, although I would have been quite capable of walking.

When I had got back to my old bed in the ward, I began a week of intensive organisation. I had already converted my store of marks into three thousand drachmæ at the Greek canteen. I also saved up odd scraps of food which I scrounged from the kitchen. A wounded padre had an ordnance map of Greece of which we all took a tracing on lavatory paper.

The main problem apart from the actual escape was how to acquire civilian clothes. I dyed a suit of pyjamas dark blue with the gentian violet ointment used for sprained ankles. Somebody sold me a white shirt and I obtained a pair of Australian brown boots in exchange for my overcoat (or rather the overcoat which Jim Crewdson had put over me when I was first wounded in Crete). The boots were too obviously new, so I cut them about with an old razor blade. A Greek plumber was repairing a pipe in the hospital and I tried to persuade him to give me his panama hat. He was terrified, saying that the Germans would shoot him,

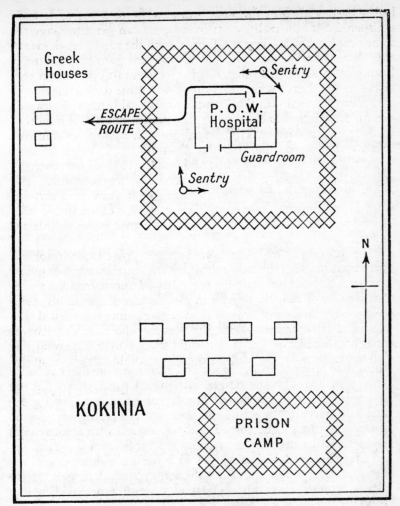

PRISON CAMP, 1941.

but later in the day, when he took it off for a moment, I stole it.

All these items of escape kit I concealed in a pillowslip under my bed. My first idea was to hop into the ration truck which came in every day through the main gate. Although we were not allowed to sit on the front steps, I used regularly to sit there on my pillowslip, half-reading a book and half-contemplating the chances of getting into the truck. The sentries would move me away at first, but I always came back, and I think the blank look on my face eventually convinced them that I was a harmless lunatic. If I could get into the driving seat and start the truck, there was little doubt that I would be able to steer it through the gate. But I could never face the possibility of the engine not starting with the first press of the button.

I was taking a course of sunbathing on the roof in the afternoon to try to cover myself with enough tan to pass as a Greek. One afternoon in the middle of August I suddenly noticed that the sentry on the gate (who was also responsible for the west side of the wire) was gazing at some Greek women digging for food in a rubbish heap. He seemed half-asleep and I knew him of old as a rather stupid man with one eye. This was an opportunity which I would never forgive myself if I missed. I ran down to the ward, grabbed my pillowslip, scurried down the stairs and out through the back door. I was still clad only in a pair of shorts and I think the sentry on the back must have thought me a member of the fatigue party about to put some rubbish in the dustbin, although we were not allowed into the compound until four o'clock.

I walked out of his sight round the corner of the building. The sentry on the gate was still looking in the opposite direction. I walked straight up to the wire and crawled through it. Something had snapped in my brain and I cannot remember actually wriggling through the tangle, although I think that I did not touch it once with my body. The dressing had come off my leg and I limped slowly across the open space, keeping one eye on the sentry. Just as he turned, I threw myself into a convenient rivulet, but by then I was five hundred yards from the wire.

I lay there panting, overjoyed with the astonishing ease of my escape. After a few moments the sentry turned to gaze at the Greek women once more. I stood up and ran, half-limping, towards the nearest Greek cottages. I glanced back once to the hospital and saw somebody wave a handkerchief from the roof. I waved back.

I was too far away to be recognised now, so that I began to walk. I came into a narrow unpaved street behind the cottages, where some women were bargaining around a fruit barrow. At any other time I would have been embarrassed, but now I was too excited to care. I began to change into my civilian clothes in the middle of the street. The women stopped their chattering and stared at me, transfixed. An old peasant came up to me and beckoned for me to follow her. I walked behind her into a cottage, holding up my trousers with one hand, and finished my changing under cover. In sign language she asked if the Germans had seen me escape. I shook my head. A little girl with trachoma in one eye took me by the hand and led me out into the street.

I walked with her, preceded now by a boy, to another little two-roomed cottage in the centre of the village. A rather attractive peasant woman, whose name I gathered to be Maria, was painting the ceiling from the top of a pair of step-ladders. She evinced no surprise at the news and led me into the front room, where she left me alone with about eleven babies.

Most of the room was occupied by a brass-knobbed double bed, which was crawling with babies of all ages. There seemed to be children everywhere. A mantelpiece was decorated with empty shellcases and I noticed that one of the babies was playing with an anti-gas eyeshield of English manufacture. I sat there on the chair, waiting and still panting with the excitement of my escape.

She had pulled the curtains and locked the door, but I was suspicious and started up at every sound. Once I heard a truck outside, and thought that they had sold me to the Germans, but it turned out to be only the sewage truck from the camp.

After about an hour visitors began to pour in with presents. The first was Maria's husband, who was an orange-seller and could say "oranges very good one bob" in English, which was not much of a help. I explained by means of a diagram on the back of a cigarette box how I had escaped. Others came in and kissed me on both cheeks, hugging me with joy. They pushed an enormous plate of macaroni before me and filled my pockets with packets of Woodbines. Some sang a national song and danced a sort of jig around me. Then they brought in another pretty girl, who unfortunately only had one eye, and pointed out the most attractive parts of her body. She rubbed both fingers together and pointed to the bed. It seemed that she had lost her husband in Albania and wanted me to till the garden. Maria noticed that I was looking embarrassed (for, after all, it was a bit fast) and told her husband to wait until later. They seemed very pleased when I said that a blonde baby was "an inglesi."

I felt that I was too close to the prison camp to be safe and, in any case, I was in no mood for settling down to married life,

115

so I decided to pay a visit after dark to the friendly house near the prison camp. The orange-seller was broken-hearted and Maria wept, but I was quite adamant about wanting to find my friends.

In the evening I walked with the orange-seller past cafés full of carousing Germans to a street near the prison camp. I made one navigational error in the dark and nearly ran into one of the sentries on the wire. At last I climbed over a stone wall at the back of the house. A man in a white cloth cap was pruning a tree in the garden and he dropped his shears in amazement when I crept up and whispered "English" into his ear. He signalled to me to beware of the large house next door, which apparently contained fascisti, and pushed me into a small gardener's cottage. The most beautiful girl I have ever seen came into the room. She was dressed in a neat, white summer frock and was barefooted. I suspected that she was the girl who used to sing "South of the Border, Down Mexico Way," to the prisoners. At first they were suspicious, but when I asked them if they had seen my friend Maxwell, they went into peals of laughter.

The girl caught me by the shoulders and, pulling me towards her, kissed me full on the lips. I blushed scarlet like a self-conscious schoolboy. She whipped my panama hat off my head and gave me a new cloth cap. Then she explained to the chagrined little orange-seller that I must go to join my friends. I was sorry to leave him, for he was the first of many kind helpers. I think it is true to say that we would have received the same help at nine Greek houses out of ten in Athens at that time. It is, without doubt, the kindest and most hospitable race in the world. If I could do anything to save them from the agonies they are undergoing at this moment, I would gladly give my life to do so.

They went into a huddle in the corner and whispered plans in Greek, with shrugs of their shoulders and waves of their hands. After a few moments I found myself in the street with the girl and her mother. Her brother went on ahead.

We walked a long way down lighted streets and past the Italian barracks, where a soldier was playing upon a trumpet at the gate. One Italian soldier cast a keen look at us and I began to fear that he had seen through my disguise, when I suddenly realised with relief that he was more interested in the girl than in me. We came to a shopping centre, where the streets were full of people and the windows were brightly lit. The brother came back with another Greek, who told me that his name was

Sortires, and who put some very shrewd questions to me. He asked me where I lived in England and I said Birmingham, which was untrue, but sounded more convincing than any other town he was likely to have known. He asked me where I had been captured and the name of my unit. At last he seemed convinced that I was not a Gestapo spy and told me to follow him. I had walked several paces before I remembered that I had not said good-bye to my new-found friends, but when I turned round they had gone.

Sortires led me up a flight of stairs, opened the door and pushed me into a room. I was still blinking my eyes to accustom them to the light when somebody shouted my name. All I could see was a polished table around which sat three Greeks, none of whom I could recognise. And then one of them was slapping me on the back. It was Maxwell, who had dyed his hair black and had grown black sideboards and a thin moustache. It was a perfect disguise, and I was staggered by his transformation.

I was overjoyed at my astounding luck in meeting up with my old friend once more. It was nearly a month since the others had escaped and Maxwell was full of their experiences. We exchanged reminiscences far into the night, while the Greeks fussed around us. It was explained that the fat man was a dentist called Tino, who owned the house, and that Sortires was a coster, who had organised his friends into a gang to aid escaped British prisoners. I learned later that his patrons were one Valisaki, a captain in the Greek Navy, and Papastratis, the famous cigarette manufacturer. Tino's wife was a good-looking blonde, who seemed to me to be making a dead-set at Maxwell, which could not have been good for the success of our schemes. She had a bonny child, which Maxwell made a great fuss about, teaching it to say "Kakomania" or "Bad Germans" in Greek baby talk.

Robin Savage was in a jeweller's house in Piraeus and Sinclair was hiding in a house by the harbour. It seemed that they had great hopes of obtaining a caique to take us to Turkey or Egypt, but the plans fell through before I had been there a day. Altogether, during my month in hiding in Greece we had fifteen different false alarms for escape by caique or submarine. Our disappointments became so regular that we began to suspect that the Greeks were not interested in our escaping to Egypt, but rather they wanted us to stay to be of use in a rebellion. I now think that these suspicions were unjustified, but when one is in hiding for long periods at a time one's ideas are liable to get out of proper perspective.

After I had had an enormous meal, my hair was dyed black by the dentist's wife with some sort of quick-taking dye which oxidised into a metallic black as soon as it had been applied. The colour lasted for the whole of my sojourn in Greece and caused me great embarrassment when it began to grow out in Egypt two months later. I can still remember the shocked whispers of Gezira lovelies, who thought that this "frightful subaltern" had dyed his hair. The piebald colour did not altogether disappear for another six months.

Ken Maxwell and I talked long into the night, but at last we went to bed. We were aroused at an early hour the next morning by Tino, who said that German soldiers were searching Kokinia. He did not seem in the least bit alarmed and told us that we could watch them from two deck-chairs on the balcony if we wished.

I was quite apprehensive, since it was quite obvious that this search was consequent to my escape, but Maxwell stilled my fears. Italian soldiers in tin hats were patrolling the streets in fours, while Germans were debussing from trucks to search the houses at the end of the street. We saw them turn out all the idlers from the coffee houses and arrest those who had not got identity cards. When the searchers reached the next house but one, Tino told us to come inside. He showed us a drain-pipe through an open bedroom window and then hid us under some floorboards in the room. But there was no need to worry. Tino told such convincing lies to the German officer at the door that he did not bother to search the house.

Sortires arrived later in the morning in a very agitated state. He said that a German officer had called at his brother's house at four o'clock in the morning while Sortires was away from home. Elias, his brother, had been arrested, while his wife, who was seven months gone with child, had had a miscarriage from the shock. Sortires was now on the run and he said that it was important that we should move to another house in Athens without delay. These two brothers were good brave boys, but they liked to endanger our position by bragging of their achievements in the cafés. Elias endured unspeakable tortures at the hands of the Gestapo, but refused to talk, so convincing them that they finally released him. There were many cases of Greeks withstanding torture rather than disclose what they knew of the

118

whereabouts of British prisoners. One woman had matches thrust up her finger-nails, and was later released. She came to see us in Athens and we were horrified by the sight of what the Gestapo had done to her. I have never quite understood why the risks Greeks underwent for British soldiers were not more publicised in the newspapers at home.

In the evening a girl called Dolly arrived to guide us to our new home. She was an ugly girl, but the stories of her bravery were legend. She was said to spend her spare time in manufacturing coloured paper "V's," which she put on the seats of German staff cars. Maxwell went with another man and I followed with Dolly out into the street. We walked down to the bus-stop in the market-place past hundreds of soldiers taking the air. I at first shrank away from the Italians, but Dolly led me right up to them until our shoulders brushed. We got into the bus and she bought our tickets. I noticed a man in a white gabardine coat who was staring at me with blue, penetrating eyes, so that I began to fear that he might be a Gestapo agent. Dolly dug me in the ribs and told me to "look out," whereupon I became very agitated until I realised that she meant me to look out of the window. I am afraid I am very stupid.

When we left the bus at Piraeus, I noticed that the man in the white coat was following. We took a turning to the left and he turned as well, keeping about fifty yards behind. I told Dolly and she bade me to keep on walking, while she dodged into a shop window. A few moments later she caught up with me, saying that it was all right. I did not dare to ask her what she had done, for she was quite capable of sticking a knife in his ribs.

We arrived at the house of Mr. Kazarsis, the jeweller, where Robin Savage and I met again for the first time in a month. He apologised for having left so suddenly without warning and lauded Kazarsis to the skies. He was an old man of about sixty, with grey hair and a faultless appearance. His shoes were so brightly polished that you could see your face in them. He prided himself on being more English than the English, and his conversation was like a quaint old Victorian book. He had served as an interpreter with our armies at Salonika in the Great War, a record of which he was very proud. Savage agreed that Kokinia was getting too hot to be safe and suggested that we spend the night with Robin Sinclair, before moving on to Athens the next day. He himself would stay in Piraeus to maintain contact with our friends.

It was explained that a rival society in Athens had been agitating to replace Sortires and Co. as our protectors. We did not understand why they should be so anxious to have us (not realising at the time that they were part of the same organisation), and when the leader, a Madame Kareeyani, sent her ravishing blonde daughter Electra down to talk us into moving, Savage's suspicions were aroused. I cannot quite remember the details of the intrigue, but it was something to do with a Greek Air Force officer called Angelo, a shining light in the rival society, who had been arrested by the Gestapo. However, it was agreed that beggars cannot be choosers and that it would be better under the circumstances to accompany Dolly to Athens.

It was a long walk to the house in which Robin Sinclair was staying and by the time we had reached it the wound in my leg was bleeding profusely. We rang the bell at the heavy iron gates of a large house overlooking the harbour. It was opened by a funny old man in Asiatic clothes, who proved to be Mr. Constantinedes, an Albanian charcoal merchant and our new protector. Inside we met Robin Sinclair, who had dyed his hair red and was wearing a blue shirt with white flannels like a Hollywood film star. It was plain to see that he was having an awkward time with Aliki, the patron's daughter, who obviously adored him. She was the rather spoilt daughter of a rich man, but was quite attractive in a way in spite of her large tummy. I felt very weak—too weak in fact to eat the splendid meal they had prepared for us in the palatial dining-room. Mr. Constantinedes retired upstairs to leave us to the tender mercies of Aliki. We had long resolved to avoid amorous entanglements, appreciating the risk of betrayal by a jealous suitor, but it was not always easy. Ken Maxwell and I were quite relieved to reach the seclusion of our bedroom.

The next day was spent in frivolous games with Aliki and her girl friends, amongst whom was a beautiful brunette called Felicity. Only by dint of the greatest tact did we avoid complications, which might have wrecked all our plans. It was easy to understand the setting for an ideal romance—young British officers being sheltered by brave, beautiful women. It was indeed fortunate that the pain from my wound prevented me from responding too much to their overtures. We played a game called "the bottle," which consisted of the girls spinning a bottle on the table and kissing the man to which it pointed when it came to rest. Sortires arrived in the afternoon and it was obvious that he intensely resented Aliki's attentions to Sinclair. Here were the first smoulderings of a fire and only our move to Athens saved us from a large conflagration.

When evening came, Dolly arrived with two other boys to take us to our new home. I was to play the urchin with one of the boys, which suited me well. We set off walking in three pairs, the boy and I leading by some fifty yards. Contact was maintained by whistling "Koreetho Mussolini," a patriotic song to the tune of "The Woodpecker Song." Dolly was a great expert, because she had a broken tooth in front.

We passed many sailors on the water-front, two of whom stopped us to ask the time. The boy was quick to answer. I made a careful note of the number of destroyers in the harbour in case it might be useful. At the underground railway station the boy bought our tickets and gave me a Greek newspaper. We swaggered about with our hands in our pockets on the platform, occasionally spitting nonchalantly on to the track. We took pains not to recognise each other when we got on the train, although all the pairs were in the same coach. I unfolded my newspaper and sat in a corner, but I was completely nonplussed when a Greek tapped me on the knee to ask a question. Again the boy quickly intervened to answer.

At the terminus we passed many German soldiers before we walked across Ammonia Square to the tram-stop. We kept on the outside of the tram where the lights were dim, but, even so, I felt that the Greek opposite me was staring rather hard. I began to calculate my chances if I jumped off while the tram was on the move. Still the Greek stared, until my face went scarlet and it seemed that his eyes were boring through to my back collar stud. Suddenly he dismounted at a stop (in point of fact the one before ours), and as he swung off the tram, he winked one eye and put up his thumb. So much for my disguise!

We walked down the streets to the bungalow in which we were to spend the next ten days. It was already occupied by five other escaped prisoners—the renowned Pipe-Major Roy, two Australians, a Polish Jew called George Filar and another Palestinian called Christo. All these escapees were being looked after by Dolly and her mother under the supervision of Madame Kareeyani. They had various incredible stories of escape to tell.

121

George Filar had been a sergeant in a Palestinian Pioneer Company and had led a party of Jews to escape down a sewer from Corinth Prison Camp. He had also demonstrated his bravery by aiding the escape of four New Zealanders from our own camp in Kokinia. He was to prove a trusty and reliable member of our party, especially since he had learned to speak Greek so rapidly. I little thought at the time that I was to fall out so much with the Jews six years later. The two Australians had swum ashore off a prison ship bound for Salonika. They had been forced to kill a German with an iron bar to effect their escape from the docks at Piraeus.

So many friends came in with presents of clothing and food that we began to fear that our new home was less secure than the last. Madame Kareeyani was a splendid woman with enormous breasts, who could not do enough for us. She was executed by the Gestapo on the day that the Allied parachutists landed on Megara airfield. Since her death there has been great controversy as to whether she really was a brave woman, but all I can say is that I vouch for the fact that she took great risks on our behalf.

I was much amused by the pains Pipe-Major Roy took to preserve his other-rank status. He frowned on attempts at familiarity, obviously believing that it was bad for discipline. The Greeks loved him.

We had a lot of trouble with Christo, who would insist upon going abroad at night, although all the others had agreed not to take unnecessary risks. Even worse, we could not cure him of expectorating out of the window.

After about ten days, a Cypriot stranger arrived with news of a submarine and promised to take us to the rendezvous in a taxi the next night. We could not wholly trust him, although he was probably quite genuine. During the day a Greek Intelligence Officer called "Jackson" arrived with certain information which he asked us to memorise in case we should get away. When the appointed time drew near, our nerves were so frayed that we were all ready to bolt out of the back door at the slightest suspicious sound. As it happened, a perfectly innocent motor car did precipitate two of us into the back garden. The taxi did not turn up, thus leaving us all in a state of agitation. Robin Savage had concocted a plan for stealing an E-boat from the harbour, which I considered to be not worth the risk. He planned to row out to the torpedo-net in a dinghy and there to pull the plug out of the boat. He calculated that this would call down a patrol boat, which he intended to capture with grenades and pistols (all of which were available). Consequent upon this small disagreement and the failure of the submarine venture, we decided to split forces. Four was too large a party in any case. I asked Madame Kareeyani to find a new billet for Sinclair and myself, while Savage and Maxwell moved off to new friends. We still maintained contact through the medium of George, the Polish Jew.

Robin Sinclair and I were lodged in a new home owned by one Aristedes. His two half-sisters, Elpice and Kathia, and his mother were living in the same house. Elias, his brother, was a merchant captain whose ship had been sunk and who occasionally called in to see us. It was a pleasant home and we were very happy. Every morning the old mother would wake us up with two figs and a glass of milk. "Kalli mera," she would say, "how are you?" By then we had obtained bogus Greek identity cards and each morning Elpice would put us through a catechism of questions. I was Costas Nicholaides, a bank clerk from Samos.

"What is the name of your father?"

"My father's name is Giorgio."

"What is the name of your mother?"

"My mother's name is Maria."

"Where do you live?"

"I live at Number Six, Stadium Street."

"No, Costas, you say it like this . . ." and she would mouth a difficult Greek word.

We were becoming quite proficient in the language and could already carry on a simple conversation. We played cards all day, becoming great experts at a version of "Piquette." In the evenings we sometimes went out for exercise. Once we went to the cinema and I sat next to a German officer. They were ridiculous films— a newsreel about Russians being mown down in thousands, and a stupid melodrama in which a flower-girl sang a song called "Bloomen." We had great fun throwing cigarettes in the air on the way back, when they told us that it was bad luck not to stamp them out. They were laughing, happy days. Elpice conceived a great attachment for me, which was difficult to resist. I can remember now how we sat on the roof in the moonlight, looking at the stars behind the Parthenon, while she stroked my hair and softly crooned a Greek love song.

123

One night there was a big R.A.F. raid on Tatoi airfield, which received heavy damage from bombs bursting in the hangars. We watched it all from the roof and were overjoyed at the fires which were started, although our friends' faces fell a little the next day when they learned that many Greek civilians had been killed. Even so, they tended to exaggerate the German losses. The extraordinary thing was their never-failing conviction that the English would soon return.

It was about the middle of September when Elias, the merchant sailor, first spoke to us of the chances of an escape. He said that several Greeks desired to get to Egypt, but had not enough money to hire a boat. They would be prepared to take us if we could raise some cash. George, the Polish Jew, who could speak Greek so well by now that he was able to walk about in daylight, was our only contact with the outside world. I instructed him to contact all the heads of the organisation to see if he could raise money on the strength of promissory notes signed by me on behalf of the British Government. Our chief benefactor was a polished gentleman called Averoff, once an officer in the Greek Navy, and he was good enough to give us something in the neighbourhood of a hundred and forty pounds in drachmæ. The President of the Anglo-Hellenic League, an old Etonian called Palis, also visited us with offers of help. I paid a visit by day, wearing dark sun-glasses, to Robin Savage, who was living in great luxury in a flat in the centre of the town. His female ward also gave us a large sum. Savage and Maxwell did not wish to accompany us for some obscure reason (I think because they had little faith that the caique would ever materialise), and we said good-bye to each other. Robin continued to take an interest in our venture up to the moment we embarked and even sent down Mr. Kazarsis to make certain that we were not being sold a pig in a poke.

When all the plans were ready, we moved down to a fisherman's cottage in Piraeus. There we met Lefteris, the engineer who was to coax the engine across the Mediterranean. He was a handsome, hefty Greek with a captivating smile and quite an air of solidity about him. We drank coffee in his house for some hours, discussing the details of the voyage. Our old friend Elias was to accompany us as the captain. We moved to the house of one Pantorelli, who was another friend of Lefteris. He was living in a house in great poverty with his aged mother and a young brother, who was christened "Spike" by virtue of his close-cropped hair. I have omitted to say that during these preceding two days we had picked up two other British passengers for the boat—an Australian sergeant and a staff-sergeant in the Service Corps called Charles Wright. The Australian was a tough egg who had run a dance-band in Sydney in civilian life. They had both walked across the mountains from Corinth and Wright had contracted some terrible sores from bad water. Spike became very attached to the Australian, who used to sing to him in a rich bass voice.

Then began the usual mist of politics and intrigue which surrounds all Greek schemes. Yani, the owner of the caique, said that he would not part with the boat unless we gave him another hundred pounds. He came to see me in the house and I pleaded with him to see reason, but he was quite adamant. I offered a promissory note but he insisted upon cash. He was a horrible-looking rogue and he stank of fish and wine. I feared that he not only wanted to bleed us dry, but also intended to collect the reward for our capture from the Gestapo.

Averoff came to the rescue again with a promise that the money would be paid in cash in Athens the moment he received a code message on the Cairo radio to say that we had safely arrived in Egypt. After a petulant show of ill grace, Yani agreed, fearing to incite the wrath of a powerful man like Averoff.

In the evening Pantorelli arrived in a great state of excitement to say that Lefteris and another Greek had been arrested by the police. We gathered at first that it was because they had been loading black market diesel oil on to the boat, but I believe from what I have heard since that it was for drunkenness. It seemed that all was lost.

The next day Lefteris arrived with a Greek policeman, grinning all over his face. As soon as Lefteris had told them that he was aiding some British officers to escape, he was released. All they wanted to know was why he had not told them in the first place. The policeman brought us some loaves of bread, and, with tears running down his face, gave me his pistol. He also promised to picket the docks while we stowed away on board the boat. I was very pleased at the turn events had taken, for it meant that there would be no further monkey business from Yani.

We sneaked down to the quay in ones and twos at about eleven o'clock, long after curfew. It was important that we should make no noise, since German sentries were sleeping on an army caique two boat-lengths away. The ten Greek passengers had got there before us and were crouched together in the tiny hold. They whispered that they were having some trouble with the boy, Spike, who had stowed away during daylight. I tried to persuade him to land, but he told me through his tears that he was only a burden on his mother, that he was only another mouth to feed and he wanted to be a soldier. I tried pulling him out by the legs, but he threatened to awake all Athens with his screams. Pantorelli pleaded with him from the shore, but he clung tightly to the front stanchion without saying a word. Another attempt to drag him out met with the same result. In desperation, I assured his brother that I would take care of him like a son when we got to Egypt.

"But you do not understand, he is very sick."

"I will pay for all the doctors in the world."

"Yes, but he must have injections every week. He has syphilis."

"Whatever he has got, I will see that he is cared for."

Pantorelli turned abruptly on his heel and stalked up the hill.

Just before dawn we cast off and allowed the tide to take us out into the middle of the harbour. When we were well clear of the shore, Lefteris started up the engine with the aid of a blow-lamp.

It was only a small vessel—perhaps thirty feet in length—and the fourteen people were crammed tight in the hold, their mouths amongst the cockroaches. There was a gaping hole where the mast should have been, so that we were relying entirely on our diesel motors. We calculated that we should have just enough fuel to reach Alexandria in four days if all went well. For navigation, we had an old school atlas which showed the shapes of the islands we were to follow as far as Crete. From there it would be plain sailing due south. There was only a sack of crusts and a few onions on board, for the famine was already tightening its grip on Athens. We christened the ship *Elpice*, which not only reminded us of our benefactress in Greece, but also represented the spirit of the voyage.

Most of us writhed in the agonies of sea-sickness in the first two hours, but we soon became accustomed to the roll of our tiny craft.

Off the first island, we sighted a patrol boat, which sent us all scrambling into the hold. Elias cast the nets overboard and we safely passed the danger point without incident. On the second day a German aircraft dived down to look at us, but it must have been satisfied because it resumed its course.

We glided happily through the calm sea between the islands, lying on the deck and trailing our hands in the water. Everything was going well until the second night, when Giorgio, another Greek, had taken the tiller from Elias. He mistook the shape of an island and took us far out of our course. I suddenly noticed that the islands were not corresponding to the shape of those in the atlas and woke up Elias. We held to the same bearing for some time, until at last he agreed. We decided to anchor in the lee of a rock until daylight. Just as we were chugging into the shadows, somebody noticed a dark shape which looked like another boat. Lefteris switched off the engine and we sat there for a long time, holding our breaths, but the shadow did not move. Daylight revealed it to be another rock.

It was a serious business this loss of course, since our fuel supply left no margin of safety. Anxiously we counted up the cans. To our horror, we discovered that someone—presumably Pantorelli—had stolen three tins. There was no turning back now and all we could do was to pray that we might meet up with a British ship on the other side of Crete. For the next two days we made good headway through the beautiful calm seas of the Aegean. There is no place in the world which quite reaches the beauty of the Greek islands in the spring and the autumn. We lay back on the deck, basking in the sunshine and thinking how infinitely better this was than our clandestine life in the suburbs of Athens. As a novice to the sea, I was quite astonished to find how long it took to reach an island which looked comparatively close. The sunsets were breath-taking in their loveliness. As the shadows lengthened, the rocky islands took on a purple tint and our tiny craft became a speck of gold on a shining lake. I thought of Flecker and expected the caique to burst into a rose at any moment. The most moving thing was the all-pervading silence, only broken by the "phut phut" of our motor.

In the planning stage, we had always reckoned that the danger point would be the straits between the east end of Crete and the Rhodes Islands. We knew it to be patrolled by E-boats and had therefore decided to pass through during the hours of darkness. The mistake in our course had taken us a full day off our bearing, so that we were already completely out of schedule. I was beginning to regret that I had voted against sailing for Turkey on the grounds that it was highly probable that she would soon be invaded by Germany. Now there was nothing for it but to soft pedal so that we would pass through the straits on the fourth night out from Piraeus. We badly needed more water and food and I therefore agreed with Elias that the best course was to sail for Santorini, a large island commanding the entrance to the straits.

We reached what we thought to be the island early on the morning of the fourth day. There was no sign of any movement on the side from which we approached, so we took the caique right up into the calm sea between the rocks at the base of the cliff. There was no question of going round to the port which the atlas showed to be on the east side, since it was extremely likely that there was a German garrison on the island. Christos, a young Greek sailor, dived over the side with a knife in his mouth, bent on climbing the cliff to kill a sheep. He looked like an ancient pirate as his naked body swarmed monkey fashion up the rocky cliffs. He was gone some time and when at last he reappeared, the news he hailed down to the boat was most disappointing. The island was not Santorini, but was an uninhabited islet four miles to the south. There was a better anchorage on the east side.

Elias guided the boat round to the other side of the island and we all waded ashore to see what we could find. It was plain that the place had been inhabited at some time, perhaps only seasonally during the harvest, because a large part of its surface was covered with recent wheat stubble. By now we were very hungry, so that we were pleased to collect odd ears of corn we found on the ground. Over on the south side, I found definite signs of habitation. Rude square dwellings had been carved out of the rocks and were fitted with wooden doors. There was even a tiny chapel on the hill with all its equipage in a fine state of preservation. I genuflected and said a short prayer before the altar, putting my remaining drachmae in the offertory box before I left.

A delighted shout from Christos heralded the discovery of a cistern full of sweet fresh water. We filled up our olive oil barrel and the stone chatty we had brought from Piraeus. We all drank long draughts, throwing the cool water all over our bodies, until our bellies were distended with the pressure. Looking out over the sea towards Crete, we could see two tiny fishing boats tossing on the waves. The Australian sergeant found two baskets full of fruit hidden in the rocks by the shore, which obviously belonged to the fishermen. All my prayers had been answered. I was for taking both baskets, but Elias insisted upon our only taking one, firm in the conviction that we would be violating some unwritten law of the sea. We left all our remaining Greek money in the other basket as some compensation for what we had stolen.

We resumed our voyage and during the fourth night we began to pass through the straits. A lighthouse could be plainly seen on the eastern tip of Crete and we could also see aircraft landing on the Heraklion airfield. When we were half-way through the dangerous stretch, a thick fog came down. At first we blessed it, but when it developed into one of those sudden storms characteristic of the Mediterranean at this time of the year, we began to fear for the safety of the boat. The sea grew from a slight choppiness to a boiling cauldron in under an hour. Elias grimly held the tiller so that our bows struck the enormous waves as our tiny craft was driven before the wind. We were carried at will by the storm for a day and a half, riding the forty-foot waves like a celluloid ball in a shooting gallery. If any of those waves had hit us broadside, we would have certainly capsized. Elias held on to the tiller for forty-eight hours without rest. Only an expert sailor could have brought us through to survival in such a sea. He would give the tiller a flick on the tops of the waves to take full advantage of the movement of those great walls of water. As it was, many waves crashed over the side to fill the hold with water. While we held the sides with one hand, we tried to bail it out with jam tins with the other. At times it was all we could do to remain in the boat. She would be carried along on the white foam at the top of a great mass of water, her propeller threshing madly in the air, and then we would crash forty feet below into the slough in the writhing sea between two towering white-flecked cliffs. It was plain from the sun that we were being carried too much to the south-west towards Benghazi, in spite of Elias's efforts to bring her round on the tops of the waves. What was even more serious, our diesel oil was being rapidly consumed with the rough usage the propeller was receiving. We could not turn off the motor because it was only our small amount of headway which enabled us to run with the waves.

After a day and a half of pure misery, the storm abated as quickly as it had risen. We found ourselves once more in a calm sea, but with the difference that now we were drifting powerless with the current. Our last stocks of diesel oil had gone. I was completely dismayed to find that almost all our water and every scrap of food had also disappeared. I cursed myself for my carelessness in not rationing it more strictly. We were all in the depths of despondency and lay half-conscious in the sun, overcome by our exertions in the storm. I ordered strict rationing of the water to one-third of a jam tin per man per day and set myself down with a drawn pistol by the barrel. It was cold in the night and we fought for a corner of one of the two blankets.

Our lethargy degenerated into argument on the morning of the sixth day. George, the Polish Jew, was disappointing for the first time since I had met him. He hurled recriminations at Elias for not having checked the oil before our departure, and even accused Lefteris of having had a hand in stealing it. When the time came for the water ration, I quarrelled with the Australian, who swore that he had not had his share although I knew full well that he had. He struck me on the chin and the Greeks threatened to throw him overboard. Most of the Greeks seemed to collapse in resignation to their fate, but Lefteris just sat in the stern staring moodily out to sea. He roused himself sufficiently to help me make two square sails out of blankets at about midday, constructing a mast from boards torn from the bottom of the boat.

In the afternoon we divided ourselves into two parties and tried to paddle with boards and planks, but we soon collapsed exhausted into the bottom of the boat. We tried again in the evening, but we were too weak to make it effective.

We were all very weak by the seventh day, when the time came round for the last water ration. I was quite touched by Spike's trying to refuse his, saying that he had no right to it since he had embarked without permission from Piraeus. It was a brave gesture, especially since he was the most sickly member of the crew. Of course we made him drink it, even giving him more than his ration. I hope he is happy now. When I last heard of him he was an apprentice in the Greek Air Force.

The most active member of the crew, in spite of his sores, was Staff-Sergeant Charles Wright. He timed how long it took for a cigarette packet to pass from the bows to the stern and thus calculated that we were making about one and a half knots with the current. He also made a rough estimate of our position with the aid of an angle made of two sticks. According to the shadows, he judged us to be about a hundred miles north of the African coast.

Those who bothered to move spent most of the day keeping themselves cool by dousing themselves under a bucket of sea water. We also tied soaked shirts round our heads. Some of the Greeks gave in to the temptation to drink sea water, but I think they regretted it. One at least developed some form of madness and sat on the side rolling his eyes at the sea.

By the eighth day we were all far gone with thirst and exhaustion. Our lips were cracked, our tongues were swelling and we could only crawl about on our hands and knees. I have always heard that when one is expecting imminent death, one dreams of the loved ones at home, or of heaven and the happy days of one's youth. I did not. All I could think of was a glass of cool Pilsener beer with a plate of steak, fried tomatoes and chips in a little café in Alexandria. So much for romance.

As the sun was going down on the eighth day, we suddenly heard the sound of aircraft engines. We waved white towels and handkerchiefs over the side, and I scrawled "no water" with dirty oil on our white blanket sail. We had already decided to signal to any craft we heard at night, German or British, aeroplane or ship, since it was now not only a question of escaping from prison, but was more a matter of saving our lives. We had tied oily rags round pieces of wood as torches for the purpose. A seaplane came over and we laughed to see the circles on its wings. It saw us and began to circle round. It dived twice over the caique and the pilots waved. We waved back, stuck up our thumbs, shook each other by the hand and grinned helplessly at each other in our joy. It looked as though it was going to land, but I think the sea was a little too choppy. Instead it waggled its wings and flew off into the sun.

We were all confident that in an hour or two destroyers would appear on the horizon. When night fell and there was no sign of rescue, our spirits fell a little, but we all felt sure that daylight would bring help. As the ninth day dragged on with no sign of the destroyers, we sank from the heights of joy to the depths of despair. We were all so weak now that we could only move

131

with the greatest effort. Our mouths were so deformed that we could only croak and even that was sheer agony.

I had suggested the possibility of making a distiller earlier in the voyage, but the others had poo-poohed the idea with a mass of figures to prove the great quantity of heat energy required. I mentioned it again—not so much as a suggestion, but more as a faint hope of something which could never be. Staff-Sergeant Charles Wright pulled himself along on his elbows without saying a word, until he was alongside the engine hatch. I noticed that he was trying to unscrew a copper pipe from the engine and, hopefully, I moved along to help him. We hacked a petrol tin in half and punctured it with holes to make a stove. Another closed tin was half-filled with sea water to make the boiler. We led the copper pipe from the boiler into a stone chatty, sealing the junctions with pieces of rag. Then, around the outside of the pipe, Wright made a cooling jacket with a piece off the bilge pump. The chatty was cooled by wrapping a wet shirt round it. We stuffed pieces of wood and oily rag into the brazier and set a match to it. After a few minutes steam began to escape from the junctions, but some must have been going through the pipe. Frantically we poured cool sea water into the water jacket and held the pipe tight into its socket to get the maximum amount of steam. We could hardly believe it when drops of water began to trickle into the earthenware chatty. When the others saw it, they all roused themselves to help by gathering fuel. For an hour's work we made enough to give us each about three mouthfuls of water. We were saved. There was no doubt about it, we were saved. We felt that we could go for weeks without food now that we had water and sooner or later we must strike land.

Three nights before, we had heard German aircraft flying over to bomb the canal and we resolved to signal if we heard them again during the night. We divided ourselves into watches and all the flares were made ready. At about one o'clock in the morning I was shaken by one of the Greeks, who said that he had heard the throb of engines. I listened and thought that I too could hear aircraft in the distance. We lit the first flare, waving it backwards and forwards.

After a few minutes, when the engines were growing louder, our hearts nearly stopped to see two long black shapes coming towards us out of the darkness. They were ships. We shouted as loudly as our swollen tongues would admit. We lit two more flares and waved them back and forth over the stern of the caique. The long ghostly shapes, which were now quite plainly men o' war, glided slowly by, keeping to their course. They seemed to ignore our signals completely. We screamed and wept to see them pay so little heed to us and then at last the rear destroyer of the three turned back towards us. It came close enough to hail.

"Ahoy there! Who are you?"

"British prisoners-of-war escaped from Greece."

There was a pause for a few moments as the searchlight was swung on to us.

"How many of you are there?"

"Four British, a Pole and ten Greeks. Who are you?"

"The *Jackal*. Stand by, we are coming aboard."

The destroyer came close alongside and blue jackets came aboard to carry us up the gangway. Lefteris elected to stay on the caique, which was brought into Alexandria under naval supervision. We were surprised to learn that we were only forty miles north of the port. I had ten rashers of bacon and eight eggs for my breakfast the next morning.

CHAPTER EIGHT

IT WAS typical of Britain that our first few hours in Egypt should be spent in an office, waiting for some pompous Intelligence Officer to interview us, for whatever else her merits she is a hidebound, ponderous nation. At first he was unwilling to accept the truth of our story and we were followed all over Alexandria by an escort until an officer of my regiment could come up to identify me.

There were also the normal difficulties with the Pay Office, which refused to believe that I was not still "missing, believed killed," until they had seen a Part II Order.

I took Spike along to see the Greek Consul, who managed to find him a home with the Hellenic Press Attaché. We had great fun buying a suit of clothes for him in the shopping centre. The poor little devil was heart-broken to leave us, but when I tried to find him a few months later, he had left to become an apprentice in the Greek Air Force.

After a few days' leave in Cairo, I was readmitted to hospital, since the rigours of the journey had not been good for the wounds in my legs. Strange to say, I was less troubled by the hole in my thigh than by a piece of shrapnel in my right heel bone.

After I had languished for a long time in the 63rd General Hospital, Helmieh, receiving diathermic treatment daily, the doctors decided to operate. They drilled the metal out of my heel and I have never since been troubled with it.

In January I was appointed to the 7th Armoured Division as an Intelligence Officer, but it was not long before I was attached as A.D.C. to the new general, General Jock Campbell, V.C., who had recently taken over command of the division. The 7th Armoured Division was at that time refitting in the Delta with new General Grant tanks, having secured Cyrenaica at the Battle of Sidi Rezegh for the second time within a year. The ground they had won was lost by fresh troops from England in a parallel fashion to the previous spring.

Jock Campbell was not the sort of man to rest idle for long in the Delta and within ten days of receiving command he resolved upon a tour of the desert to inspect the new defences at Gazala. I picked him up in his famous cut-away Humber staff car from the aerodrome at Sidi Barrani, where he narrowly avoided being shot down by long-range Me 109's. It was a pleasant trip up through our old battlefields to Tobruk, for there is no better job in the world than being A.D.C. to a nice general. And General Jock was the hero of every officer and man in the Middle East. It was more a question of his looking after me than of my running about after him. Before I had even time to think what there was to be done, the General would be cutting the sandwiches or lending me his towel. He loved the Western Desert as no other man could love it, and all the way up from Alexandria he recounted stories of the fighting in the past two years. He pointed out Conference Cairn, first named after a conference between Straffer Gott, Dickie Creagh and Jock Campbell at the time of Graziani's first advance, and Fig Tree Grove, where he had once had his guns. They were all interesting revelations to me, who had only previously known these places as names on the map.

The General loved to drive his car at fantastic speeds, but he was kind enough to hand over the wheel to me when he felt that he was tiring. We visited all the various headquarters and spent a night with General Gott. The most remarkable thing was the new technique of digging trenches for vehicles with bull-dozers. Another feature which was quite new to desert warfare was the enormous minefield stretching from Gazala to Bir Hacheim. I felt that the General (like me, for what it is worth) disapproved of the idea of locking brigades up in defensive positions called "boxes," which were nothing more than the same type of perimeter camps that the Italians had been so ridiculed for using. Mobility is the essence of desert war, and for that matter, all war. It seemed to us that the newly constituted 8th Army had gone a long way towards losing it.

After we had traversed the length and breadth of the mine-field, we drove back towards Cairo. At first the General had contemplated flying from Gambut, but I persuaded him that the presence of long-range enemy intruders made it unnecessarily risky. I think he was more influenced by a cable he had received from his wife, congratulating him on his V.C., but asking him to take great care of himself.

We set out to make the long distance to Alexandria before dark, which was an impossible task from Tobruk in any case. Near Bardia we ran into a thick dust-storm, which slowed us down to about ten miles an hour. The stretch of desert between the wire and Tobruk had been converted into a gigantic rubbish heap by the passage of three armies in countless battles. It was quite depressing to notice the transfiguration since the First Wavell Campaign. Every so often down the coast road we would come across a tiny group of graves and the debris of war lay everywhere—tin hats, empty cans, derelict vehicles, bits of clothing and the scars of weapon pits. The surface of the sand had been so much disturbed that the desert was now cursed with constant dust-storms, never before experienced.

Near Halfaya Pass the storm lifted and so we stopped for lunch at the foot of the cliff near Sollum Bay. General Jock opened the bully-beef tins and passed round the sandwiches. He asked me to take the wheel and to drive fast, still hoping to make Alexandria before dark.

Although I am not excusing myself, it must be recorded here that the steering of the car had been loosened by the hard wear it had received over bad desert going. Near Bug-Bug the metalled surface of the road had never been completed and instead it was paved with soft, blue clay from the saltmarsh. Until this clay has been rolled and dried in the sun, its surface can be very slippery.

The car must have been going at about forty-five miles an hour when I hit a fresh patch of clay, recently laid. Somehow, I lost control of the wheel and the car skidded from side to side of the road over about two hundred yards. I just had time to hear the General say "Keep the bloody thing straight," when I felt myself falling through the air. I never lost consciousness in spite of the force of my landing on my back. I picked myself up to notice with horror that the car had overturned, the four wheels still spinning helplessly in the air. I ran round to the other side to find the General lying on his back with blood coming from his mouth. He had been killed instantly. His servant and his driver were both lying unconscious beside him. I did not know what to do. The country all round was deserted and I contemplated suicide. How could I face the world with the news that I had killed the greatest man in the desert in his hour of triumph? I began to run down the lonely road towards

30 Corps Headquarters. After I had run about three miles, I came across a little South African padre, who took me back to the scene of the accident in his truck. The two men had both recovered consciousness, little the worse for their fall, but there was nothing to be done about General Jock. I sat there with my head in my hands, unable to bear the accusing glances of his servant. From then onwards I lapsed into a sort of coma from which I barely roused myself for a fortnight. I went through the courts of inquiry as if in a trance, dreaming that it had all happened. For it was a grievous loss to Britain. If Jock had been alive, we might not have suffered the terrible defeats we did in the withdrawal to Alamein. He had been the driving force of the Division, whoever was commanding, and without him we were like a man without a soul.

The new general, Frank Messervy, was good enough to take me back into my old job as Divisional Intelligence Officer. The G.I., Peter Pyman, was very sympathetic and realising that I would like to be away from the gossip of the Delta, he sent me up to the desert to reconnoitre the new Divisional Area. I had ten days alone in the sand with my servant, a Cockney called Shean, and we had great fun in our wanderings. We coursed a gazelle one day and only caught it south of Sidi Omar after a thirty-mile chase. We had fried liver for breakfast the next morning, which resulted in Shean's being evacuated to hospital with a tape worm. I suffered no ill effects.

The division moved up to the Sidi Azeiz area at the beginning of March. The desert was resplendent with blue flowers after the heavy rains and I found for them a leaguer area which was like a garden in Holland. The scent of the flowers was strongest in the early morning and the late evening, when the heat of the day had died and all the desert seemed fresh and clean.

The troops were in fine fettle. For the first time in the war we were equipped with a number of American tanks designed to take on the Germans with something like an equal gun. At Sidi Rezegh our cruisers had won the battle through the gallantry of their crews, although they had been out-gunned, out-telescoped and out-ranged. The new General Grant tanks had a 75-milli-metre gun, which could knock out a German tank at 1500 yards. No longer was it necessary to close to the suicidal distance of 800 yards before we could open effective fire. Even if the new guns could only be traversed through thirty degrees, they were guns and not pea-shooters, and we reckoned to give the Boches a big surprise.

By the middle of April the division was ready to move up to its position in the line. Rumour had it that we were building up for a full-scale offensive in June and that we would be the spearhead. The new divisional leaguer was north-east of Bir Hacheim in reserve behind the minefield. It was a dull stretch of desert made worse by the seasonal hot winds called "khamseens." We witnessed two phenomenal sand-storms during this period, the like of which I had never seen in the desert before. In the middle of the afternoon the sentries reported a great mass of orange smoke rolling towards us from the west. We gazed upon it in amazement, fearing some new device of chemical warfare. It was about fifty feet high with well-defined edges and the base was flecked with black and red smudges. It came upon us quite slowly, enveloping the leaguer in something worse than a London fog. I was sensible enough to drive out of its way on the next occasion.

The next month was largely spent in battle exercises with our new weapons. On one such demonstration I was instructed to explain the scheme to a Free French Brigadier from Bir Hacheim. I had almost given up hope of finding him in the spectators' stand, when I was accosted by a scruffy little man wearing corporal's stripes. My manner was quite off-hand, until I discovered that this was the commander of a demi-brigade. This gallant little soldier, called Colonel de la Roche, became my firm friend before he was killed in the subsequent fighting.

In my role of Intelligence Officer I was ordered to pay a visit to the Free French Column and the South African Armoured Cars, who were at that time harassing the enemy around Rotunda Segnali, the southern extremity of their position.

One of my clearest memories is a dinner with Tomcol, as the Free French were known. The officers were seated under an awning on the top of a hill and all around were Senegalese and Legionnaires, stripped to the waist. There was a fine old-world flavour to their methods. Every so often a runner would come up to salute the Brigadier, who sat on a pile of cushions under the awning. Trumpets were blowing in the leaguer and there was colour everywhere. Their cooks had brought desert cuisine to a finer art than we British had dreamed possible. All the many herbs were used and they could make an excellent potage of boiled snails. The French officers filled me with large draughts of strong arak with which my head was reeling by the time I went to bed. I remember that we had a great argument on the respective merits of the twenty-five-pounder and the famous soixante-quinze. Their achievements a month later at Bir Hacheim amply justified their faith in the French gun.

I visited the 4th South African Armoured Car Company, whose reputation was now only second to the 11th Hussars. They were patrolling a ridge called Teilim from which it was possible to see the Germans on Rotunda Segnali. One of their troop leaders gave me a justified rap on the knuckles for being so stupid as to drive fast near his position. The great secret of remaining unobserved when there is no cover is to cut movement down to a minimum. A cloud of dust is a sure way of attracting attention. He pointed out the black bobs on the skyline which were German vehicles. I crawled up to one South African position to draw a panorama sketch of the German feature. While we were there several shells lobbed round about, but the "Springboks" were not in the least bit perturbed. Only crass stupidity on somebody's part caused this fine unit to be disbanded. I came to know their Intelligence Officer, Harry Oppenheimer, quite well before I left. He is a delightful character and I would like to meet him again some day if he would deign to talk to such a notorious "anti-semite."

All the Senussi bedouin had been moved back out of the danger area in April. Picturesque caravans of heavily-laden camels, donkeys, women in red robes and proud bearded sheikhs moved back through our lines towards Egypt. At the beginning of May the armoured cars arrested a lone Arab near the minefield. Peter Vaux, the G3 (Intelligence), made him strip under the powerful light of a reading-lamp in our armoured control vehicle. The poor fellow was terrified: even more so when he revealed Italian uniform under his Arab robes. We always reckoned that Italian Intelligence was more shrewd than the German, who relied mainly on wireless intercept. However, this was the only occasion of which I heard when a spy was actually caught in our lines in the desert.

I was on leave in Alexandria with Colonel Cowley, A.Q. of the 7th Armoured Division, when the battle finally burst. On 27th May the Germans outflanked our minefield with the entire Deutsche Afrika Corps. The Italians pressed all along the front to contain our infantry, and the Ariete Armoured Division launched fierce attacks against the French at Bir Hacheim. Although the armoured cars had reported the German movements hour by hour from the moment they quitted Rotunda Segnali, there was some staff hitch in the dissemination of the information, which resulted in two armoured regiments being caught unawares by heavy panzer attacks. The 7th Armoured Division was driven back in disorganisation to the old battlefield at Sidi Rezegh near Tobruk. In spite of this, none of our strong points were taken (except the unimportant Retima Box) and General Messervy, commanding 7th Armoured Division, escaped from German hands to reorganise his tanks.

We had no idea that all this had happened when we left Alexandria. All we had heard was a vague rumour that the Germans had launched an attack. We hastened to get back to the Division before we missed the victory we felt certain would be ours. Such was our faith in the powers of the General Grant tank.

Our confidence was no little shaken by a collection of deserters at the petrol point at Daba. They told us that the Division had been wiped out and that the battle was lost. Having heard similar rumours before in the fog of battle, we put them under arrest before driving on at full speed towards the front.

Near Bardia we met some R.A.F. pilots who told us that the Germans had cut the road at Gambut, which meant that Tobruk was surrounded. Fortunately, soon after this we met up with an army officer who gave us the true picture, which was far from discouraging. The block at Gambut had been broken and the Germans had been beaten back from El Adem. They were now confined in the area between the El Adem Box and the minefield, where a fierce tank battle was raging. None of our positions except the small outpost at Retima had fallen.

We made our way in the dark to the position of Divisional Headquarters on the Duda Ridge. They were full of amusing experiences, but not in the least bit downcast by the shaking the Division had received. German tanks had got in amongst the headquarters, capturing the General, who later escaped by posing as a sanitary man and jumping off a truck during an attack by our guns. The only harm had been to his sense of smell when constrained to share a slit-trench with a big Basuto pioneer. Peter Vaux, my fellow Intelligence Officer, had actually commanded the Division for a spell. The 4th Armoured Brigade had rallied under Brigadier Richardson to drive the Germans away from El Adem. The situation was by no means bad.

In view of the fact that I was now completely out of touch with the situation as far as Intelligence was concerned, the General gave me command of a small composite force, whose duty it would be to protect the Headquarters from a similar surprise. It was a large command for a subaltern—ten armoured cars of mixed varieties, eight Bofors guns, a two-pounder portee and a tank. Aptly, Jim Richardson (of Beda Fomm fame, who was now G2) christened it Frigforce.

For the next two days a tank battle raged between us and the minefield in which 1st Armoured Division splendidly regained any laurels they might have lost in their retreat from Agheila in the spring. The result was that a large number of German tanks were destroyed and Rommel's army was penned into a pocket in the minefield, which came to be known as "the Cauldron."

Then began certain miscalculations by the Generals, which turned victory into defeat. I do not know what other facts have come to light, but no soldier who fought in that battle can ever excuse those high-ranking officers who at the time were damned but have since been resurrected. Perhaps the term "Cauldron" led to a misconception of the true situation from the start. The Germans were at first receiving their supplies through a narrow channel in the minefields. All the weight of the R.A.F. was turned on to this gap and the 150 Brigade of the 50th Northumbrian Division was put in as a "cork to stop the bottle." Quite naturally, they were crushed from both sides. The trouble was that certain people mistook what was obviously a widening bridgehead for a watertight trap. Instead of cutting off the Germans by a powerful outflanking movement south of Bir Hacheim, which would have been the normal desert technique, they were reluctant to expose Tobruk by moving our armour. This meant that we had partly lost the initiative which was ours by right of battle. Then we proceeded to launch the sort of attack which has brought disaster to British arms throughout history. We began a frontal attack on the Germans' strongest defences in the "Cauldron." If the attack had gone in immediately it might have been successful, but instead there was a fatal delay of three days while we made our intention painfully obvious.

When the attack was finally launched, I was patrolling on the edge of the minefield near Bir Harmat. The assault was made by an Indian Division with the 22nd Armoured Brigade. Although the troops fought bravely under the direct command of General Messervy (who himself went up to the front), they recoiled in disorder from the strength of the German positions around Got Aslagh. Tanks foundered on their old enemy, the concealed anti-tank gun. By the second day it was obvious that the attack had failed.

Then began a period (I forget how long, but it must have been nearly a week) of errors being heaped upon errors. Bir Hacheim had quite plainly become the key to the battle. It was some way south of the "Cauldron" and was the southern extremity of the minefield. Rommel was not prepared to advance so long as this stronghold remained to menace his flank. He launched the whole of his weight against the gallant garrison, while the major part of the 8th Army concerned itself with small skirmishes around the "Cauldron." The French pleaded for help but all they received was the assistance of harassing columns from the 7th Motor Brigade, who had already demonstrated how easy it would have been to cut off Rommel by their shelling of German transport west of the gap. One or two other stupid little columns (aptly named after fish) were formed by the Indians, but they only contributed to the further frittering away of our strength. After ten days of gallant, heroic, fantastic resistance, Bir Hacheim fell. Rommel immediately swung into the outflanking attacks which were to beat us back to Cairo. There was no "black day" in which the battle was lost by a fluke. Every day was a black day from this moment onwards, because the Generals had lost control of the battle.

I was still in the Harmat area when Rommel emerged from his lair intent on the kill. The first intimation we received was a few shells bursting near the Divisional Headquarters leaguer. I could see no sign of the enemy and was amazed when I turned round to see the huge armoured control vehicles of the headquarters withdrawing at top speed to the east. I was amazed and furious, because I had been given no warning. There is nothing quite so damaging to morale as to see a large headquarters retreating rapidly away from the battle. The General, who was still battling with the Indians in the "Cauldron" at the time, quite rightly ordered them to return. But not for long. In the middle of the afternoon, German tanks burst through from Bir Harmat. I could see them plainly through my glasses with the panic-stricken trucks of the Indians retreating like a flock of geese before them.

A few better-aimed shells fell in our leaguer, and in a matter of moments we had upped sticks for a big "harouche" to the east. Behind us, Knightsbridge was still holding out in the face of fierce attacks and the 4th Armoured Brigade was fighting one losing battle after another on the edge of the escarpment.

It was dark when we at last called a halt astride the Trigh Capuzzo west of El Adem. Several units had straggled into our column during the retreat, including some Sikh two-pounder anti-tank guns, a company of sappers and a platoon of the West Yorkshire Regiment. With this motley assortment, I formed a square box across the track. A German patrol bumped into us at about eleven o'clock, but sheered off when we opened fire.

Just before dawn we moved down the escarpment into the valley between El Adem and the main Tobruk escarpment. We sat there all day (having been joined by part of 30 Corps Headquarters), while the 4th Armoured Brigade were worsted in a tank battle south of Knightsbridge. By now a general retreat had been ordered. 50th Division again proved how the battle might have been fought by causing great damage in their withdrawal across the German lines of communication. The 1st South African Division withdrew via Tobruk to Egypt, while the 2nd South African Division busied themselves about preparations for the defence of the Fortress. The Guards pulled out of Knightsbridge, suffering great losses in a delaying position near Rigl, and also withdrew into Tobruk. The attempt to hold Tobruk was the final error in a grossly mismanaged campaign. Tobruk has never been a strong place and with no threat to the Germans from the 8th Army outside, they were able to fall on it like a wolf on the fold. The attempt to recover the hundred-odd tanks in the Tobruk workshops was not worth the loss of 25,000 men.

The next day we withdrew to the foot of the escarpment between Tobruk and El Adem. I placed my armoured cars on the top of the escarpment, while the Headquarters remained at the bottom. Even before it had reached its position, one of my armoured cars ran into a German four-wheeler coming down one of the precipitous tracks. They faced each other with no room to manœuvre at twenty yards' range. Fortunately, my Daimler was quicker on the draw and knocked his opponent out with one two-pounder shell. I was on the top of the escarpment when I noticed large German columns swirling around the outside of the El Adem box. Some of my cars were already being fired upon. It was the end. The General ordered a complete withdrawal to the wire. The 4th Armoured Brigade fought a last battle near Sidi Rezegh, but were decisively beaten. With shells bursting all round the cars, we withdrew eastwards into Egypt. The odd thing was that there were still negroes working on the railway line, who did not cease work when we passed. I wondered if they continued to work diligently for the Germans.

Tales of retreats in the desert are pretty much the same: trucks breaking down and being sabotaged, deserters breaking off to run away to the Delta and dumps being rifled, but this retreat was more orderly than most. Although the 8th Army only had about twenty-five tanks left out of seven hundred when it reached the wire, there was never the same air of panic we had known in 1941. Perhaps it was because we were not hard pressed, Tobruk having been left behind like a golden apple. We paused for a day or two at Sheferzen on the Egyptian Frontier until we received the awful news that Tobruk had surrendered. I remember receiving a reprimand from the General for chasing a gazelle with the whole Division behind me when I was supposed to be navigating. It was a thoughtless diversion but at least it proved that there was nothing wrong with our morale.

A long protracted retreat is even more tiring than a long advance. We were holding off the Germans with harassing columns and small patrols by day, while at night we would trundle back to a new position. This particular battle lasted six weeks from the time the Germans first attacked at Bir Hacheim. During this time we never had a proper night's sleep.

At Mersa Matruh the 1st Armoured Division had been reformed to fight a delaying battle, while the 7th Armoured Division was supposed to pass into reserve behind their front. We all had a certain confidence in the strength of Matruh Fortress, which was manned by a brigade of the 10th Indian Division. The New Zealand Division had also arrived to hold the southern part of the line around a place called Calder.

I had never been as far south as Kanayis before and when the Division passed across the Siwa Track, I was struck by the beauty of the large cliffs and broken ground. By then I had only six armoured cars left in my squadron. But the Germans were hard on our heels and we were just passing through the New Zealanders near Calder when they struck. Heavy Stuka attacks were launched against our tired transport, setting many trucks on fire, while the German armour split our line in half by crossing the Charing Cross minefield as though it had never existed. By nightfall they had cut off Matruh by blocking the road at Garawla. The Egyptian mines in that minefield had never been much good and the field had been so long laid that it had become ineffective. In any case there is little use in a minefield which is not covered by fire and this one had been left completely open. Matruh garrison was captured, adding another five thousand or so to the long list of prisoners. We were heartened by the tremendous show of courage by the New Zealanders, who were said to have charged German tanks with 15-cwt. trucks.

We drove back all night, once having a scene where we found ourselves on a parallel bearing to a German column. There was a short delay at Fuka, where we tried to stem the enemy rush. British aircraft were appearing in ever increasing numbers, two squadrons of Bostons going over several times a day to bomb the German spearheads. I remember one terrible night when there was supposed to be a hundred Wellington raid on German leaguers south of Matruh. We were ordered to light fires in the shape of a "V" pointing towards the German lines. The effect was that all except the leading aircraft mistook these fires for damage caused by other bombers in their squadron and dropped their deadly cargo on our own troops. We were in a tight close-leaguer at the time when the sky was suddenly lighted up by a number of flares. Only our vehicles seemed visible in the surrounding darkness. Some of the truck-drivers panicked, driving in all directions away from the danger point. After a few bombs had been dropped, knocking out two cruisers and about five trucks, we all withdrew to safety in the south.

The German aircraft were less active at this time—possibly since the rapid advance of their ground troops had outstripped their aerodromes, and also because our own Kittihawks had caused so much damage to their fighters. The pilots of our fighter planes, who were mostly South Africans, put up a tremendous show in spite of their inferior aircraft. We saw many dog-fights in this campaign and the whole desert was

145

strewn with wrecked aeroplanes. The Germans had, however, developed an annoying technique of sending over lone aircraft at night to cruise about over our leaguers, dropping a bomb wherever they thought they saw a sign of movement. I do not think that they did much damage except to our nerves. Sleep was rare enough in this retreat, but when one was forced to keep one ear open for the ominous throb of a wandering aeroplane, tempers rapidly frayed. Towards the end we always dug a hole before lying down to rest and I never heard of any one being so stupid as to use a camp-bed, thus poising himself for the reception of the full effect of a bomb.

When at last we reached El Alamein, the 1st South African Division was entrenching itself in the north, while the New Zealanders were digging in around Abu Dwyis in the south. There was nothing impressive about the strength of the line, except perhaps that it was in a narrow neck of bad going between the Qattara Depression and the sea. Those are talking nonsense who say that the success of our last stand was due to the foresight of someone who had prepared fortifications long before. Alamein was artificially no stronger than any other line we had tried to hold in the desert.

The retreat was orderly to the last, as it had always been in spite of the fact that vehicles were crammed nose to tail on the coast road. Nobody attempted to pass another and military policemen in white gloves told units where to go as they came along. The R.A.F. must receive great credit for staving off air attack at this time.

The middle of the line was held by Indians plus the 1st Armoured Division in the north and by the mobile columns of the 7th Armoured Division in the south. Our Divisional Headquarters was located near Qaret el Himeimat, astride the Barrel Track—a route much used by deserters in previous battles. There was a story that one petrol truck had made its way down the Barrel Track as far as Khartoum during the Sidi Rezegh battle, only stopping to refill with petrol from their supply. The sand is very loose in this part of the desert and we had to struggle with sand-trays and mats to make the last few miles to the leaguer area. It was not a very inspiring line of retreat to have behind one.

Although there had been no panic in this long withdrawal, we had no confidence in our ability to stop the Germans. Every other line we had tried to hold had folded up and we could see no reason why this one should be any different. There was talk of a new sort of fighting on the canals in the Delta and orders were even issued for use in the event of a withdrawal to Khartoum. There was no question of surrender. We were determined to go on fighting even if it was to be with mules in the mountains of Abyssinia. We heard rumours that there had been a run on the banks in Cairo and that G.H.Q. was burning its files. The Navy was said to be evacuating Alexandria. The only ray of hope was a story that Straffer Gott had torn up the plans for a retreat, saying that we would fight on this last line to the end. Somebody also said that the Australians had been cheered on their way through Cairo. We were not to know that Rommel had already out-run his supplies.

The first attacks came early in July. The Germans made a thrust with two columns—one just south of the coast road, which was checked by the 1st Armoured Division and the South Africans, and the other along the top of the Qattara Depression, which was halted by the New Zealanders at Abu Dwyis. These successes gave us more hope for the final outcome.

One day at the end of the first week in July, two aircraft were seen coming over very high towards our leaguer. There had been several other raids during the day and the men were in no mood to stay for confirmation of their nationality. People began to run away from the vehicles in all directions. I was convinced that they were Bostons and I stood in the middle of the leaguer shouting those famous last words: "Don't run. It's all right. They're ours!" Too late I saw the black crosses on their wings. They both unleashed a basket of butterfly bombs and before I could throw myself flat I had been hit in the arm. Ironically enough, I was the only one in the leaguer to be hit.

They carried me off to a Field Ambulance Unit nearby and then began three of the most miserable days I have ever spent. The ambulance was full of wounded, including a loudly complaining Italian, and there was no proper medical attention. We started off in convoy but since our vehicle had no sand channels, we were soon wallowing in soft sand far behind. We must have bellied down at least once in every twenty minutes. Seriously wounded men (one with only one arm) dug with spades, pushed blankets under the wheels and shoved at the back until we were once more on the move. We passed two staging points where we were given a mug of tea, bully and biscuits. In all it took us three days to cover the seventy miles between Himeimat and Cairo.

We were lodged in the 15th Scottish Hospital at Giza, where I shared a small ward with a squadron-leader of the 9th Lancers. He was a very knowledgeable sort of chap, who took the precaution of bribing our sister with a bottle of gin and a bunch of flowers. As a result, we were able to spend most of our days near the swimming pool at Gezireh Sporting Club. Even so we crossed the path of the Colonel when we were late back for our dressings one day.

On 19th July I was put on a train in Cairo bound for Suez and final evacuation to South Africa. Even on the hospital ship at sea, we heard tales of the new firebrand of a general who was going to put everything right in the Middle East. There were many amusing stories about his efficiency, including one about his not allowing coughing at lectures. It did something to dispel the gloom caused by the news of Straffer Gott's death. All who knew this newcomer said that Montgomery was the man to shake up the 8th Army.

CHAPTER NINE

OUR HOSPITAL SHIP was staffed by Indians and called the *Taiorea*, a name which lent itself to obvious parody. We were well cared for on board in spite of our having to weather rough seas in the face of the monsoon. The Anglo-Indian nurses could not have been more gentle. I struck up a friendship with a gunner called Robin Dunne and a Cameron Highlander called Ralph Campbell, who had been wounded on some soda-water bottles in a traffic accident near the N.A.A.F.I. at Daba. We were allowed to go ashore in Mombasa, where we were taken out to see the jungle by some of the residents. Kenya seemed to be an amusing place in which to live, although I suspected that some of our new acquaintances might have slightly sordid backgrounds. We were quite sorry to have to board our ship once more.

The voyage was uneventful apart from the rough seas and certain scares about Japanese submarines in the straits off Madagascar. By the time we reached Durban my wound was almost healed, although I had lost the use of my middle fingers.

We were moved by train to Oribi Hospital near Pietermaritzburg, the "Sleepy Hollow" of Natal. Our six weeks' stay in South Africa was like a holiday of which people only dream. The South Africans threw open their homes to us and never ceased to contrive new plans for our entertainment. The hospital itself was like an Eddie Cantor film—full of glamorous blondes in trim white uniforms. And the country round about had a majesty unchanged by the ages. They said that it had once been the camp of the Zulu King, Cetewayo (pronounced with a click of the tongue), and it was not difficult to imagine the stamping feet of the impis, the swaying ostrich plumes and the rumble of the drums.

I was not greatly incapacitated by the wound in my arm and so was able to enjoy these pleasures to the full. We spent several days on a farm near Merrivale where I disgraced myself by shooting the only duck on the lake. It was all a wonderful change from the dust and dirt of Egypt; stalking guinea fowl through the wattles, hacking about on a half-groomed country pony and sipping tea on the grass under the rhododendrons.

Many of us only avoided marriage by a narrow margin in these happy days, while others fell by the wayside. It was as if we had settled on the fresh clean petals of some wild rose growing out of the dross of war. Well I remember paddling bare-footed in a rocky stream in the Botanical Gardens or sucking an orange with a gurgling maid from the University or dancing on the crazy paving of an open-air café on the outskirts of the town.

One would have thought that with all this happiness we would have been loathe to leave the Union, but towards the end of our stay we began to feel a restlessness, an urge to get back into the battle and a desire to escape from this idyllic backwater. The new General was leading the 8th Army to great victories and we felt a certain annoyance at having been cheated of our share in the glory. We began to agitate for either a passage back to Egypt or evacuation to the United Kingdom.

At the beginning of December I found myself on a troopship bound for home. It had been necessary to refuse an operation to restore the tendons to my middle fingers, but I considered that since there was nothing I could not do except play the piano (which I had never learned anyway) it was a waste of time. At length we reached Liverpool, where we were infuriated by a long wait in the estuary. We heard on the wireless that we had been preceded by a ship bearing refugees from Singapore, who had been accorded a great welcome on the docks, so that we were somewhat disappointed to find that our reception party consisted of four military policemen and a horde of petty staff officers. The voyage from South Africa had not been exactly pleasant in view of certain quarrels we had had with merchant sailors who were being repatriated after losing their ships. There had been a cargo of oranges on the decks for children under nine at home, and when we discovered that several crates had been rifled, bitter accusations were bandied between us and the sailors. Finally, we mounted a guard of wounded soldiers armed with batons over the cargo, which had led to a number of brawls with the seamen. The whole affair was most distasteful. Our temper was not improved by the gloomy atmosphere of our homecoming. We had all got the stupid bee in our bonnets about our being some of the first wounded heroes home from the wars, and we had half-expected the band to be playing, with weeping relations waving handkerchiefs from the quay. Instead we were met by sheaves of forms and the sombre gloom of smoke-begrimed Liverpool in the pouring rain. We consoled ourselves with the thought that all England is a factory—a dirty teeming workshop—and therein lies the source of her greatness. It was unfortunate that the authorities should have decided to move us to a transit hospital on the outskirts of Liverpool, for there is nothing more difficult to deal with than a band of British soldiers who think that their rights have been abused. We chafed at the regulations which prohibited us from going into the town. At last, after we had openly rebelled against authority for three days, we were given railway warrants to take us home.

At first we revelled in the joy of being home again; in the familiar sight of green fields and red-roofed cottages; in the pleasure of living again with our people, of meeting old friends; in the relief of hearing our own native tongue on the lips of everyone, great and small; and in the fresh wind and the rain which is England.

After I had been on sick leave for a month, my spirit became restive once more. I managed to fight through the sea of forms to appear before a Western Command Medical Board, which I persuaded to upgrade me to "A" category. They were astonished at such a request, having hitherto only been concerned with downgradings or applications for pensions.

My one desire was to get back to the regiment in the Middle East. It was not that the people at home were out of touch with the reality of war, but more that the years of battle had made us out of step with them. There were none of the bands, the flags and the colour one associates with a nation fighting its way to glorious victory. Rather there was an air of grim, sombre determination—the atmosphere of the factory. Their amusements, the giggling women and the flowing alcohol, seemed artificial, and yet it was no different from our own leisure in the past two years. I was irritated by the emphasis on "the blitz," when anything I saw of the damage did not begin to compare to, say, the devastation caused to Canea in Crete. And "music while you work" was not martial tunes calling patriots to arms, but was the heartsick sludge of "Darling, won't you go romancing?" I wrote to solicit help from any Generals I knew, but it was easier to get into England than to get out of it. I was posted to three separate units, all of which were bound for the Middle East, but always their sailing orders were cancelled at the last moment. I was miserable amongst the constant imaginative training of the Army in England, who were still burnishing gun barrels and marching up and down the roads in the same old way. They distrusted me as a young upstart with two medals, who thought that he was a kingpin just because he had been lucky enough to see a little action.

When I was appointed to command the Headquarters Squadron of one armoured brigade, I reported to the Brigadier and the conversation went something like this:

"Good morning, you are Farran?"

"Yes, sir."

"Why aren't you wearing proper boots and gaiters?"

"I have a wound in my heel, sir, and have to wear soft shoes."

"Hump. Well you must understand that in this Brigade personal turn-out is the order of the day. Look at yourself."

"Yes, sir."

"Now, your job here will be managing the Brigade accounts."

"But, sir, I cannot add two and two together to make four."

"Well, now is the time to learn. When I first became P.R.I., I was not good at arithmetic, but I soon learnt and became the best P.R.I. the regiment had ever known."

"Yes, sir."

"And one more thing. You fellows come here from the desert thinking you own heaven and earth. Well, you don't. Now you can get down to some real soldiering for a change."

I dropped my papers on the floor in the process of saluting and stumbled out. It was not long before I had agitated myself into a more suitable job. One day, when I was standing by my tank during a scheme, I managed to get my own back on this pompous Brigadier. He said, "Old boy, have you a cigarette you can spare?" I knew that my driver smoked horrible Woodbines in paper packets and said, "Dobson, the Brigadier would like one of your cigarettes." He pulled a battered packet out of his overalls and handed it over in his greasy, oil-begrimed hands. The revulsion on our dapper Brigadier's face was quite pretty to watch, but he was forced to accept it.

After wandering from one unit to another all over England, I at last found myself in February, 1943, with a draft bound for North Africa. It was the principle of following the ball, which brings success in all games, and had finally brought me to release from the prison that was England in 1942.

Book II

The Special Air Service

CHAPTER ONE

INTRODUCTION

THE OBJECT of almost all military tactics is to threaten the security of the enemy's lines of communication, those vital lifelines without which an army cannot exist. Attacks on lines of communication may be divided into two categories; the flanking movements made by large formations in the main battle area and the long-range harassing attacks made by small raiding parties, possibly independent of the main theatre of operations. These latter long-range attacks were, until recently, the prerogative of cavalry patrols, living off the country.

In the last great war, all theatres found a need for units which could specialise in this form of warfare. The Chindits were raised for this purpose in Burma, the Special Air Service operated in Africa and Western Europe, the Special Boat Service carried out raids in the islands of the Ægean, and the Long-Range Desert Group was an important reconnaissance unit in the Western Desert, to say nothing of various small forces such as Popski's Private Army.

The first of these units to be raised was the 1st Special Air Service Regiment, commanded by Lieutenant Colonel David Stirling of the Scots Guards. In the winter of 1941, when he was still a subaltern in the Scots Guards in the Middle East, it occurred to him that it would be easy for determined men to inflict heavy damage on the enemy's long single line of communication along the Desert Road. At this time the war situation was grim for the Allies. Greece and Crete had been evacuated and most of the ground won in Wavell's First Campaign had been lost to the Germans. The Higher Command was ready to listen to any plan which might embarrass the enemy, so long as it did not mean a large drain on their already slender resources. General Wavell, and later General Auchinleck, gave the unit their blessing and the first recruits were collected together at Kibrit in the Delta.

The unit was first called "L" Detachment, Special Air Service, as a code name calculated to deceive the enemy as to its strength and object. The first recruits came from a Commando Brigade known as Layforce, under the command of Major-General R. Laycock, who later became Chief of Combined Operations. A parachute school was formed in Egypt, and all ranks were trained in parachuting and demolitions. A high standard of physical fitness was insisted upon, and any volunteer who did not come up to the requirements in this respect was returned to his parent unit.

The first two operations attempted were by parachute, but unfavourable weather prevented their success. It was soon discovered that the airborne approach in the desert was too difficult, and in any case, unnecessary. The enormous distances involved, lack of water and the absence of ground features to aid accurate air navigation were obstacles too difficult to overcome. Infiltration from the wide, open flank to the south was a much easier proposition.

In all its early operations, the Special Air Service operated in conjunction with the Long-Range Desert Group, whose role was primarily reconnaissance. The "parashots," as they were called, were carried to within a short distance of their targets by L.R.D.G. patrols. Headquarters, transport convoys and, especially, aerodromes were attacked with conspicuous success. A technique of destroying aircraft with a timed incendiary bomb was invented by Captain "Jock" Lewis (who was later killed) and over three hundred aircraft were destroyed in the first year.

The unit gradually became independent of the Long-Range Desert Group, although an effective liaison was maintained. When the first American jeeps arrived in the Middle East, it was recognised that they were the ideal vehicles for this type of warfare. They had a tremendous load-carrying capacity, an enormous range when fitted with extra petrol tanks, a fine cross-country performance, and great fire power when modified to carry Twin Vickers Aircraft machine-guns.

When the 8th Army was beaten back to Alamein, the Special Air Service continued to harass the enemy's rear. The railway from Tobruk was continually sabotaged, keeping it out of action for long periods at a time.

When Rommel at last began to withdraw, S.A.S. patrols ambushed his line of retreat night after night. Unfortunately, Lieutenant-Colonel David Stirling was betrayed by an Arab when on an operation near Homs, and was captured by the enemy.

Although he made many attempts to escape, he was always recaptured and was unlucky enough to spend the remainder of the war in a prison camp.

It was not only in the Desert that the Special Air Service had developed a technique of guerrilla war. One branch of the Regiment also specialised in attacks from small boats, exploiting to the full the excellent opportunities presented in the Ægean. They infiltrated between the islands into enemy-held waters and landed on unguarded spots on the shore. Many useful pinprick attacks were carried out, especially in Crete.

After David Stirling's capture, the Regiment split into two halves under the two most energetic of his commanders. The squadron which had been operating in the islands became the Special Boat Service under Lord Jellicoe, son of the famous Admiral. Most of the remainder formed the Special Raiding Squadron under Lieutenant-Colonel Paddy Mayne, another dominant personality. Mayne progressed from strength to strength, earning a glorious reputation for his unit in commando operations in Sicily and Italy, until he expanded it into the 1st Special Air Service Regiment for the D-Day operations.

When the 1st Army landed in French North Africa a need was felt for a guerrilla unit to operate on the same lines as the Special Air Service in the Desert. Command was given to Lieutenant-Colonel William Stirling, brother of David Stirling, and the 63rd Commando was used as a nucleus on which to form the 2nd Special Air Service Regiment at Philipville, halfway between Algiers and the Front.

Its earliest operations were attempts to imitate David Stirling's methods by infiltrating jeeps through the mountains, with the object of attacking aerodromes in the enemy's rear. All these operations met with only limited success, owing to the static nature of the enemy's front line positions. Similarly, attempts to carry out raids by small boats on the closely guarded shores of Lampedusa, Pantellaria and Sicily were not very successful.

In July, 1943, detachments of S.A.S. parachutists were scattered over Northern Sicily and Sardinia in conjunction with the main landings in the south. Although the operation was in the nature of an experiment from which many useful lessons were learnt, communications were successfully cut, causing great confusion behind the enemy's lines. Similar detachments cut the railways leading into the leg of Italy at the time of the landings at Salerno.

The surprise disembarkation of the 1st Airborne Division at Taranto presented new opportunities for infiltration by jeeps, and many attacks were carried out by long penetration patrols behind the withdrawing Germans.

After the line stabilised north of Termoli, in the capture of which S.A.S. troops were concerned, infiltration by jeep became no longer practicable. Until the unit was recalled to the United Kingdom in March, 1944, however, many successful seaborne raids were carried out on railways running along the Adriatic coast. The total destruction of a railway bridge south of Rimini by parties landed from two British destroyers was one outstanding example.

In March, 1944, the 1st and 2nd Special Air Service Regiments were linked with two French Parachute Battalions and a Belgian Parachute Company to form the Special Air Service Brigade. Intensive training was carried out in Scotland for long operations in North-West Europe before and after D-Day.

A little after D-Day advance parties were dropped into many of the forested areas in France, sometimes to organised reception by British agents, but more often to areas selected at random from a map. After D-Day supplies were dropped in large quantities, until finally whole squadrons of Special Air Service troops, equipped with jeeps and machine-guns, were dropped in to commence attacks on the enemy's rear. Sometimes these troops supported the Maquis, but more often than not they operated alone. They destroyed transport, petrol dumps and trains all over Central France, being supplied by the Royal Air Force almost nightly. The success of these operations was astonishing.

After the crossing of the Seine and the rapid advance into Germany, the two British regiments were attached to the leading elements of the 2nd Army to engage opportunity targets. A small number of sabotage parties was also dropped in Belgium and Holland.

In December, 1944, one squadron of the 2nd Special Air Service Regiment was transferred to Italy, where it operated with conspicuous success behind the Gothic Line in conjunction with the last big attack.

Finally, all units of the Special Air Service Brigade were united for the occupation of Norway, where security duties were carried out in the Bergen area.

Plans were in train for operations in China and Siam when the atomic bomb ended the war against Japan.

All Special Air Service units, except the Belgian Company, were disbanded in December, 1945.

CHAPTER TWO

NORTH AFRICA AND SICILY, 1943

WHEN WE landed at Algiers in March, 1943, we were transported by truck to the Armoured Corps Transit Camp in a pretty little village on the far side of the bay from the town. We languished there for some weeks in the way that people always languish in transit camps. Each day I would pay a visit, always fruitless, to the Allied Force Headquarters to try to arrange an air passage back to the 8th Army. The war in Africa was in its final stages and nobody was prepared to stir himself about a detail like one stray tank officer.

I would hitch-hike on American trucks back to the village and sit in the sun watching French fishermen wading for sea urchins or repairing boats, until I thought that perhaps I would have to stay in that little French village until the end of the war. We would adjourn to a little estaminet in the evening to drink the tart Algerian wine. Perhaps the only difference between the 1st and 8th Armies was that the former dressed rather more smartly, that they painted their trucks a darker green and that the gutters in their rear areas were always full of drunken soldiers. The men drank the powerful wine like beer and suffered in consequence.

One day I was sitting on the steps of the Aletti in Algiers waiting for the official opening hours for soldiers, while Frenchmen were drinking all round, when I met an old 8th Army friend called Sandy Scratchley. I told him my tale of woe and how I thought it likely that I would spend the rest of my days in Algiers. He told me that he himself had been with David Stirling of the S.A.S. for some time and that he had now transferred to his brother Bill, who was forming a similar unit from the 1st Army end. Of course I had heard vague stories of David Stirling's exploits in the desert and how he had destroyed a fabulous number of aircraft, but I never quite knew what it was all about. Hesitating, half-expecting a negative answer, I told him that I had an introduction from General Willoughby Norrie and was it possible that there might be a vacancy for another officer. He promised to take me up for an interview with Bill Stirling at A.F.H.Q. the next day.

I made sure that I was in time for the interview by arriving two hours early with another potential recruit called Tyser. We sat on the steps of A.F.H.Q., looking down on the sunny bay of Algiers, busy now with a new convoy. The town, which ran down the side of a hill green with cork trees, was a magnificent sight from above. On one side stood the Casbah, a solid mass of hovels towering to a great height, and outside were the wide boulevards of the modern town. Perhaps it was a pity to leave it.

We were summoned to a very unconventional type of interview which rather took the wind out of my sails. An intense-looking soldier, who was introduced as Lord Jellicoe, continued to discuss a map in the corner of the room with someone else whose name I cannot remember. During the interview I tried to get a squint over his shoulder and thought that it was a map of Sardinia but could not be sure. Bill Stirling was a great mountainous man, who shook us warmly by the hand and asked us a few embarrassing questions. He radiated an encouraging aura of confidence and although he told us that we would be on a fortnight's trial, we already felt ourselves part of the team before the interview was finished. It was not terminated by the usual abrupt dismissal, but after inviting us to lunch, he turned to discuss highly secret matters with Jellicoe. We did not know whether to go or to stay, but finally compromised by hovering around the door. I am sure that this is one of the secrets of leadership and I have since harkened well to Bill's maxim of always trusting a subordinate right up to the moment that his worthlessness is proved beyond doubt.

We learned that Bill and Jellicoe had been severely shaken in a motor accident that morning, but it did not seem to interfere with their powers of global planning. We had already been transported to a world which knew no obstacles—a world in which we felt that we were doing something concrete towards winning the war. The Stirlings did not leap over red tape; they broke right through it. I have never met any who equalled their drive and, although they made many enemies by slipping round smaller fry, they always got there in the end. As a first sample of the pulsating energy they communicated to their subordinates, we were informed that we would be required to attend a parachute course at Mascarrah on the Morocco border in two days' time. I felt as though I had been swept up by a gale. Bill drove us off to lunch at a black market café on the top of the hill, driving at a speed which took my breath away. I was still dazed by it all when I was finally whisked home to the transit camp in his staff car.

We were quartered with the 2nd Parachute Battalion at Mascarrah, living in small bivouacs pulled over the sand. Except for the farm-houses and odd ploughed fields, it was an area more reminiscent of the desert than of Algeria. Each afternoon the dust swirled up in whirlies, which swept through the leaguer at great speed, covering everything with filth. The paraboys were training hard and came in dog-tired each evening after a long route march. I was impressed by the way they all gave an "eyes right" to the Colonel, John Frost, before they dismissed by the gate. (I am always infuriated by the present fashion of sneering at the discipline of the Airborne Division. If a few of the "Omdurman boys" in the War Office could have their way, there would be no airborne troops in the British Army at all. Certainly, their present aim is to reduce them to the level of any other mediocre county division.) These parachutists were mostly the seasoned troops of the 1st Parachute Brigade, which had fought its way back from Tunis unsupported, after the failure of the first thrust. I think they took a secret delight in magnifying the horrors of parachuting to us poor recruits. Whether that is true or not, we were all well acquainted with details of a Roman Candle and other ways in which a chute might not open by the time we were ready to jump.

The first five days of the course were spent in physical training on the ground. We learned how to roll in the proper way on both shoulders, how to keep our feet together and how to collapse a parachute after landing. It all seemed great fun because as yet we had not been introduced to an aircraft. After our synthetic training had finished, we were told that we would have to do our five descents in forty-eight hours to take advantage of the fine weather.

I cannot here describe the thrills of a first parachute jump; of the nervous fingers which fumble as they fasten the harness; of the constant glances at the static line to make sure that it is not entangled; of the safety pin which will never go first time into its socket; of that terrible feeling in the pit of the stomach as one stands to the door; and of the leap of your heart as the plane bounces in an air pocket. It is enough to say that the first parachute descent is always the best, because there is usually no difficulty in keying yourself up to get out of the plane. Only when you have experienced those few awful seconds before the parachute opens do you really know what parachuting means. When at last you have completed the gentle thrill of your feathery descent and felt the final bounce as you hit the ground, you are filled with supreme confidence. If you could then go straight up again, you would jump without a single qualm. But given time to think, your thoughts gradually go back to those few terrible seconds in the slipstream. For the only difficult part of a parachute jump is getting out of the hole. All sensible instincts revolt against it. It is stupid. It is against human nature. But you go on doing it just to prove to yourself that you can.

There is no great danger in parachuting and I often wonder whether it is really worth the extra pay. However, the British have the lowest paid parachutists in the world, so that the sum is so small that it does not really matter. They say that it is safer than crossing a busy street in London, and except for a run of bad luck in Palestine in 1946, I have only known of three failures since I first became airborne. The cause of the first was never discovered, the second was a fellow who neglected to wear a tin hat and split his head on a sharp stone, and the last was caused by acid eating through a static line in the aircraft. It is even true to say that one gets bored with the business if one is jumping regularly. After a time it is easy to guess the exact conversation one will hear on the dropping zone after the jump —so-and-so had a lot of twists, somebody else is convinced that he had a delayed drop and another (an equal liar) will swear that he had a stand-up landing.

Nevertheless the morning after our last night jump we were very proud to receive our new wings. Parachutists ! We were dare-devils—men playing a man's game. Now we would have something to show the pretty girls at home. We made our triumphant way back to Maison Blanche near Algiers, where we caught the troop train for the S.A.S. Base at Philipville.

In the matter of train travel, the 1st Army had the 8th Army beaten. They even had braziers burning inside the cattle trucks and the run of tea was quite continuous the whole way to Constantine. At one station a group of men was left behind while on a quest for water. They caught up the train in a few hours by hopping a lift in an Arab bus. I cannot remember how far Algiers is from Constantine, but it is certainly under two hundred miles, and yet our train was so slow that it took three days to cover the distance. Here we despaired of the railway and persuaded a negro truck-driver to convey us over the last sixty miles to Philipville. We lodged ourselves in the Officers' Club and went out to see the sights, deciding that it was too late to attempt to find the unit that night. I was walking past a second-class hotel called the Louvre, when a soldier lurched up to me and said:

"Got a light, chum?"

I answered, "I am sorry I haven't. But I should be careful of matches if I were you. You might blow up."

An officer, who was walking past, stopped and said, "You sound like a cavalryman. Are you?"

When I replied that I was, he said that he also was a 15th Hussar. He asked me where I was going and I told him that I was bound for Sandy Scratchley's outfit. Whereupon he was overcome with glee and insisted upon buying me a drink before we collected my kit. It appeared that he was the Adjutant.

There was a great air of urgency in the camp at Philipville—something I had never known before. Everything was done in a tremendous hurry. And there was a pleasant sense of intimacy with the men, who were all of a higher standard than any other ranks I had met in the past two years. Not that the discipline was not strict. If a man made one mistake or failed in any respect whatsoever, he was returned to his parent unit. There was little punishment except the axe of dismissal—a supreme disgrace for men who longed for the day on which they could go into action. The team spirit was developed to a high degree. There were, of course, the minor difficulties of a rapidly expanding unit. The nucleus of old hands from the 63rd Commando had recently carried out raids on Pantellaria, Lampedusa, Sicily and Sardinia, and they rather resented the flood of new arrivals. Camped nearby were two other veteran S.A.S. units—Popski's Private Army, which was resting after its drive round the Gabes Gap, and Lord Jellicoe's men, who were planning a parachute raid on aerodromes in Sardinia.

It was a pleasant tented camp pitched alongside a wonderful beach. Behind were the towering hills of the Jebel, covered with thick green cork forest. All day one could hear the rattle of small arms or the thud of explosive from training cadres on the beach. There seemed to be a complete disregard for the normal army safety precautions, but nobody appeared to get hurt. The physical training was very rigorous. Before a recruit was accepted, he had to run to the top of a six-hundred-foot mountain and back again in sixty minutes. Failures in this final test were returned to the Infantry Depot on the other side of the hill.

There were long route marches with sixty-pound packs, practice in night infiltration and various schemes to encourage self-reliance in the men. It was emphasised that the method of approach to the operational area was of secondary importance. That which really mattered was what you did when you got there. We were trained to land by sea in a fast surf using West African dories, to infiltrate overland by foot or in jeeps, and in the normal parachute drill in an old fuselage. We experimented with all kinds of sabotage devices, and close-quarter shooting was taught in a style which would have shocked old instructors in the Small Arms School at Hythe.

For the first ten days my body ached so much that I could only listen with open mouth to the tales of the old hands in the mess, but gradually I became fit enough to be restored to my normal low intelligence. My seniority gave me a post as second-in-command to Sandy Scratchley, who was commanding a newly raised squadron then in training for a landing in Sicily. About a fortnight before the Allied landings in Sicily, Bill Stirling revealed the exact nature of our task in a lecture in the Operations Hut. We were to land a short time ahead of the Highland Division to seize a certain lighthouse which was suspected of housing a number of machine-guns so sited as to be able to sweep the beaches on which the landings were to take place. He showed us an air photograph of the island on which the lighthouse was situated and left us to work out our plan. He had a great knack for appreciating the crux of a problem and we readily agreed to his wise modifications. At the time most of the unit was much more concerned with large parachute operations in Northern Sicily, Sardinia and Italy, so that we were left very much to ourselves in our minor task.

While Sandy Scratchley was away arranging for the details of our reception near Sousse, where the Highland Division was to concentrate before D-Day, I took the forty-odd men who had been selected for the operation up to Djelli for a dress rehearsal. Up to that moment we had never seen a landing craft, but we had trained on a model made out of sandbags on the beaches at Philipville. An exact rehearsal was carried out from our mother ship, the *Royal Scotsman*, and the trial went completely according to plan, except that having taken our island in a mock attack and sent up the success signal, the Navy forgot to pick us up. We sat on that tiny deserted island for a whole day, frantically sending up Verey lights, until somebody at Djelli suddenly remembered "the Commandos."

About a week before the big day, we moved down by road through the famous Pichon Gap to Sousse. Whilst we moved along that beautiful road, winding between the towering green mountains, I was struck by the great difference between the 1st Army country and the desert. It was remarkable that the 1st Army had been able to take so many of those commanding features by direct assault. However, it was noticeable that their battlefield was not strewn with the rubbish of war as were those of the 8th Army, either because the scale of the battles had not been so great or because it had mainly been a campaign fought by infantry. There were few derelict vehicles and shell-holes, and none of the tangle of barbed wire or minefields one can see to this day anywhere between Alamein and Mareth.

We were bivouacked in an olive grove near a place called Msakin not far from Sousse and the Highland Division was encamped all round us. From dawn to dusk the skirling of the pipes never ceased. We continued with our rigorous training, but almost as soon as we arrived disaster fell upon the squadron. In spite of the beautiful scenery surrounding our camp at Philipville, it had been the beauty of a fickle jade, for the undergrowth had hidden a dangerous malarial swamp. Now, at the most inconvenient moment, this dread disease began to grip the regiment. I had heard before of armies being laid low by malaria overnight, but only when one has witnessed the disastrous effects of the disease oneself can one really appreciate what a menace it is. Our force was reduced from forty-five to thirteen in under two days. At first we were contemptuous of the new boys, who, we thought, could not stand the sun, but when older hands began to go under, it was plain that something was seriously wrong. A doctor pronounced it to be a dangerous brand of recurrent malaria. The regiment was troubled by fresh outbreaks of the disease even in France and Italy, over a year later, and we had to insist upon mepachrine tablets being taken by operational parties right up to the end of the war.

It was clear that Sandy Scratchley was also infected, but he refused to relinquish command until the last day, when he had been laid so low that walking (to say nothing of a scramble landing) was quite out of the question. He therefore passed over command of the party to me. We were determined not to ask to be relieved of our task so long as there was a fair chance of success. The trouble with "private armies" is that they have so many malicious critics that they cannot afford to have a failure. I knew how important it was to Bill Stirling, who was fighting the most important battle against a dead weight of staff officers to keep the unit in being, that we should produce a clear-cut victory.

We embarked on the *Royal Scotsman* in Sousse the night before the party. We were housed in all the luxury of a modern Irish Channel packet and the food was better than anything I had experienced since South Africa. The few remaining men were in good heart, quite confident of success in spite of their reduced numbers, and spent most of the next day in cleaning their weapons for the fight.

It was a brave display of strength. All around, as far as the eye could see, ships of all sizes were tossing up and down on the waves; rakish L.C.I.s rolling sideways, waves washing over their bows, clumsy tank-landing craft, gunboats, motor torpedo boats and the larger hulls of the mother ships (all converted Channel packets). On the horizon were the watchful shadows of lean, wolfish destroyers and to the south-west we could see the comforting silhouettes of the big ships of the Fleet. Although the weather was fine and the sun set in a crimson glow behind the masts, the sea was so rough as to cause us to be anxious that the operation might be cancelled.

In the afternoon I developed a serious headache and began to sweat on my bunk. Boris Samarine, my Russian second-in-command, who was one of the many foreigners in the S.A.S., borrowed a thermometer which showed that I had a temperature of 102°. It seemed clear that I also was in for a bout of malaria. Boris scrounged a quantity of quinine from the doctor and I took about four times the normal dose—so much that I fell back into a deep sleep from which I was not roused for eleven hours.

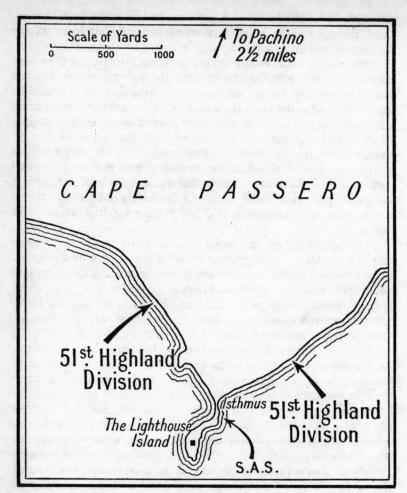

HIGHLAND DIVISION BEACHES IN SICILY.

At three o'clock in the morning Boris shook me and told me that the boys were already in the boat. I buckled on my equipment and staggered out of the cabin. The ship was at rest, tossing silently on the waves, and round about I could just see the shadows of other vessels through the darkness. Over on the shore, which was a thick black smudge at the foot of the dark-blue sky, a searchlight was probing the water. The barge was lowered down the last few feet to land with a bump in the sea. And then we were being thrown about in confusion in the bottom as we were caught up in the angry turmoil of the waves. It was rough—too rough for a landing. Flynn, our Naval lieutenant, put her blunt nose into the rollers, which crashed over the end to swamp everybody sitting forward. The men crouched under the sides, bent over their weapons to keep them dry, while the spray dashed against their faces. They were just black huddled shapes, immobile and silent in the dark.

I reeled over the metal deckboards, trying to recapture my footing, to where Flynn was sitting, face into the wind, dressed in black shiny oilskins. I saw that he was trying to follow a small launch with a red tail-light. And then he shut off the engine and we wallowed for a little, being tossed about at will by the waves. Behind were the bobbing shapes of the first flight, who would idle there at the rendezvous until they had given us our proper start. He glanced at his watch, and looking up, gazed once behind and once at the shore before giving the signal to restart the motor. Our bows began to carve into the white, splashing crests once more. The searchlight momentarily lit up the faces of the men, but passed on mercifully without pausing. Overhead the drone of hundreds of aircraft became louder. I could see by their black silhouettes that they were Dakotas, heavily laden birds of the night bound for the bridges at Syracuse. Then red tracers shot up dotted lines into the sky as the anti-aircraft guns opened fire from Pachino.

We were getting in closer to the shore now and we could see the colour of the sand sloping up from the water's edge. There were little white houses and fields of cabbages beyond the beaches. Everything was ominously quiet. The landing craft swung into calmer water north of the island and then she turned to approach the place where our objective was joined by a sandbar to the shore. Still there were no signs of hostility. She ground to a standstill some five yards from land, her hull stuck hard on the bottom. I told Flynn to lower the ramp. Dropping myself into the sea, holding my carbine above my head, I found myself in water to my waist. I waded steadily ashore and the others followed behind, breaths bated. One fool slipped on a rock and dropped his Bren-gun into the water. Then we were wriggling on our bellies up the slope towards the lighthouse, white and gleaming now in the moonlight. I saw three shadowy figures come out of the front door and disappear round the back. We took the last few yards in a rush, fingers on our tommy guns ready to fire. I kicked open the front door to find the house deserted, although the uneaten meal on the table showed that the occupants had only recently left.

While we were searching the rooms and the outhouses, firing started from the Argylls' beach on the left. The first flight was ashore. Odd tracer bullets zipped into the lighthouse, shattering the glass. I walked out of the front door and fired our success signal into the sky. There were lights going up on both sides now and further back there were the occasional flashes of mortars fired by the enemy. Tracers were criss-crossing into the dunes. I walked back into the building and sat down, deciding to change my socks. Boris came in after a few moments to report that a further search of the island had revealed three terrified little Italians, crouching in holes in the ground, and an abandoned machine-gun. I directed a party to take up fire positions on the neck connecting us with the shore, while we resumed our search of the lighthouse. Suddenly there was a tremendous roar, which shook the broken glass out of the tower and sent us diving under the tables, thinking that the end of the world had come. It was some time before I realised that it was not the biggest bomb in the world, but that the new rocket barges were firing their first salvoes at the shore. One cannot wonder that the Italians put up so little resistance.

There were still odd machine-guns firing at an L.C.I. off Amber Beach when dawn came and we endeavoured to pick them out from our positions in the isthmus. Randolph Churchill, our go-between with the Highland Division, walked up through the bullets and told me that our orders were to return to Bizerta as soon as we could get a ship, since we might be required as reinforcements for the parachute operation in the north.

Flynn's landing craft was still aground beyond all immediate hope of salvage, but at about ten o'clock we managed to get a lift back to the *Royal Scotsman*. Amongst their trophies, the boys had got an enormous Italian flag and a turkey. When we reached North Africa we heard that the Jocks had already taken Pachino. At last we had a firm foothold on European soil.

CHAPTER THREE

JEEP OPERATION IN ITALY, 1943 (PART I)

I SPENT the months between Sicily and the first landings in Italy in a trip to Egypt—half for business and half for pleasure. At that time we were scraping for men, being forced to accept quite inferior material from the Infantry Depot. One of the most usual criticisms of a volunteer unit is that it steals the cream of the best soldiers from the regiments of the line. This is largely untrue in view of the many ways in which a Commanding Officer can block an application for transfer, no matter how many authorities you might hold. With large campaigns in Italy impending and with the fighting still going on in Sicily, while the Army at home was already piling up its material for a second front, Commanding Officers were more loathe than ever to let their best men go. If some of those critics had only seen a few of the men with whom we had to make do during this period, they would have swallowed their arguments and produced a few more on the spot. Bill Stirling, ever intriguing to by-pass an obstinate check, guessed that the Middle East was a better ground for recruitment in view of the fact that it at that time contained several idle units. Knowing well that the D.M.O., Middle East, was a member of my regiment, he thought that I would be the best person to talk him into supplying a few recruits. As it happened, I failed.

I broke all records for trans-desert travel by covering the two thousand-odd miles between Philipville and Alexandria in four and a half days. With my servant, Dover, I drove for eighteen hours a day in a jeep, only sleeping between midnight and dawn. Before the war such a feat might have earned a mention in a geographical magazine, but, as it was, only Dover and I knew that we averaged over fifty miles an hour the whole way.

In the first half day we passed through the green defile of the Pichon Gap and over the plain to Sfax. We slept on the beach near a place where Sandy Scratchley had had an unpleasant argument with a drunken soldier before Sicily. The soldier had reeled back from the town (then out of bounds) overfull of red wine and in an aggressive mood. After calling Sandy a common little jockey, he attempted to strike him. Sandy told the guard to chuck the man into the sea to sober him up. The fellow decided to give us a really good scare while he was about it, and must have swum at least two miles from the shore before he responded to our pleadings to return.

We passed through the Gabes Gap to Tripoli the next day, driving through the vast minefields around Mareth. I was amazed at the strength of the pill-boxes and wire on the line itself, and thanked God for Britain that General Montgomery had not been forced to attack it frontally. Medenine village had a quaint house structure, with roofs consisting of tiny domes like wasps' tails. I have since seen similar houses in Southern Italy and Northern Syria and wondered if there was any connecting link between them.

Tripoli is a large empty modern city with wide avenues and boulevards, little changed by the war. We began to bed down on one of the ornamental lawns on the promenade, but were brusquely ordered to leave by a military policeman. It occurred to me that the 8th Army had changed.

We spent the next night alongside Marble Arch, that ridiculous monument that Mussolini had built way out in the desert near the Tripolitanian frontier to be a gift from the Second Roman Empire to posterity. The R.A.F. ground staff on the landing field there must be some of the loneliest people in the world, for there is not a single British unit between them and Tripoli or Benghazi on either side.

The next day we motored north through Benghazi, which was much more badly damaged than at the time of my last visit, and past the rich red fields of the Barce plain, through the cool green hills of the Jebel Akhdar, and up Derna Pass through our old battlefields to Tobruk. I was shocked by the way the Senussi had pitched their tents outside and were using the trim little colonists' houses as stables, although I now realise that you can no more despise the Bedouin for leading a simple life than rate a Connemara peasant for not using Colgate's tooth paste. Equally the fact that they do not yet understand the doubtful attributes of Western civilisation is no excuse for stealing their birthright.

From Tobruk to Alexandria the tide of war has completely transformed what in 1940 was a pleasant, if barren, land into a continuous junk-strewn dust-heap. I was appalled by the change wrought by Montgomery's advance even in the last year.

It was good to see old friends in Egypt again after so long an absence. Although I failed in my official object of securing recruits, I had a very pleasant holiday. The Seidls welcomed me with typical warmth and we spent many happy hours together at the races or the Sporting Club swimming pool.

The return journey was in marked contrast to the speed of our arrival. I had so overstrained the jeep by my break-neck driving that we had a constant series of mechanical failures, always in the loneliest parts of the desert. Into the bargain, I was forced to go into an Indian hospital at Buq-Buq with a fresh attack of malaria. We eventually arrived in Tripoli on tow behind a convoy of new vehicles, three weeks after our start from Alexandria—an ignominious contrast to our previous four and a half days from Philipville to the Delta. I left Dover with the remnants of the jeep in Tripoli and completed the remainder of the journey by air. A "private army" has not only to live on its wits behind the enemy lines, but also has to resort sometimes to sharp practice to get its way with our own forces. We had evolved a wonderful system for by-passing a cumbersome machine known as the "priorities board" as far as air passages were concerned. We would walk up to the clerk in the "courier's office" and whisper some mysterious code word such as "frog-spawn." The clerk would gaze at you in an awe-stricken, uncomprehending sort of way, and you would say again, "You know, top secret, frog-spawn. Must get to Algiers right away." Usually you were ushered to the aircraft without the formality of papers or ticket.

Soon after my return I was given command of a new squadron equipped with jeeps mounting Twin Vickers Aircraft machine-guns. Before we were properly organised as a unit, we were hurled into frantic preparation for a new operation in conjunction with the landing of the Airborne Division at Taranto.

After working all night on the loading of kit on to the jeeps one day early in September we drove via Souk el Arba to Bizerta. Even the guns had to be tested "en route," there having been no time to fire them in the camp before we started. We were lodged overnight in a large American Transit Camp called "Texas," near the harbour, and the next morning our jeeps were loaded on to the decks of a U.S. cruiser. Bizerta town seemed to be much more badly damaged than Tunis, obviously having received a greater weight of bombs. I remember that there was a scare over some German parachutists who had destroyed a Flying Fortress on the airfield during the night. They were eventually captured when they attempted to queue up for rations at an army cookhouse. The confusion caused by this small raid was a revealing pointer to the effect of our own operations behind the enemy lines.

We steamed towards Taranto with a large fleet of British and U.S. warships, not quite understanding how we were going to land from such large vessels on a hostile shore. Only when we were out at sea, sitting round the table in the wardroom enjoying American hospitality, did we hear the startling news over the loud-speaker that Italy had surrendered. It was an announcement which filled us all with tremendous excitement, and which started a great wave of speculative rumour. We heard that the Italian fleet had come over to the Allies and even saw visible evidence of the fact in Italian men-o'-war under naval escort sailing past us towards Bizerta. People said that we would be in Rome in a week. We heard that Scorcenzy, our German counterpart, had successfully rescued Mussolini by a daring raid off Capri. And then at about three o'clock in the afternoon we sighted the shores of Italy around Taranto Bay. The loud-speaker said that there might be opposition to our landing, but that they were not expecting it, in accordance with a treaty concluded with the Italian authorities.

It was a sunny day and the tiny red-roofed villages around Taranto looked more European and more like home than anything we had seen in North Africa. It was quite plain that our fleet was still suspicious of Italian intentions, and the destroyers nosed first into the harbour with the utmost caution. As we moved slowly down a line of buoys through a calm sea, we passed several tugs flying Italian flags, whose crews lined the rails to regard us with the same curiosity with which we regarded them. Our cruiser was one of the first in, and tied up to the jetty on the west side, the lines being seized by heavily armed Italian sailors. As soon as we had touched the quay, the first wave of S.A.S., dressed in cap comforters and overalls, swung down the ropes to take over the town. They moved forward with their tommy-guns cocked ready for any opposition, but reports soon came back to say that it would be a peaceful occupation.

It was dark before my jeeps were unloaded ready for action,

but Brigadier Hackett, under whose command we then were, told me to push inland as far as possible up the main road. There was an uncanny air about our silent advance up that deserted highway. We had a vague idea that there might be Germans somewhere inland from the port, but we could not guess how many or where. There was nobody on our flanks and we were half proud to be the advance guard of a new army on foreign soil and half afraid of the unknown ahead. I had scattered the jeeps on alternate sides of the wide, tree-lined avenue with Big Jim Mackie, my second-in-command, in front and me behind in the second jeep. With the long shadows of the trees running across the road in the moonlight, only the faint throb of the jeep engines could be heard in the silence of the night. Our maxim was that good reconnaissance is done by the eyes in daylight and by the ears at night. Obeying orders to the letter, Big Jim frequently stopped to listen. He was a tall, sandy-haired Scot from Edinburgh, who was to be my stand-by in many encounters to come and who must be one of the most loyal men in the world. I do not believe that Jim has ever harboured an evil thought in his life. I used him so often in the leading jeep that it is a wonder that he survived the war.

Suddenly he stopped and beckoned me forward. A number of armed figures were standing around a bridge a few yards ahead. As we were peering into the half-light, an Italian sentry shouted a challenge. I called back that we were "Inglesi" and began to walk towards them, telling Sergeant-Major Mitchell, my gunner, to cover me with his Bren. I had just reached the bridge, on which stood a group of excited little men in green uniform, when a sentry rushed towards me with a brandished rifle and fired a round through my legs at under five yards' range. The Sergeant-Major filled him with a whole magazine of Bren bullets. And then there were profound apologies on both sides when we had established our identity. An officer produced a bottle of wine from which he insisted that we drank a toast to our new alliance. Ignored by his friends, the dead sentry lay crumpled in the dust—an innocent victim of an accident of war. Before we moved on the officer gave me his address in Rome, but all his hospitality could not make us forget the body of a dead Neapolitan, lying unmourned on the bridge with his life blood running in the gutter, killed after the armistice.

A little further on Big Jim became uncertain of the route.

He asked a figure at the side of the road how far it was to Massafra. The fellow answered with a grunt and, pointing to his chest, said "tedesco.' Jim turned slowly to his gunner, a well-educated boy called Clarke, and said, "Corporal Clarke, what does ' tedesco ' mean?" Clarke stared for a moment, mouth agape, then shouted "German" as he swivelled the guns. It was indeed a German, who did not seem in the least surprised to be captured. With a gruff "Ach-so," he climbed into the back of the jeep. Four more Germans were captured in this fashion before a hail of schmeisser bullets began to pour into us from an olive grove. The Vickers, perhaps the best machine-gun in the world for quick retaliation, pumped magazine after magazine of tracer into the darkness. During the confusion I ordered the column to turn round, since it was quite clear that Massafra was occupied. There were no casualties amongst the jeeps, although one prisoner had escaped because Big Jim had his tommy-gun on "safe" at the crucial moment.

We turned left down a side road, hoping to come across another route to the north, but dawn found us in a tiny village called Pogiano, unoccupied by the enemy. We slept there under the shadow of the cactus hedges while we awaited fresh orders from Brigade. During the morning most of the Brigade moved up on bicycles from Taranto. The Brigadier told me to push out to the north-west along the coast to see if I could locate the limits of the German position. If possible, I was to infiltrate through to their rear areas.

I led the column in line-ahead for about eight miles beyond Pogiano until we came to an Italian policeman on a cross-roads. He told me that German vehicles were passing all the time and usually turned left towards a village called Ginosa. I waved the jeeps into ambush positions and the last vehicle was still backing into the trees when I saw the head of a large column approaching from the west. I threw myself into the ditch, pointing my tommy-gun up the road. I half-suspected that they were Italians and the first vehicle was nearly on top of us before I noticed the German cockade on the front of the driver's cap. The squeezing of my tommy-gun trigger was the signal for the whole weight of our fire-power to cut into the trucks at practically "nil" range. Having once started such a colossal barrage of fire, it was very difficult to stop it in spite of the fact that the Germans were waving pathetic white flags from their bonnets. I remember screaming at a Frenchman called Durban to cease fire and making no impression on his tense, excited face until the whole of his Browning belt was finished. At last the racket stopped and I walked down the road towards a tiny knot of Germans waving white flags from behind the last vehicle. All those in the front trucks were dead. Still panting from the excitement of the ambush, we screamed at them to come forward with their hands up. A totally demoralised group of Germans was led up the column by an officer, bleeding profusely from a wound in his arm and still shouting for mercy. It was plain that there would be no question of further resistance from any of them. In all we took about forty prisoners and four trucks. Eight other vehicles were destroyed and about ten Germans were killed.

My greatest fear was that the Germans would retaliate from Ginosa or at least investigate the cause of the shooting. We had not sufficient strength for a pitched battle so that, after sending back the prizes with the prisoners, we sabotaged the remaining vehicles and withdrew a short way down the road.

The Germans sent down a number of infantry in armoured troop-carriers within an hour of our attack. They halted at the cross-roads and began to salvage the remnants of the vehicles and to bury their dead. I sent up two men hidden in the back of an Italian hay cart to get a better view of their activities and they returned later to say that the enemy had withdrawn to Ginosa.

For the next two days we tapped in with patrols around Ginosa to try to discover the limits of the German position. Once one of our jeeps destroyed a motor-cycle and a truck by shooting on the move, quite a creditable feat. It appeared that the enemy was holding a line running east to west from Cioia delle Celle through Castellaneta and Ginosa. It could only have been a delaying position since the roads were weakly held by small sections of parachutists.

Still trying to work round to the left, I moved my squadron headquarters another four miles down the coast road to a railway station from which I pushed up three troops on different minor tracks to try to find a way round the German right flank: one through Pisticci, another through Bernalda, and a third to Riverella Railway Bridge. It was amazing how well our heavily-laden jeeps travelled even over the most mountainous goat tracks.

The first reports were from the centre troop, which said that Bernalda was clear although they had run into a German anti-tank gun north of the town. I decided to move my headquarters into Bernalda to lessen the wireless range. We drove into the village through cheering crowds of women and children who threw bunches of grapes into the jeeps and roared "Viva truppa alliata" into our faces. They were a gay happy throng and the girls had obviously put on their best dresses for the occasion, but the words "DUCE" and "REX" on the walls were only crossed out with a single negligent stroke. The temper of these people changes very quickly. The Italian commander of the carabinieri struck me as being an untrustworthy type of man and he did not seem in the least bit impressed by the number of troops we had landed at Taranto. I suspected that he would soon find a way of informing the Germans of my positions.

The centre troop returned in the evening to report that it had scattered a number of Germans laying mines and that it thought that it had been pursued into the town by a German patrol. I decided not to leaguer in the village square as I had planned, but to return to the open country to the south. The streets were crowded with civilians taking the evening air, and when some German infantry opened fire on us on the outskirts of the town we were unable to retaliate.

We leaguered around a cross-roads near Pisticci, mounting a strong guard and keeping one eye open for a withdrawal route to the south. It was all a cat-and-mouse sort of game for I dare not risk an involved battle with my slight strength.

There was a small concentration camp nearby which I officially liberated, putting the Italian guards under the custody of their Polish wards. It did not seem a very awful place although the internees fêted us with tears running down their faces. They were quartered—men, women and children—in drab wooden huts, but I could see no signs of whipping blocks or excessive malnutrition. Their main crimes seemed to have been "anti-fascist" sympathies or communism—little enough cause for an imprisonment of over six years. It gave us a grand feeling of goodness to liberate these wretched people, although I had not the heart to tell them that we were already over fifty miles ahead of our main forces and that their freedom might easily be short-lived if the Germans should come in our direction.

At first light I again pushed up patrols towards Riverella

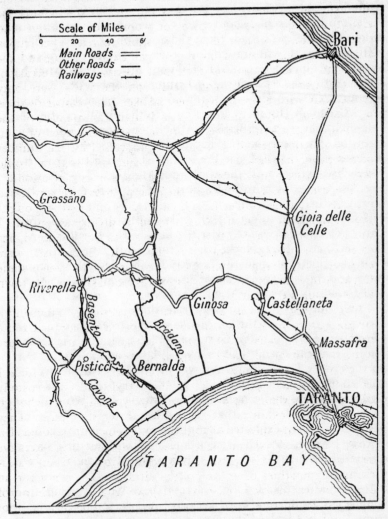

Scale of Miles
0   20   40   6'
Main Roads ═══
Other Roads ───
Railways ─┼─┼─

Bari

Grassano

Gioia delle
Celle

Riverella

Basento

Ginosa

Castellaneta

Massafra

Bradano

Pisticci

Bernalda

Cavone

TARANTO

TARANTO BAY

SCENE OF OPERATIONS, ITALY 1943.

179

which the left-hand troop had reported clear. We were gradually moving further west in an attempt to find a weak link in the enemy line. Squadron Headquarters was having breakfast around its three jeeps when Durban, the French gunner, gave the alarm in an excited shout. A large armoured car was nosing up towards the cross-roads from the direction of Pisticci. There was no hope of withdrawing unobserved and so we crouched behind our guns, determined to hold our fire until the range had decreased to one at which the Browning might be effective. The armoured car was almost on top of us when I realised that it was a Canadian Humber. Running into the middle of the road, I shouted that we were British. After a few moments of mutual suspicion, we were shaking hands and clapping each other on the back. The first link had been established with the 8th Army which had come up all the way from Messina. The Canadians gave us packets of gum and a bottle of gin before they left to return to their squadron.

I had no desire to get myself linked up with the main forces again. Our object was to twist the tails of the Germans, and if the Canadians became locked with the enemy rearguards there would be much less opportunity of finding a hole in their armour. In those days we wanted a shoot and were determined to get one.

I found my patrols held up by a blown bridge near Riverella Railway Station. The railway ran along a deep ravine and through a tunnel to the other side of a feature on which the Germans were reported to be stationed in strength. The Italians told us that the enemy had many pill-boxes and anti-tank guns on the crest. The only answer was to tap even further west. I sent an officer called David Huggett to try to get across at Grassano, where there was a small railway bridge. While he was away it occurred to me that the tunnel through the German position might be exploited at night. I was reluctant to commit a party of men to such a hazardous raid without first having estimated the chances of success by a personal reconnaissance of the tunnel.

In the afternoon I dodged across the ravine, moving from boulder to boulder, always keeping one eye on the ridge in front. Slowly I stalked my way up to the mouth of the tunnel. Near to that gaping black hole there was a small railway worker's cottage. I sat looking at it for a long time through my glasses before I dared a closer inspection. Leopard-crawling on my stomach, I came close enough to see several chickens pecking about near the door. An upturned German steel helmet was rocking in the wind like a top about to overbalance. There was no sound except the fluttering of the hens and the rustle of a single eucalyptus tree in the wind. I wriggled up to a window and peered inside. There were no signs of life. The front door was gently banging on its hinges. I plucked up courage and moved boldly round to the front. A cough at the back of the house sent me scuttling back to the shelter of the rocks. I cocked my carbine and waited for the reaction to the clatter of my escape. Nothing happened. I wormed round to the top of a knoll from which I could see the back door. Then I kicked myself for a fool. An aged, fly-blown mule was tied to a stake in the garden and was coughing away like an old man with asthma. Abandoning all caution, I pushed my way into the front door. The house was unoccupied, but the odd items of German equipment showed that it had not always been so. I moved on towards the tunnel, keeping my back against the sides of the cutting. A heavy tree-trunk had been dragged across the line. I had sidled about halfway along the tunnel and could see the sunshine at the far end, when a rattle of machine-gun fire came from above as if someone were dragging chains across sheet tin. Stumbling over the lines, I ran back towards the cottage, my heart pounding against my ribs. The bullets were whistling across the cutting, bouncing off the rocks on the far side. I heard the rapid fire of the Vickers between bursts of Spandau and guessed that the troop covering the bridge was being attacked. Making my way from rock to rock, I traversed the steep slope towards the road.

A gully ran down the hillside across my path and I was able to walk up it without further fear of discovery. Peter Jackson, one of my troop leaders, was engaged in a fire fight with two Spandaus on the top of the crest. Both sides were just wasting ammunition although Peter claimed to have hit two Germans. His grandfather had won two Victoria Crosses and I feel sure that Peter would also have deserved one had he not been killed in a jeep accident a month later. He loved a fight and was very hurt when I told him to withdraw to the station.

Back under cover of the buildings, I briefed Jim Mackie for the offensive patrol through the mountain. He was to take twelve men through just before dawn, leaving two to guard the route of escape at the far end. Once on the other side he was to appreciate the German strength, kill as many as he could with a few surprise bursts and then withdraw back the way he had come. As far as I could see, the tunnel was unguarded but it might not remain so. On no account were the two men to abandon the mouth until the main patrol had returned.

In the evening David Huggett returned with the important prize of the office truck of a German parachute battalion. In addition to the papers, the truck was full of loot and the Orderly Room Under-officer had also been captured. David, who was justifiably proud of his success, had driven halfway into Grassano before he had realised that it was occupied. He killed several Germans in the street in a brief fight before he made off with this valuable trophy. The cigarettes and food were most welcome since we had already been forced to resort to requisition from the local population for rations.

Daylight produced another troop of Canadian armoured cars. Their Commander was as furious as I at being held up by the blown bridge. We drank coffee together in the station-master's office, champing on the bit at our enforced inactivity. Jimmy Mackie had not returned by midday and I was becoming very worried about the fate of his party. The only way in which we could help was by making a last attempt to push jeeps up the road since I hesitated to commit any one else to the tunnel.

The Armoured Car Commander was a thrustful sort of chap who was only too ready to help. I got him to cover the hillside with one Humber whilst the other towed up some telegraph poles from the station. Working under the cover of his Besas, we made a ramshackle bridge over the gap by laying concrete railings across the poles. When at last we had finished laying sods on top of the railings, we looked on our handiwork with great pride. There was surely nothing that could stop us. One of the men stuck up a crazy sign with the words "S.A.S. Bridge, Sept., 1943," painted on it with tar. It was just strong enough to take an unloaded jeep, so I pushed Peter Jackson across with his troop. He came back thirty minutes later with a broad smile on his face. Apparently the Germans had blocked the road with an anti-tank gun, but Peter had made hay of its crew before it could come into action.

At about two o'clock Jim Mackie's tired little party trooped back through the tunnel. He had had a skinful of adventure from which he had only emerged by the breadth of a hair. Passing through the tunnel without mishap, he had found himself in the middle of a German battalion. He had time to inspect their defences at close range before he bumped a sentry. It was fortunate that both Jim and the German forgot to extract the pin from the grenades they threw. The alarm was given and the Germans fired in all directions, not knowing from which side the attack had come. The patrol fought its way back to the tunnel to find the mouth occupied by a German section. The two men he had left on guard had fled back to safety. After a rather lucky little action, Mackie's party fought its way back to our side of the mountain. I could imagine the confusion of that fight, with grenades bursting in the cutting and tracer bullets whinging into the darkness of the tunnel.

Mackie was furious with the two men who had abandoned their post. He demanded that I should deal with the senior one on the spot. Our discipline in these things was necessarily harsh for we could not afford to have a single weak link in the chain. I held a short trial by my jeep in the olive grove. It was even more distasteful to me that the culprit should be my old Cockney servant, Smith. The poor boy wept as I told him that he had behaved like a coward and would have to be returned to his parent unit. I wished that I could have taken those words back, but our code was inflexible. His failure had almost resulted in the death of ten others. He would have to go. I could see that the men fully agreed with my decision and would give poor Smith no sympathy. I hope he succeeded elsewhere. He left that night on the captured truck—a broken, dispirited little man.

I decided to move even further west to try for the last time to by-pass Grassano. We halted in a small village overlooking the valley while Jim Mackie took his jeeps down the same route by which David Huggett had entered to seize the Orderly Room truck. In the village the jeeps were surrounded by the usual horde of helpful Italians. Pretty girls, barefooted children, wizened peasants and patronising ex-Americans all fought each other for the honour of touching our equipment. There were many offers of bottles of wine and the backs of the vehicles were piled high with bunches of grapes, walnuts and flowers. The troops doled out German cigarettes to all who asked, occasionally scattering the crowd with the sudden false alarm of "Tedescho."

Perhaps the greatest nuisances were ex-Americans who insisted upon giving us inaccurate information.

"You English. Speaka da English verra good. O.K. Bud. Pittsburgh, that's me. Americano citizen. Yeah!"

"Americano or Italiano, you push off. And leave that blanket alone."

"O.K., Bud. No offence. Mighta glad to see you boys. Say, you got a real American cigarette?"

"Push off, I said."

"O.K., Bud. No offence. Maybe you like a little vino. No goddamned beer around here. Them German bastards taka the lot."

"Push off!"

A wave of a pistol might finally encourage him to withdraw a few yards, but it was only to recuperate before another attempt at friendship. Non-frat would never have worked in Italy. All this hospitality was understandable and very welcome at the right time, but we were trying to fight a battle. When the confusion was at its height a German lorry entered the village. It was impossible to shoot through the panic-stricken multitude, which was perhaps fortunate for we secured its capture undamaged. The vehicle was loaded with sacks of flour, soap, combs and other little toilet trinkets. The stuff was of no use to us so I ordered the Sergeant-Major to distribute it to the crowd. A great surging mob fought for the presents around the tailboard of the truck. I was amused to see that the Sergeant-Major was giving the best items to the most attractive girls. Of such stuff are soldiers made.

Jim Mackie entered the village on a bullock cart. He came up to me with a miserable apologetic look on his face. He had been ambushed on the road to Grassano and, although he had managed to withdraw without casualties, both his jeeps had been destroyed. He described how two machine-guns had opened up at close range from the corn and how they had fought back at a disadvantage since they could not see the German positions. He was heart-broken at having lost his jeeps. It was really my fault for I should not have been so stupid as to send two troops down the same road on successive days.

It was clear that there was no further hope of infiltrating through this sector of the front. We had achieved a certain success in shallow penetration but the results were not sufficient to justify our remaining in the area any longer. We were now eighty miles beyond the nearest airborne troops and our supplies were running short. The Canadians were advancing now in all their strength. I decided to return to Taranto for further orders.

The password in the Taranto area was, "Are you Airborne? No, Seaborne." When we reached the first knife-edged road-block, the leading S.A.S. driver was challenged. "Are you Airborne?" He replied, "Not bloody likely. I'm in D Squadron."

CHAPTER FOUR

JEEP OPERATION IN ITALY, 1943 (PART II)

SOON AFTER our return, we were ordered up to Bari to await the arrival of the 4th Armoured Brigade, under whose command we were to fall. We moved up the road in a medley of jeeps, requisitioned cars and trucks. I travelled with John Syms, our Force Commander, and several miles up the road from Taranto we passed our French Foreign Legion Squadron, all smiles beside their broken down bus. John bet me five pounds that they would pass us within thirty minutes in a different requisitioned bus. He won his bet.

Bari had been taken by Popski's Private Army and was now only occupied by a sprinkling of airborne troops. It was thrilling to be in a large city, newly taken. All the Italians were friendly. The streets were full of stalwart Bersaglieri in plumed hats and tight shorts, who claimed to be itching for a fight with the Germans.

We were billeted on the northern outskirts of the town in a large school overlooking the sea. It was the first time I had been lodged in a house during a campaign, and in spite of the luxury of proper Christian lavatories, I think I would have been happier on the ground under the olive trees. For several days there was little to do except to clean our guns and maintain our vehicles in preparation for a new advance. The men much enjoyed their evenings of pleasure in the big town. It has always struck me as odd that in the first fine flush of occupation the girls should prefer foreigners who might barely speak a word of their tongue. Even if the Americans and the Canadians were more popular at home, Tommy Atkins could hardly complain when he had the run of half the countries in the world. Perhaps the female mind is more intrigued by mystery.

Our first task was a long-range patrol to Melfi to report upon the progress of the Canadians, who were advancing on a parallel axis further inland. I plotted the route on which we would be least likely to meet the enemy—along side tracks, minor roads and small villages to the west. In each village along the route we were met by the same happy liberation scenes. Gay bouquets of flowers adorned the bonnets and we were for ever eating fruit and drinking wine. Most touching of all was the gratitude of the old mothers, tears streaming down their wrinkled faces. The Italian flags and Union Jacks appeared like magic. I sensed a certain disappointment in some places that we were not American, which was understandable in a country with such strong ties to the United States.

Sometimes the hospitality could be more than annoying. Presents were always thrown at the jeeps, but although we did not mind an odd bunch of grapes in the face, we thought hard apricots or walnuts was going a little too far. I was once so infuriated by a direct hit on the nose that I stopped the jeep and began pelting the crowd with small apples. Far from being offended, they thought British humour wonderful. At least I was lucky enough not to stop a wet fish, which was poor Peter Jackson's fate.

After we had gone about thirty miles the diminishing welcomes made us proceed more warily, it being a fair assumption that the presence of Germans was keeping the people to their houses. We approached the village of Rovreto, which crowned a hill like most Italian villages and overlooked a wide, undulating plain. The peasants did not seem at all sure that there were not Germans in the village. It was a long open approach and we could not fail to be observed from the hill. We moved cautiously, stopping at every rise for another look through the glasses. We were mounting the last spiral path to the village, half-expecting to be received by the burst of a "rack gun," when I noticed the tell-tale dust of an approaching column. Soon we saw a line of armoured cars and trucks moving up from the south. We were just moving up to better defensive positions in the narrow streets when I noticed that the armoured cars were Humbers, which made it almost certain that they were Canadians.

Some minutes later we were coffee-housing with French Canadians in the streets of Rovreto. In the excitement of this meeting I had foolishly neglected to post look-outs. Only the prompt action of Sergeant-Major Mitchell saved us from disaster when about fifty Germans entered the village from the other side. The first notion of danger I received was a sudden burst of Bren from the tail of the column. Rallying the crews of the last jeeps, who had all dismounted to talk to the civilians, Mitchell seized a Bren and charged the German platoon. Firing from the hip, he drove them out of the village and down the hill on the other side. His party pursued the enemy until they were pinned in a river bed by his fire from above. Four wounded Germans were captured in the streets.

The French Canadian Company then launched an attack down the side of the hill with some of my men running well in the van. They returned when they had driven the enemy back some three miles, capturing several more prisoners.

The Canadian method of mixing infantry companies with reconnaissance units in an advance is a very sensible one for European country. Armoured cars can so easily be held up by a small block on a road which an infantry platoon could clear in a matter of minutes.

After this small skirmish at Rovreto we turned north again towards Melfi. We proceeded along a white dusty road past lonely farm-houses and down into a deep valley. Here a bridge had been partially destroyed by the detonation of a quantity of Teller mines which showed that the Germans had neither time nor material for a proper demolition. When we had filled up the hole with rubble, we manœuvred our jeeps across the gap.

We were motoring along happily at about twenty miles an hour between a series of interlocking spurs, when a spare man in the back of the second jeep gave the alarm. I ran forward to inquire the cause of the halt, and Nock, the boy who had spotted the enemy, pointed out a number of men in khaki caps lying on the high ground covering a defile, barely a hundred yards ahead. If he had not been so alert we might have run straight into the trap. As it was, there was a chance of turning the tables.

I waved the last two jeeps on to a ploughed field on the right, ordering them to try to appear from an unexpected direction to a flank. Peter had to be content with the cover of two small bushes on the road, while I led a foot party up the slope in the centre. The Germans were very idle and not yet aware of our presence. Some were sunbathing near an Italian cottage, their white towels hanging on the hedgerow, while others were on duty behind a machine-gun in a weapon pit. The first shot came from them, but we returned the compliment with the whole of our tremendous weight of fire, at least seven machine-guns pumping in tracer at the sort of range at which you cannot miss. We had been shooting for about twenty minutes when another enemy automatic weapon opened up from a flank to which we were fully exposed. We only escaped heavy casualties by dragging ourselves back along the furrows. I thought my fighting days were over when their bullets threw a clot of mud into my face. When a mortar also opened up from the direction of Melfi, sending bombs whistling down vertically into the plough, I thought it time to withdraw. As we were backing out, I caught a glimpse of Nock, grinning at the enemy from behind a telegraph pole. His ammunition exhausted, he was sticking his tongue out at the Germans, slapping his hand on his empty magazine as much as to say, "Hah! Hah! Jerry. We've had you again."

The Canadians had quitted Rovreto but we found evidence of their action in the shape of a badly wounded German in a ditch. His face was as yellow as old parchment and it was clear that he had lost a lot of blood from a wound in his side. His blue Luftwaffe uniform was sodden with dark red blood and only urgent medical attention could save his life. I pulled his tunic aside and bound him up with a shell dressing. We found some wooden planks in a barn and my gunner tied him to this rude stretcher on the back of the jeep. It was nearly dawn when we arrived back in Bari. The poor fellow must have suffered agony in that drive across bumpy, unmetalled roads. He kissed my hand when I left him in the Airborne Dressing Station.

The squadron was left in reserve near Canosa while the 4th Armoured Brigade was engaged in an operation to cross the River Ofanto. Peter and I went into the town in the evening to see if we could find some amusement. It was not long before we were surrounded by all the celebrities of the village who pressed us to go into their houses for a drink or something to eat. We could not possibly satisfy them all, so we compromised by accompanying the mayor to a café in the village square. It was a great party. Bottle after bottle of wine was produced. There was no question of refusing and before long we were as garrulous as any Italian. All the belles arrived in their party frocks and we danced on the cobbled floor to the tune of a piano accordion. Delicious fruit, fried chicken and spaghetti were thrust in front of us and everybody talked at the same time, filling the room with their babble. I shook hands with so many people and was so often kissed on the cheeks that I was quite exhausted by it all. Or perhaps it was the wine. It must have been about eleven o'clock in the evening when Peter and I were sitting each with an arm round a girl, singing "The troopship was leaving Bombay." My lady friend had been a fan-dancer in Rome, which gave her certain prestige over the others. Suddenly I heard the engines of jeeps outside in the street. My heart leapt. It could only be the squadron. I dropped the fan-dancer unceremoniously on the floor and dashed for the door. I was just in time to catch Sergeant-Major Mitchell in the last jeep.

It appeared that they had been ordered at the last minute to carry up Ramon Lee and his Frenchmen to the other side of the river, whence they would carry out a patrol into Cerignola, the next town on the axis of advance. I felt a fool. I would never have forgiven myself if Jim Mackie had been forced to take the squadron into action without me. But I was so drunk that until I had worked off the effects of the wine I would be in no position to take command. Sensibly the Sergeant-Major kept me in the rear jeep and politely told me to be careful every time I made too much noise.

Big Jim handled the column perfectly according to the rules. Every few yards he would stop to listen and we never exceeded a walking pace. Each jeep was loaded with grim little legionnaires, dressed in American overalls and woollen caps, their hands clutching their tommy-guns and carbines.

At last the Frenchmen debussed. Ramon gathered his men around him and swiftly hissed his final instructions. Half the party went off to the left under his second-in-command, Louis de Sablet, and were swallowed up by the black shadows. Drunkenly, I insisted on going with Ramon. I have never seen a night patrol handled with such skill and, drunk though I was, I learnt a lot from Ramon that night. His instinct for direction was uncanny. We cut through some woods on the right to approach the town from the rear. The men moved along noiselessly in tight, Indian file, never putting a foot in a wrong place. Each time I stumbled over a branch or a rock, Ramon would curse me with muttered French expletives in the way only Frenchmen can swear. Sometimes he would halt and all the shadowy figures behind would collapse on to the ground as if a ball had been rolled into a pack of cards. Ramon would click his fingers and a face-scarred legionnaire would double off on tip-toe through the trees to reconnoitre some suspicious object. The silent speed with which he moved over the ground pointed to a thoroughness in training unknown in the British Army. When Ramon became more sure of his ground the pace quickened.

It was something of a shock to me when houses suddenly appeared in front. The legionnaires split equally on each side of the street, silently moving from one doorway to another. Two scouts moved on ahead and seized a man sitting on a chair on the pavement. Quite calmly he said:

"At last you have come. I have been waiting here since midnight. The last Germans left at eleven o'clock."

Ramon was obviously angry at having been deprived of his kill. He vented his spleen on this poor friendly Italian by cross-examining him in broken, would-be sarcastic, English. The Italian protested that he had always been an anti-fascisto. In fact he would prove it. There was an American airman in the hospital, whom they had sheltered for months, refusing to turn him over to the Germans. After sending back a runner for the jeeps Ramon rudely ordered him to conduct us to the hospital.

At first the sisters refused to open the door but Ramon threatened that he would shoot in the lock if it was not opened in five minutes. A frightened doctor opened it enough to allow a shaft of light to fall upon our faces. He was so overjoyed to discover that we were not Germans that he hugged us all on the spot. He led us into a small lighted room. A young airman was lying on a bed in the corner, naked except for the paper bandages covering terrible burns on his legs and arms. As we came into the room in all our battle array, his eyes lighted up and he said, "Gee I'm glad to see you. Where've you all been to. I've been hoping you would come for days. Are you British?"

He was a little puzzled by a single British officer amongst so many Frenchmen, but I assured him that we were really friends. I would report his presence on my return and make arrangements for him to be evacuated back to the hospital in Taranto. I gave him an English cigarette, leaving the remainder of the packet by his bed. The poor devil was loud in his praises of the Italians, but I could see that even the slightest movement gave him pain. We left him with the promise that daylight would bring our main forces but I could see that he followed us to the door with doubting eyes, afraid to believe that his miseries were over.

The 4th Armoured Brigade was commanded by an old desert friend called Brigadier John Curry, who pushed me out to reconnoitre on the left flank as he drove up the road to Foggia.

We passed through a very casual infantry patrol along a side road to a village called Stormarella. We were greeted on the outskirts by the usual spontaneous welcome so that I was even less prepared for a sudden outburst of firing from the front jeep which had just turned a corner into the main street. I halted the rest of the column under cover of the houses and moved forward to try to find out the cause of the trouble. One of the leading crew, who was lying flat on the pavement shooting down the street, told me the story. They had almost collided with a German staff car on the corner and had immediately opened fire. Only then did it become apparent that half the village was occupied by the enemy.

There was no hope of extricating the front jeep from its position in the High Street, so I tried to outflank with a foot party through the houses to the right.

Leaving only the drivers in the jeeps, we ran down a side street parallel with the main thoroughfare. About two-thirds of the way down the line of houses we encountered small-arms fire from a German section on a roof. I hurled myself into a doorway followed by three other men. Once inside the cottage, we made our way up a rickety ladder to the flat roof. From there we fired tracer bullets into the enemy house.

Street fighting went on all morning with many bullets being fired by both sides, although I think that the enemy did not suffer much more than we did from the wild shooting. Towards noon the enemy began to pull out of the village, moving slowly back from house to house. In the last dash I found myself crawling across a dung heap with three other officers and no men. A schmeisser was chipping the plaster from the last house behind us, its bullets ricochetting off with a whine to the other side of the street. In the odd glances I obtained between crawling through the barbed wire and throwing myself face down in the dung, it appeared that the firing was coming from the corner of a fig grove. Most infuriating of all, I had lost my Luger. Peter Jackson threw a grenade and then we all stood up and poured a fusillade into the suspected bushes. They were the last shots of the skirmish for the Germans withdrew from the area. I rallied the squadron in a farmyard full of black-and-white Friesians. We only had one wounded prisoner to show for the morning's work.

It was clear that we should continue our advance to Castellerano, on the edge of the foothills. The Germans would certainly be in a state of readiness on the roads so I decided to take the squadron across untracked country for the first time in Italy. If we were lucky enough to find a good track later on, there was a chance that we might be able to approach Castellerano unobserved from the north.

We moved in desert formation with large intervals between the cars. As I watched the jeeps bucking across the plough, I thought of similar days years before. The ground was hard enough to reduce the dust, but I feel certain now that we were watched the whole way across. It was more the gratification of an old soldier's whim than a sound tactical move. It is not always a good thing to fight a battle on the lessons of the past.

We had motored four miles across the fields, breaking through the fences with our wire-cutters, when we came to more hilly ground, thickly covered with young hazel trees. The jeeps laboured up a stony track through a flock of sheep until we came to a steep precipice. Below I could see enemy trucks moving like dinky toys on the road. Peter Jackson, who was leading, beckoned me forward to a crest on the left. We were perhaps three hundred yards from a village perched on the top of a round knoll. Through my glasses I could see Germans running out of what appeared to be the school, and we heard one or two rifle shots. It was clear that the alarm had been given.

I had just given the order for the jeeps to turn round when Roach, Peter's Irish driver, spotted a German steel helmet in the bushes about fifty yards away. Almost immediately a tremendous hail of machine-gun fire was directed towards us. At least four spandaus were firing simultaneously. My own jeep had not yet turned round. Leaping into the driver's seat, I set her nose at the wood of young saplings, charging them at top speed.

We crashed down one tree after another in a desperate attempt to get under cover. One other jeep followed me but there was no sign of the others. All round us the bullets splattered into the trees. My last view of Peter was of his crew still fighting the guns from a blazing jeep. It was a gallant attempt to cover our withdrawal and typical of the grandson of a double V.C.

Our two jeeps crashed down the slender tree trunks until we were halted by a ditch. Behind us we thought that we could hear sounds of pursuit. The men worked with the desperation of terror to fill in the trench with brushwood and sods. We were across and the trees began to thin when we heard the sound of engines to the left. Fearing a chase by tanks, we switched off our motors until we laughed at each other with relief when two other jeeps came into the glade. We all returned to Brigade together, our hearts heavy at the almost certain death of Peter, Roach and Durban. After I had reported to the Brigadier, we leaguered for the night in one of those red carabinieri stations which one comes across at intervals all over Italy.

I was just folding my maps for the next day's run when Peter walked in through the door. For some moments I could not speak. Then all I could say was, "I thought you were dead." He explained how they had avoided being hit by a miracle. Durban had fought his guns until the flames reached the petrol tank. Then they had run under the cover of the black smoke into the woods, pursued by several Germans. They ran non-stop for over three miles until they came to a farm where they borrowed a pony trap to complete their journey. I poured out two glasses of brandy and we sat back, German cigars in our mouths, exchanging versions of the battle.

We moved on to Foggia the next day in a motley collection of captured lorries and jeeps. One squadron had left for Molfetta to fit out fishing boats for landings up the coast, but the other squadron was still with us. Foggia was unoccupied by the enemy, although a German staff car made the mistake of driving into it during the day. The devastation caused by American pattern bombing was terrible to behold and I can well believe that it was the last straw which broke the camel's back. There was hardly an undamaged house in the city. Most of the streets were blocked with rubble and some of the railway engines in the station had been carried over three hundred yards. The power station had been completely destroyed and I found a large piece of transformer four miles away. The civilian casualties must have been appalling. The only inhabitants left in the ruins were a few gutter rats engaged in looting the little that remained. In the main shopping centre, valuable goods were spilled into the street. Some of my men found a store of clean shirts which were very welcome, since we had only landed with one change of clothing. There is not much room for personal kit in a jeep.

We were surprised to notice a staff car flying an R.A.F. flag well in the van of the advance. It stopped one of our jeeps and the officer in the back said, "I am Air Marshal Coningham. Have you been to the aerodrome yet?"

"No, sir. We have only just arrived."

"Well in that case you must go in front of me. Go on, it's the Army's job to be there first."

It was easy to understand his delight at the easy way in which the valuable airfields around Foggia had fallen into our hands. Now we would be able to step up the bomber offensive against the whole of Southern Europe.

We were entertained to dinner that night by Ramon's company of Frenchmen. From somewhere they had produced table-cloths, proper cutlery and china plates. They set out the table in the moonlight under the olive trees, and while we sat waiting one of them entertained us with a piano accordion. Ramon was always quick to search out the best wine, but this night he excelled himself. First we had velvet vermouth as an aperitif and with our meal he served an excellent chianti. There were four courses: no little achievement in open-air cooking without proper equipment. The chicken was cooked as only Frenchmen know how and I felt sure that the potatoes and beans must have been scrumped from the garden next door. If there is one feature to be admired in an old soldier it is his ability to make himself comfortable under even the worst conditions. To steal articles to increase a soldier's comfort is scrounging, not looting, and there is a wealth of difference between. Any fool can be uncomfortable; a wise warrior takes a little trouble to improve his lot.

The next afternoon the Brigadier ordered two parties to reconnoitre the towns of Lucera and San Severo. I was fortunately allotted the Lucera task for I believe that four scout cars were destroyed by an anti-tank gun on the outskirts of San Severo. We had moved slowly westward through fields of vines, travelling line abreast for about five miles, when I first noticed German guns through the glasses. We found a good hidden position in a half-moon wood where the jeeps were quite secure from observation. Creeping up to the edge of the trees, we could clearly see three German 88 millimetres firing airburst over Foggia. In view of the artillery it was probable that the Germans were there in strength. I decided to stay in our present position until dark, and then to lead a foot patrol into the town. As soon as it became dark we moved off in column. We had not gone far before we heard the sound of a large enemy transport convoy moving up the road. Having committed myself to the plan of infiltrating into the town, I decided to carry on in spite of the excellence of this new target. I have since regretted that I missed this opportunity to inflict real damage on the withdrawing German columns. My proper course should have been to return to the jeeps and to lead them in an attack upon the road. Although our orders from the Brigadier had been to reconnoitre Lucera no plan should be so inflexible that it cannot be changed to take advantage of an unexpected situation.

It required all one's concentration to maintain the proper direction in a long night march in Europe. Many obstacles forced one to tack one way or the other, and of these obstacles tall grape vines running in lines across the bearing were the worst. Over near the railway station, a building was burning furiously, lighting up the sky—another pointer to an imminent German withdrawal. We crept round a party of talkative Germans and began to mount the last slope to the town.

I was quite surprised to see the white houses so soon. As we were crossing the last ploughed field, there was an enormous explosion. We threw ourselves trembling to the ground, fearing that our presence was known. It flashed through my mind that we must have exploded a trip-mine. And then clods of earth and bricks came whistling down from the sky above. I was hit in the side of the face by a large lump of masonry. Blood poured over my shirt and I thought my jaw was broken. The others helped me into the shelter of the vines. I felt ill—very ill. Someone produced a hip flask and poured neat cognac down my throat, for I could not swallow.

In a voice which must have been very difficult to understand, I told Jim Mackie to see if he could find a safe house in the town where we could base ourselves and where I could recover from the shock of this blow.

He seemed to be gone a very long time but there was no sound of shooting. I staggered to my feet and led the remainder of the patrol into the outskirts of the town. Jim met us in the first street and told us to follow him, keeping very quiet for there were many Germans about. Padding softly along behind him in the shadows, we turned into a larger street. He pushed open a lighted door and told us to hasten inside before we were seen. It was the home of an old priest who was terrified that the Germans would discover our presence. His sister bathed and bandaged my wounds while we worked out further orders for the patrol.

I sent out three pairs with orders to snipe at Germans but not to get involved in a fight. During the night the patrols covered most of the town while I sat in the priest's drawing-room receiving the reports. The last Germans left on a motor-cycle at about one o'clock, but met disaster at the hands of one of our patrols near the Town Hall. It appeared that the explosion which had caused me so much pain had been a German demolition of the road. The amusing thing was that we watched the Germans laying mines and had them all plotted by the next morning.

It was a busy night. I could not have slept with such a swollen jaw anyway. My face was lopsided for weeks afterwards. It was certain by the morning that there were no further Germans about so we sallied forth in our great strength of twelve to take over Lucera. The Italians turned out in their thousands to welcome the conquering army. I felt very proud for it was the first large town we had captured alone. If only old, ugly women had not tried to kiss my bruised face I would have been completely happy.

I ordered the mayor to release all political prisoners from the gaol, which was a very foolish move because it only meant that they were transferred to the Town Hall, where the administrative arrangements were inadequate. The wretched fellows were so broken in spirit that they remained in their new billet all day.

Our jeeps arrived during the morning and I sited them tactically around the cross-roads. We were joined by two companies of infantry in the afternoon. When they had been relieved of their responsibilities most of the men were entertained in Italian houses.

It poured with rain during the night, catching us all by surprise. We carried our soaked bedding into the Town Hall and slept alongside the newly liberated prisoners. It was still raining hard the next morning, soaking all the kit in our jeeps into a miserable sodden state. When the sun came out in the afternoon all the bushes in the ornamental gardens were adorned with towels, blankets and items of clothing.

After we had been in Lucera for two days I obtained permission to move on further north. Using our old trick of creeping along narrow paths, always stopping to observe all round before we moved across a patch of open ground, we moved north to the San Severo-Castelnuova road.

I set a trap on the road for a short while but no transport came along. Just after we had crossed on our route across country to the north, a motor-cycle flashed along behind us going from Castelnuova towards Torre Maggiore. I told Peter Jackson to pursue it, knowing well that it could not escape if our troops were indeed in San Severo. He cornered the crew in a house in the village and after a scuffle in which a little chap called Downey (who was afterwards killed in France) had to knock out a big Fascist on the stairs, they captured four prisoners.

Meanwhile I moved north past the corner of a farmyard wall. Suddenly two armour-piercing shells landed very close to the jeeps. I could not see whence they came but it was quite clear that we were in the sights of a German 88 somewhere. As we backed into cover behind the farm, many more shells were fired at us. I did not stay long in the farmyard since high-explosive shells were tearing big lumps out of the masonry. Hoping that the buildings would hide us, we moved back across ploughed fields on to a reverse slope. Shells were bursting behind us over the farm long after we had gone.

I met Peter on the road, triumphant with his prisoners. It was plain that the front was becoming too stable for our game of shallow infiltration and I decided to make my way back to the main forces.

We pulled off the road a short way to a small homestead for a brew of tea. Peter's German was even more limited than mine. When a prisoner came up to him and said, "Ich bin krank," he put out his hand and said, "Oh, how do you do. Ich bin Jackson."

We motored slowly back through the fields. There were handsome white oxen carving furrows in impossible slopes; peasant women in bright 'kerchiefs were bent over their hoes; here and there the brown earth changed to green where the grapes grew; some of the stony ground was shaded by orderly lines of olives; and from the crests of the hills neat white cottages looked like rosettes sewn on a patchwork quilt. This was a land of peace. If war is civilisation, you can keep your flush lavatories, your nylon tooth-brushes and your vulgar motor cars. Give me rather a two-roomed casa with a strong wife, salami sausages hung from the rafters and strings of onions from the windows; two pigs in a sty, three oxen in my stable and a plot of land which is my own.

CHAPTER FIVE

BATTLE OF TERMOLI

AFTER OUR last patrol at Castelnuova we were ordered back to Bari, where the whole direction of the S.A.S. party was undergoing a change. Hitherto our operations since Taranto had been no more our proper role than the original sea-landing had been the normal task of the Airborne Division. Now that the line had stabilised before Termoli it was no longer necessary for us to continue to plug along as an offshoot of the main forces. 78th Infantry Division had landed at Taranto and the time had come to leave this main battle business to the experts. Our job lay behind the enemy front.

The other two squadrons, including the French, had become somewhat jealous of our success in the jeeps. It was only fair that they should have the first chance of a new operation. They had commandeered a small fleet of fishing boats, including a two-masted schooner, which was to transport them up to our new base at Termoli.

The first operation had only an indirect connection with the war. Many British prisoners had escaped at the time of the surrender and were now at large behind the enemy lines. In response to pressure brought to bear by politicians at home, a force was organised to do what it could to facilitate their rescue. We were the tools. A number of small parties equipped with wireless sets were dropped in the foothills all along the Adriatic Coast from Ancona to Pescarra. Their job was to direct ex-prisoners to beach parties who had been landed from motor torpedo boats on the coast. Between the beach parties and the parachutists in the hills, foot parties of S.A.S. would act as guides. Periodically landing craft or motor torpedo boats would come into the beach parties in answer to a torch signal to pick up the refugees. The operation went on for two months but was never an outstanding success. There were many reasons. Sometimes large parties of ex-prisoners got down to the beaches alright, but they were usually scattered by the Germans before they could be picked up. The Navy found it difficult to make exact landfalls on a featureless beach, and above all most of the prisoners were so demoralised that they were not prepared to exert themselves. Contrary to popular opinion at home, many of them preferred to stay in comparative safety in an Italian farm than to risk their necks in a hazardous escape.

Termoli had been seized by a landing carried out by the 1st S.A.S. Regiment, No. 3 Commando and 40 Marine Commando. I was ordered to make speed towards the port in my jeeps with the object of requisitioning a good house near the harbour for the main party.

78th Division was also heading fast for Termoli with the object of joining up with the Commandos. We drove up long columns of trucks and guns, badly dispersed on the road, through Foggia and San Severo to the north. I noted the new tendency to advance along a single road with certain disapproval, and it was not long before the Germans took advantage of the weakness.

North of San Severo we were attacked by enemy aircraft for the first time since the landing at Taranto. Me. 109's swooped down on the packed convoys to set several trucks on fire. I over-rode an obstinate military policeman who refused to let me pass, determined as I was to beat the infantry to the town. Peter and I forged on ahead; we were held up by a flooded river but found a bridge further inland; we drove on until we reached the final river line before Termoli where the sappers were con-structing a pontoon bridge. I told a captain lies about the urgency of my mission and we were ferried across in a pontoon.

Then we drove into Termoli—the first connection the Com-mandos had had with the main forces. It was good to see our own winged dagger flaunted on the sand-coloured berets of the S.A.S. in the town. They had had a great victory. Two hundred German prisoners had been taken by surprise and the Parachute Divisional Commander had only escaped capture by a narrow margin.

I selected a rather slummy building near the harbour where we waited for our tiny fleet to arrive. They came in just as the sun was setting in a golden ball in the west, casting a gilded sheen on the water. Four little caiques heeled over against the wind led in by a tall schooner. I envied the others their oppor-tunity to play pirates. The smaller craft anchored by the jetty while the schooner tied up alongside the Naval torpedo boats off the shore.

For another day Termoli was quiet. 78th Division was taking over from the Commando Brigade and everything seemed normal. We were engaged in settling into our new billet while the first parties were landed up the coast, and one night we were entertained to dinner by our comrades in the 1st S.A.S. Regiment. There was nothing to indicate an impending enemy attack.

By the next morning the whole situation had been transformed. Reports came in about an enemy counter-attack developing and shells began to crash all over the village. Several landed in the street outside our billet, wounding a number of civilians. As the day went on the weight of the bombardment increased.

All I did was to improve the safety of our billet with sacks of corn as protection against blast. As far as we were concerned the battle was somebody else's affair. The regular infantry with several tanks had arrived in Termoli and I could not see where we could fit in with our twenty-odd men. It may have been a weak view but we had had a good run from Taranto and were supposed to be resting.

Several times during the day a pair of Focke-Wulfs swooped in at ground level to bomb the shipping in the harbour. They landed one small stick astride the jetty, sinking one of our fishing boats with a direct hit. I dived into the water to rescue a wounded man but neglected to remove my German jackboots. In consequence they filled with water to weigh me down so much that I also had to be rescued.

The bombardment had become if anything more intensive by the next morning. It was impossible to get a proper perspective on the situation from behind our corn sacks, so I sent off Peter Jackson to see if he could find some news at Brigade. He came back at about midday, after an adventurous drive through bursting shells, to tell a comic story of his encounter with the Infantry Brigadier. Apparently a rather pompous man, he had said, "Don't worry, old boy! Nothing at all. Everything perfectly under control." At that moment a spandau had begun to fire into the Brigade Headquarters at close range, forcing the Brigadier to cut short his interview by diving under an armoured car. Peter did not seem at all sure that the situation was under control. He said that 78th Division was fighting off fierce counter-attacks between the bridge and the brickworks, that whole units were fleeing in panic from the village and that the Commandos had been called back into the line to hold Termoli itself.

In the afternoon when the bombardment was at its height, Sandy Scratchley arrived in the billet, having recently come out to Italy from North Africa. He quite rightly reprimanded me for sitting idle like a rat in a hole while Termoli was in acute danger of falling to the enemy. I sheepishly collected twenty men with six Bren-guns and followed him down to the Commando Headquarters. Even the short walk down to their billet was extremely perilous. I got in a burst with my tommy-gun at a Focke-Wulf diving low over the houses and shells were bursting everywhere.

The first hour was spent in the cellar beneath Brigade Head-quarters, where we found some delicious apples. The building had been hit only a few minutes before by a shell which killed the Staff Captain. Brigadier Durnford-Slater, and especially the Brigade Major, Brian Franks, struck me as being incredibly cool amongst it all. German tanks had approached to the edge of the railway line, overrunning the Commandos, who neverthe-less stuck to their ground although hemmed in on three sides. It appeared that the counter-attack was being made by a panzer and an infantry division—a formidable force in view of the fact that 78 Division had not got all its heavy equipment across the river. I am sure that if the enemy had been less half-hearted, he would have taken Termoli.

When we were led out to a position in the windows of the hotel, it was humiliating that I felt forced to duck at every shell, whereas Sandy only half-ducked and Brian Franks walked on as though nothing had happened.

We chose positions on the second-floor balconies, but it was fortunate from our point of view that in less than an hour Sandy arrived with fresh orders for us to hold the railway goods yard. When the battle was over I noticed that not a single balcony remained intact.

Our first position was on a crest at right angles to the coast, perhaps a mile north of the village. We had not been there long when the Germans advanced on our left to seize the cemetery, which forced us to fall back on the last ridge before the goods yard.

Although we only had a strength of twenty men, our fire power was quite abnormally strong. In all there were six Brens and a two-inch mortar. I covered our thousand-yard front between the 1st S.A.S. and the sea by putting ten men with three Brens on each side of the railway line. Our main trouble was that we had no tools with which to dig weapon pits.

In spite of the fact that heavy fire was directed on us from the cemetery and that constant attempts were made to advance down the line of the railway, we held our positions for three days. Mortar bombs swished down all the time but most of them crashed harmlessly in the engine sheds behind. Only one man was wounded although I am sure we inflicted heavy casualties on the enemy. The range was so short that we could not fail to hit a man advancing in an upright position.

Crossing the railway from one side of the position to the other was a most perilous venture. A sniper cracked bullets dangerously close to our heads as we raced across the open track. We had been in our position for nearly a day before we discovered that the railway engine and truck in the middle of our front was loaded with high explosive, ready to be detonated. I was terrified during the entire battle that it would be hit by a mortar bomb.

We were short of rations and the nights were bitterly cold. It was the only pure infantry battle I fought in the war and I never want to fight another. Our spirits were low until we were encouraged by a County of London Yeomanry Sherman tank which came up on our left. It scored a beautiful direct hit on a dome in the cemetery and the green marble disintegrated like the atom at Bikini. Everyone cheered loudly for it had contained an annoying sniper.

On the third day the Irish Brigade landed in the harbour. The London Irish moved up to our position for a counter-attack and I pointed out the enemy guns to the Company Commander who was to pass through my sector. He asked me to fire everything we had down the railway line while he advanced from the left.

It was a perfect shoot. Only when the fools stood up and began to run back down the beach did I realise their great strength. Several hundred figures in blue overcoats began to double back, tacking this way and that to avoid our bullets. The 1st S.A.S. on the left were having the same kind of harvest. I think the enemy must have been surprised at our fire power for we had conserved ammunition carefully until this last moment. It was a reward which made our miserable three days in the cold worth while. The London Irish Company Commander came back on a stretcher, but he was cheerful enough for he had been wounded in the hour of victory.

CHAPTER SIX

MY LAST operation in Italy in 1943 was a true S.A.S. operation behind the enemy lines. The squadron had moved back to a billet in Goia delle Colle near Taranto, where we were engaged in absorbing new reinforcements. It was a lovely old country house with a spacious garden. The furniture was still in the rooms upstairs and there was even a horse in the stables. I used to take this old bay mare for a hack through the lanes every morning. All Southern Italy was at peace and we were very happy. An Italian cook provided excellent food, supplementing the rations by local purchase.

The men were given transport to take them into Taranto or Bari three times a week, and they were not driven too hard for they deserved a rest after their exertions of the past two months. Once indeed we went for a nineteen-mile route march, and arrived back with blistered feet, for we had deteriorated a lot from the hard condition we had reached at Philipville.

Colonel Grant-Taylor, the famous pistol shot, stayed with us while he instructed some of the men in close-quarter combat. He was a wonderful teacher. I can hear his patter now.

"First I must tell you that murder is my business. Now you see this. This is called a tommy-gun. Well, it isn't. It's a musical instrument and you play it like this—tacktack, tacktack. All shooting should be done with the navel, like this. Get it right, for a gunman is worth his weight in diamonds. Diamonds!"

One night in a pleasant little restaurant called the Miramare in Bari, my dinner was rudely interrupted by a whole chicken hitting me in the face. Grinning at me from the opposite side of the room was Sandy Thomas, my old New Zealand friend. We were so overjoyed to see each other again that we rushed across to pummel each other in the ribs between the tables. After the wound he had received on the opposite side of the street from me in Crete, he had been moved from the hospital in Athens en route for Germany. He had hopped over a wall in Salonika and had made his way to Turkey. Now he was covered with medals and bidding fair to being a colonel at the age of twenty-four. Soon after dinner the hotel was shaken by the crash of bombs in the harbour. A surprise raid by JU 88's sank a number of ships then in the process of unloading by the light of arc-lamps. Sandy always brings trouble in his wake.

The day after our long route march, when everyone was limping about the billet in gym shoes, Esmond Baring, our staff officer at 8th Army H.Q., arrived to brief us for a new operation. He explained that the object was to make a feint against Pescara and that a mock landing party would demonstrate off the shore, while we blew the railway line to the north. Sixteen men were to land in rubber boats from an M.T.B. between Ancona and Pescara. They would stay ashore for approximately a week, causing as much damage as they could, and would then be picked up again further down the coast. Only one officer would be required because one party of four (included in the sixteen) would be commanded by Grant Hibbert of "B" Squadron, who had already done an operation in the area.

It was natural that there should be great competition amongst the officers for the honour of leading the party. Knowing that Peter's blisters were worse than mine, I proposed a race to decide it. I did not play the game, because although Peter beat me, I asserted my right as Squadron Leader to go anyway.

We moved up to Termoli by road and waited in the old Commando Brigade Headquarters for the night. When the time came we embarked on an Italian motor torpedo boat under the command of a British Naval officer.

The launch started north at high speed, throwing up great showers of spray behind. I can remember little of the voyage except that it was remarkably smooth and we were not allowed to smoke. The efficiency of the Italian sailors was most impressive. When at last the engines cut out, we glided in slowly to the dark coastline. I could see the lights of villages and, occasionally, a pair of headlights travelled along the coast road.

I whispered to the men to get their rucksacks ready. There was only the hiss of hushed whispering as I moved up to the control tower. There was what appeared to be a large rock in the river mouth, not far from where we were due to land. The skipper, after looking at it through his glasses, ordered the engines to be switched off completely.

The battery of pom-poms was swung round towards it. It began to rain heavily, soaking our overalls. We sat there for a long time, the skipper observing the rock.

"What is it?" I whispered.

"A submarine charging its batteries. I don't think they have seen us," he answered.

My nerves were so tensed that I could barely speak. It was incredibly bad luck to run into perhaps the only submarine on the coast. But the sailor seemed quite happy to go ahead with the plan.

He signalled one engine to start up gently, and we floated in even closer to the shore. The order came to put out the rubber boats and there was awful confusion in the dark. People grabbed the wrong rucksacks, dropped the paddles and stumbled over ropes. I felt that the Germans would be certain to hear the noise. The first flight pushed off from the side and seemed to land safely. My turn came, I nearly upset the dinghy and we were off. We helped the sailor to paddle for the start, but he would have to take her back alone. There was only the sound of the paddles and the patter of the rain in the stillness of the night. I kept one eye on the submarine and the other on the sandy beach ahead. Never have I known a night so black.

When the rubber bottom rasped on the shingle, we leapt into the water and waded the last few feet to the shore. Already at the beginning of a long march, we were starting with the disadvantage of wet feet. Before we had gone far, not only our feet but the whole of our bodies were sodden by the rain.

I did not know exactly where we were, but I stumbled inland, intending to cut north to the river bank later. We blundered into a small village where the usual dogs started barking, and I kept walking straight through the street, hoping that any one who saw us would take us for Germans. A light came on in one of the cottages and I quickened my pace. The rain was beating into our faces and our rubber-soled boots were slipping in the mud. Over a stile we lost ourselves in a maze of muddy fields and dykes. The going was terrible. For every two paces forward we must have slipped one backward. Twice I fell into a deep ditch and had to be rescued by the others. Our rucksacks seemed to weigh at least a hundred pounds, and if I had a guinea for every time I fell over that night, I could buy a motor car.

The hours were going by and we still had not found a place

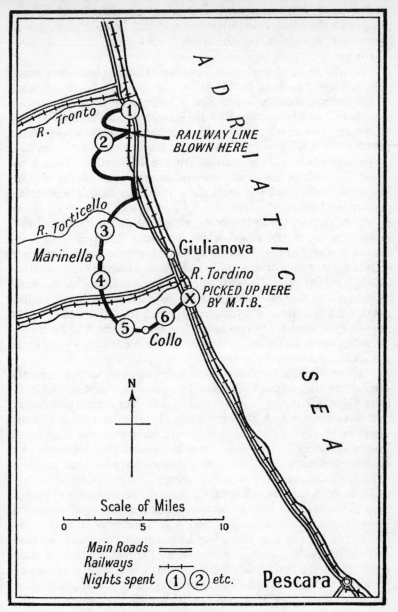

OPERATION NEAR PESCARA, 1943.
207

in which to hide during daylight. It was hopeless. I had expected to get to the other side of the railway line before dawn, but we were still struggling in the mud by the river mouth at three o'clock.

After finding the river, we walked along a tow-path where the ground was more firm. At last, worn out by our exertions, we crawled into a thick patch of bamboo. Pushing through on our hands and knees, we cut a little clearing in the middle. Still the rain came down so that, tired though we were, we could not sleep. Corporal Linton lighted a tommy cooker under his gas cape and made a little coffee with the rain-water. It was too near the village but there was no alternative. There we lay, four miserable, half-drowned men, shivering in our wet clothes under the bushes.

Throughout the next day we were kept on tenterhooks. First a man came to saw wood between us and the river. We could see him plainly enough and only hoped that he could not see us. Then a party of workers, male and female, started digging about thirty yards away towards the village. Their chatter never ceased all day. Once a man stood facing our patch of bamboo and we felt certain that he had spotted us. If he had said so much as a word we would have shot him, for he was covered by four carbines, but when he began to urinate we laughed at each other in relief.

There were bright spells during the day, but mostly it rained. In the evening I sent off McPhail to see if he could get a look at the diggers, because it was possible that they were constructing defences for the Todt Organisation. He came back some minutes later with the report that they were only peasants digging an air-raid shelter. More important, he said that we were only five hundred yards from the railway bridge on which he could see two German sentries. At last I had got my bearings.

The torrential rain started again before dark. It was a mixed curse for at least it reduced our chances of being spotted. As soon as the twilight was finished, and there were so many black clouds in the sky that there was little enough of that, we started off on our march to the rendezvous. We followed small tracks and narrow lanes, making a detour round the sentries on the bridge, until we reached the railway; we scrambled up the embankment, crawled across the lines and down the other side; Corporal Clarke lost his boot in a midden but we found it after a long search; keeping into the shadows, we reached the wet. black tarmac of the main road.

Quite unexpectedly, we came face to face with an old man bearing an umbrella. Pretending that we were Germans, I asked in broken Italian the way to the cross-roads. He conducted us down to them and then said good-bye to us in English.

We huddled under the trees for some time before Grant appeared. He had been lucky enough to stumble upon a deserted farm-house so that his party was drier than mine. Seddon appeared at about eleven o'clock but there was no sign of the other party under Sergeant Rawes. Grant was all for postponing the blow until the next night on the grounds that we were too miserable to do the job efficiently and were in no condition for the long escape march. I was inclined to agree. All the time I was thinking of the importance of not missing the rendezvous with the M.T.B. If we postponed the attack until the next night, we would only have four nights in which to cover the seventy miles to the beach. As far as the main plan was concerned, it would not matter if we blew the line a day late since the mock landing was scheduled to take place several days after our attacks. The suggestion that our charges would be better for a thorough drying won the day. Grant, who had previous experience of the area, advised that we should hide for the day in a lonely farm, where we could confine the occupants to the house.

I walked off with my party through the rain to the west. After we had gone about a mile, I took a turning to the right up a hill. Although the operation had only been in progress twenty-four hours, we felt as weary as if we had been doing it for weeks. There was a ramshackle cottage a short way off the track—a high, barnlike affair with a dilapidated roof and worm-eaten doors. It is an infallible rule that if one is seeking shelter, the poorest dwellings will always give refuge. Rich houses are unreliable.

I knocked on the rickety old door, but there was no answer from within. Pushing my hand through a crack, I lifted up the latch with the tips of my fingers. A frightened male voice said, "Who are you?" but I waved the others into the room before I answered, "English parachutists. We want food." I shone my torch on a wooden bunk in the corner. A young peasant boy was sitting up on the bed in his shirt-tails, staring at the light in bewilderment. I turned the torch on ourselves and said

again, "We are friends—English parachutists—we want help."
He gave us a nervous smile and assured us that he would do
what he could. He leapt off the bed, pulled on his trousers and
boots, put a match to a carbide lamp and told us to follow him
into the rain.

On the other side of the building there was a somewhat larger
door. The boy woke up his father, with whom he carried on a
long conversation through the cracks. An old man pushed open
the door with a squeak and pulled us inside. His wife, a dear old
peasant woman with a wrinkled face, was already down on her
knees, blowing up the ashes of the wood fire into flames.

They hastened to give me the only chair, while the others
slumped down on the bare stones. At first they were a little
hesitant, but when at last they were convinced that we were
English, they fussed about us as if we had been their own children.
The old lady was crying to see how bedraggled and tired we
were. She built up the fire with young brushwood until the room
was lighted up by the blaze. All the time she kept muttering
"Mamma mia" under her breath. The old padrone signed to us
to remove our sodden footwear and soon the little room was
filled with steam from our drying clothing. I told him that
nobody must leave the house while we were there. He roared
with laughter and beat his chest, saying that he had always been
an anti-fascisto.

The boy came in with a plucked chicken which the old lady
cut into little pieces and fried with tomatoes in a large pan. I
sat in the light of the fire, studying the remnants of my map
and watching the cooking with longing eyes. Linton produced
some rations and explained how to make coffee. We fed sweets
to two little barefooted children who had crept unnoticed into
the shadows in the corner. They advanced diffidently until they
were about a yard away, stretched out their tiny hands for the
sweet, and then scampered back into the corner to conceal their
embarrassment.

After we had eaten the delicious fried chicken and the padrone
had uncorked a bottle of vinegary wine, we were shown to a
great double bed in another back room. After dividing ourselves
into watches, the remaining three cast themselves on the ancient
quilt and were soon fast asleep.

The sound of zooming aircraft brought us leaping from the
bed at eleven o'clock in the morning. Through the windows we

watched a squadron of Kittihawks bombing the submarine in the river mouth. It looked as though the information had got to the right place. They were swooping and diving over Giulianova, and we saw a large lump of metal flung into the air. We were all jubilant because indirectly it meant a first success to our operation.

During the day we prepared the charges for the big blow. They had not been as badly damaged by the rain as we had expected. The old Italian's eyes stood out like organ stops when we produced Hawkins' mines from our packs. All the time the old mother sat by the fire, rocking backwards and forwards on a stool, praying for our deliverance. Tears dripped down her wrinkled old face as she muttered under her breath.

The original plan had been for Seddon to lay mines on the road and to blow down telegraph poles, while the other three parties carved pieces out of the railway line. I had drawn a pack full of mines in the confusion on the boat, but it did not really matter for they would blow a hole as well as anything else.

The peasants gave us a last meal of pasta asciuta and we sat waiting fully dressed by the fire for the hands of my watch to move round to ten o'clock. And then we were saying good-bye. I think they guessed what we were about to do because the old man warned me about the sentries on the bridge. His wife clasped our wrists in both her hands and cried as she kissed us all.

As we plodded down the road there was no sound except the padding of our rubber soles and the soughing wind in the trees. The others were there on time, but there was still no sign of Rawes. (He eventually turned up at the M.T.B. and told us that he had blown up three trucks and wrecked the line as soon as he heard the sound of our explosions.)

We moved off to the attack, agreeing to squeeze our half-hour time pencils at exactly eleven-thirty. The rain was still driving hard in our faces as we started the old trudge over the fields. After crawling across ditches and through hedges, we scrambled up a wet, grassy bank to the railway. We dumped our rucksacks together so that Linton could lay the charges while we guarded the area. Fumbling in the storm with the wind driving the rain up in great sprays down the line, Linton tinkered about for what seemed like an age. There was a scare when a truck drove up the road. Then he stood up and said he was ready. Two minutes late, we squeezed the time delays.

Picking up our packs, we rolled down the embankment to the wire fence. Before long we were fighting up muddy paths into the hills. Our flat rubber soles would not grip in the mud and often we would slide back to the bottom of a slope after having fought our way to the top. Sometimes we had to crawl on our hands and knees, weighed down by our packs. After we had pulled our way by branches to the top of a particularly difficult ascent, we heard the sound of the explosions and saw the flashes through the rain. Altogether, excluding the effort of Rawes, we blew the line in sixteen places, demolished seven telegraph poles and blew down one electric pylon. Returning to the struggle, we laboured on through the rain until we were in the last stages of exhaustion.

In four hours we covered less than ten miles from the scene of the attack, which was not enough. I had hoped to be at least twenty miles away by dawn. The only answer was to cut down to the main road, even if the risk of capture was increased. I covered most of the way down to the plains on the seat of my trousers.

We marched along the main road, two on each side, ready to throw ourselves in the ditch at the first sign of trouble. Our carbines had fallen so often in the mud that they would never have fired. We came to a few houses, a railway station and a bridge at Porto Torricello. This was the first river line and meant that we had covered over a third of the distance to the rendezvous. Passing through the village, I noticed a German lorry in the station yard. It was too late to turn back. We padded on silently, keeping our eyes straight in front, and soon we were through. Seddon had less luck behind. His party was challenged and fired upon in the village. Two escaped but the others were captured.

I led the file over several fields to the south to a large white farm. At first we went into the ox-shed, where we smoked a cigarette, but a dog nosed us out and began to bark. I went out into the rain and threw a stone at a window. A peasant woman of about thirty-five put out her head and asked us who we were. I said that we were English parachutists. She slammed the shutters. A few moments later a young farmer came down with a lamp and led us up to his main living-room—even more frugally furnished than our last asylum. The farmer was quite pleasant, but the woman seemed very sullen. She lit the fire and brought us some chairs without saying a word. Then she put a pot of pasta asciuta on the hob. It appeared that there were no children and I was a little afraid of this quiet woman. The food lulled our suspicions and we began to eat. We were too tired to bother about confining them to the house, and in any case we were afraid to offend them. After we had eaten, we threw ourselves on the red brick floor and went to sleep.

When evening came the man agreed to show us the way across the river by a bridge further inland. He led us back to the main road and we marched along it for miles. At last I became suspicious. Whenever we asked him how much further, he replied, "Less than two kilometres, just cinque minuti." This went on for so long that I became convinced that he was leading us into a trap. If we stayed on the main road much longer we would be certain to be caught. I refused to go with him any further and cut across an unguarded railway bridge to the left. The poor Italian was so dismayed at our sudden bad humour that he wept as he said good-bye. I think he was really quite well intentioned.

We tramped on along second-class roads in the light rain, for the downpour had slightly eased although the paths were still boggy. Once we heard the hoofbeats of a cavalry patrol and dived head-first into the ditch, waiting trembling until they had trotted past. It looked as though the hunt was on.

An old man we met on the road warned us that Marinella was a Fascist village. If we did not want to be captured, we must steer well clear of it. The amusing thing was that the old fellow took us for Italian partisans, of the existence of whom we had barely heard at that stage of the war. Most of the odd people we met on the roads believed that we were German, an idea which we encouraged by shouting German greetings. Often we were able to slink past in the shadows without being spotted.

Normally we took steps to avoid villages but it was not always possible. McPhail was suffering from malaria which made him very excitable. Most of the time he was gently swearing under his breath as he marched along. When we found that we could not by-pass one village, I led the file down the main street. A figure appeared in a lighted doorway and called to us, but we kept on walking. Then I noticed an armed sentry standing by the church on the left. It was too late to duck so we kept on, but McPhail tapped me on the shoulder, telling me to look at the sentry and asking permission to shoot him. I hissed, "Keep quiet, you fool! Keep on walking! Don't look!" He continued to argue, but the others shut him up. The main street curved round to the left, and when the houses concealed us from the sentry's sight, we began to run. The alarm was given behind us. We lolloped along the first turning on the right, our heavy rucksacks bumping against our backs. After we had run about a mile, we collapsed under some bushes, incapable of further exertion. Although there was shouting in the village behind there were no signs of pursuit.

On we tramped, up and down the hills. Corporal Clarke was a brave little man, better educated than most, but he was too fat to be a marcher. He had rolled over more times since the landing than all the rest of us. In fact he rolled like a ball all the way from the Tronto to the Tortello. It did not damp his spirits and he was always ready with some funny crack.

I took the wrong turning at a "Y" junction and led the stick into Marinella, the one place to be avoided. I tried to get some information from the first house on the left of the street, but gave it up as a bad job when a dog started barking at the back. Leaving the others in the ditch, I crept alone into the village. After sneaking through several back gardens, I came to a cottage with a light showing through a french window. Stealthily I turned the handle. It was open. I leapt in through the curtains, brandishing my pistol. A naked woman was in bed with a man. She gave a shriek and, pulling the sheet up to their noses, they gazed at me with horrified eyes. I had four days' growth of hair on my chin so I must have looked like a horrible nightmare.

"What is the name of this village?"

"Marinella, signore, but I have done nothing wrong and have no money."

"I don't want your money. I am a friend. Are there many Fascists in this village?"

"Yes, signore, there are many people."

"I said are there many Fascists."

"I don't know, signore, I am a poor man."

"Look here, there is no need to be afraid. I am an English parachutist."

His wife babbled some sentences so quickly that I could not follow their meaning. He suddenly became more friendly and

214

told me that there were many Fascists in the village. It would be wise for me to go away as soon as possible. I thanked him and he swore to keep the whole incident a secret. I assured him that if he gave us away, dire punishments would be inflicted when the Allies arrived and they had already taken Pescara (which was untrue). He leapt out of bed in his shirt-tails to open the door for me.

We traipsed back the way we had come, depressed that this five miles off our course would mean an extra ten miles in all. We were all exhausted but most of all McPhail, whose malaria had so robbed him of his senses that he questioned every move. After we had gone about half a mile down the right arm of the fork, we were so tired that we turned into the first farm gate we encountered. It had begun to rain again, adding more to our misery. I left them behind a haystack while I reconnoitred the farm. It was not a good place, being so close to Marinella and the main road. It would have to do. I opened the door to the ox-shed with a piece of wire and looked around. It was a large tidy byre under the main dwelling. There was a quantity of hay in the corner, an old, flea-bitten pony and two rows of neat cattle. Best of all, it was warm.

I whistled up the others and we pulled down hay to make beds for the night. Linton made some tea on his tommy cooker and we fell off into a deep sleep. I must have moved during the night for I woke up to find my head in a patch of wet cow-dung. The others laughed heartily for the first time since the beginning of the operation, although my swearing roused them from their sleep.

An old man with a lamp woke us up at about five o'clock in the morning. We told him that we were English, but were too tired to care what he did about it.

I told Linton to go upstairs to rustle up some food at about ten o'clock. We found him sitting in front of a large fire surrounded by four pretty girls of much the same age with lovely black tresses tumbling down their backs. I cannot remember all their names except that they had a peculiar South American flavour, two being Santiaga and Argentina. If we had stayed there much longer, I am sure that one of the men would have become attached to one for life. All day they were laughing and giggling and changing their dresses. We had many fried eggs and some more of the delicious fried chicken we had tasted on the first night. The old man broached the special wine he had been saving for the arrival of the Allies. In the afternoon he told us that a boy on a bicycle had seen a German cavalry patrol in Marinella, but he assured us that there was no chance at all that we would be found.

At eleven o'clock we said good-bye to the girls and thanked the old man warmly, promising to come back one day. It was pouring with rain again and I hated having to go out into the storm, but time was getting short if we were to catch the boat.

We marched down a secondary road to a small hamlet and turned left into the fields. Our training had advised us not to march in step but to walk in pairs like civilians. We were too tired to do anything except tramp along in single file, one behind the other, only the regular crunch of our feet keeping our legs going automatically forward in step.

The path soon petered away in heavy plough. I knew the general direction and decided to cut across country until we hit a better track. Great clods of mud stuck to our boots, making them heavy to lift, and often the weight of our packs carried us forward on our faces into the furrows. After a few hundred yards, we were completely worn out; the night was very dark; and the rain blew mercilessly into our faces. I took a pace forward and found myself sliding down a steep precipice, but I managed to dig in my heels and the others pulled me back. We sat down in the mud in the rain. McPhail and Corporal Clarke said that they could not go on, but they would have to go on! We began to discard the least essential items from our packs— mess-tins, spare ammunition, and even sleeping bags. They were buried beneath the plough so that it would be long before they were discovered.

Staggering forward against the wind and the rain, we retraced our path to the village by following our own footsteps in the mud. I found a tiny one-roomed cottage and knocked on the door. An old peasant gave me a chair by the table while he went out into the rain to find the others. Pointing to the soaked rag of a map, I told him that we wanted a guide and he brought forward his son, who knew the countryside well. We brewed up some tea and dosed McPhail with quinine for he was now seriously ill.

Soon we were battling against the elements again with the youthful guide carrying McPhail's pack. We wound round the edge of the ravine to where the path degenerated into a goat track on the hillside. We crossed a stream by some stepping stones and Corporal Clarke fell into the water. I say we crossed a stream, although after a time the path itself became a minor river. Our boots were hopeless. They had been designed for silent padding along metalled roads, but up these muddy slopes they slipped so much that it was like trying to skate on glass.

Over a main road, we inquired at the house of the boy's aunt, but she refused to put us up for the night on the grounds that it was so near the highway that the Germans often came in for eggs. We followed a line of trees down a muddy lane to three farms. At the last one we discovered the shelter we were looking for. It is impossible to explain what risks these poor people took for Allied soldiers. If the Germans had discovered our presence, they would have had no scruples about burning down the farms, and their farms were their lives. If the house and the oxen went there was nothing. It was the same in Greece and France. Always the poor, the very poor, would share their last crumb. It was not that they were concerned with politics or war, but just that they pitied someone in an even worse state than themselves.

This farm housed three families who had fled from the bombing at Bologna. Some of their people had been killed in Allied air-raids but there was no resentment. They made room for us in front of the fire and filled us up with salami sausage and bread. There were children everywhere, boys and girls scampering all over the building. At first they fought each other for sweets, until they discovered that the first piece of chocolate always went to the shy one at the back. These kids had not tasted chocolate in their whole lives.

There was no room for us in the house so we bedded down in the stable amongst the oxen. In the morning we sat in front of the fire again, occasionally jumping up to look at German trucks through the window. The Italian politeness exceeded all bounds. I was doing my daily duty behind the haystack with my trousers well round my knees, when an old woman came by with a pail of water. She said, "Good morning, sir. How are you? Did you sleep well?" With a smile and a nod, she passed on to the house. What splendid old-world courtesy!

It was getting so near the time for the rendezvous that I threw caution to the winds and walked the next day during daylight. Once we startled some peasants round a well, but we swore them to secrecy. I do not think that they really understood what we were talking about. We came across a round-faced man working with some pigs near a farm. He recognised us immediately.

"Say you're British, ain't you? Well, I used to live in the States. Come in and have a drop of wine."

He warned us about Fascists in the village of Collo and we adjusted our bearing to pass by it to the right. We split up into a ragged group, carrying our carbines butt uppermost. It was Sunday in Collo and we could see all the people in their best clothes going to Benediction.

We crossed the road, now in darkness, and began to blunder through ploughed fields once more towards the coast. Italians make more use of their ground than any one in the world, and even the steepest slopes were ploughed. We went up and down for hours over the heavy going in a race against time for the boat was due in at eleven o'clock. In the same old way, we fell over, slipped and slithered in the mud. I remember once stopping with a desperate thirst to fill my rubber water-bottle from some of the muddiest water I have ever seen, but we seemed to suffer no ill effects. Only the thought of the boat kept us going.

I became separated from the others in the last stretch to the beach, after we had taken cover from an armoured vehicle on the road. It was past midnight when I arrived alone, but Grant Hibbert was still at the rendezvous, signalling with a torch. No vessel appeared and we withdrew inland, promising to meet again the next day.

I wandered about for a bit, looking for the rest of my stick but there was no sign of them.

I plodded back across the sods until I found a tiny farm, two miles in from the shore. I woke up the peasant who took me into the house. He apologised for not giving me the bed, but his wife was about to have a baby. Throwing some quilts and a mattress into the corner of the same bedroom, he signalled me to sleep if I wished. I slept until midday.

When I arose, he cut up some slices of salami and fried two eggs, explaining that the sausages were home-made from a pig presented by his father on his wedding day. I was excited to learn that there were several other parties of Englishmen in farms round about. Further inquiries confirmed that they constituted the whole of our raiding force except Seddon and one other, who had been captured.

When we had collected at the beach in the evening, I put out Rawes with a party to watch the road, telling him to lay mines just before he left for the boat. We started flashing the torch behind a blanket at eleven o'clock. There was a great danger that somebody might see the signals from a flank, yet if we shrouded the torch too much with the blanket the beam would not be visible so far out to sea. While we were signalling, two German half-tracks passed along the road.

It was nearly midnight when we noticed the long black shape of some vessel creeping into the shore. We were not at all sure that it was not a German E-boat from Giulianova, and took the precaution of hiding ourselves in the dunes. Then we saw a rubber boat coming in over the surf. It was Sandy Scratchley with the rescue party. Four trips were made by the dinghies before we were all aboard and on our way back to Termoli.

In the sober light of our old billet at Goia delle Colle, it did not seem to me that we had done so much. Holes in a railway line are easily repaired. But 8th Army Headquarters seemed satisfied. They had intercepted wireless messages which showed that a certain amount of panic had been caused. General Montgomery was so pleased that he sent us down his usual "good boy" gift of newspapers and cigarettes. Little gestures like that make the men think that their endeavours are really worth while.

CHAPTER SEVEN

INTERIM, 1943-44

THE PERIOD between December, 1943, and July, 1944, was such a hotch-potch of small incidents that it is almost impossible to connect them into a narrative.

Poor Peter Jackson was killed in a jeep accident on a wet road near Taranto when his vehicle skidded to avoid a cart. His was one of the few losses in the war which really affected me. He was such a reckless, gay person that it was impossible to realise that he was dead. As for the others, there has been so much violence and bloodshed that I am now incapable of deep emotion.

We went back to North Africa early in January, and stayed there until we went home to U.K. in March. It was a quiet period—made up of the normal run of a regimental soldier's life —squadron football matches, drunken parties, vigorous training, parachute exercises, troops' concerts and masses of paper work.

I went on a week's leave to Morocco, spending one night with the Foreign Legion at Sidi bel Abbes and the remainder of the time in the old Vizier's palace at Fez. I was most impressed by the efficiency of the Legion, although there was no evidence of the sort of stern discipline one reads about. The town itself has one of the largest red light quarters in the world. Although I hold no brief for French morals, I do think that they are realists as far as the sexual life of a soldier is concerned. How can a man be normal if he is separated from the opposite sex for six years or more without a break? If there had been a few licensed brothels in Naples, perhaps the venereal disease rate might have been lower.

In Fez we were lucky enough to witness the excitement of an Arab riot. We had been in the hotel two days, when we were aroused one morning by the sound of shooting outside. Many bullets hit the walls, and we were confined to the building. A mob gathered outside the main gates, chanting "Vive Roosevelt, Vive Churchill, en bas la France!" After the mob had been dispersed, I felt that I could no longer sit idle in the hotel.

Carrying a schmeisser, I walked down to the Medina with Ramon Lee. An excited French officer with some Senegalese was attacking the city wall. He said that although he had taken the bazaar once, snipers always reappeared behind or dropped grenades from the roofs. In spite of his protests, we walked a short way past his firing line into the Arab area. We were greeted by shouts of "Long live the English" and many smiles of friendship. Later, in the afternoon, we watched the French carry out the final sweep to restore order in the town. Kittihawks pretended to shoot up the Medina from the air, and then two battalions of Goums went in from the east. The Goums are very fierce levies from the mountains, who are said to be paid a "pro rata" rate for the number of enemy ears they produce. These tribesmen played a large part in the capture of Bizerta and the final break through the Liri Valley in Italy. They are officered by some of the best types in the French Army.

The Goums and the Senegalese closed into the bazaar with fixed bayonets. I fear that many Arabs were killed. Although I would hesitate to say that the Arabs are not correct to fight for their independence, as long as the French continue to show a firm hand in North Africa they will be respected. So long as a Western Power is in charge, it is incumbent upon that Power to maintain law and order. If the British had been as firm with the Jews in Palestine, we would not now be reaping the results of a vacillating policy—the contempt of the whole world. It is pointless to argue that the French are hated everywhere. Are we any better loved for our weakness?

We went home to England in March to prepare for the D-Day operations. I was unlucky enough to contract malaria again on the very day we were disembarking in Liverpool. After I had recovered and had had my share of leave, I rejoined the regiment in Scotland. We were stationed near Prestwick Aerodrome in Ayrshire.

The S.A.S. had swollen to the size of a large brigade. There were two British battalions, two French battalions and, perhaps the best of all, a Belgian company. We trained all over the mountains of Scotland. Mostly we marched with heavy packs from one farm to another, where we were received with wonderful hospitality. There is not so much difference, after all, between a slate shepherd's cot on the Border and a little white farmer's croft in Italy. Instead of salami sausage and chicken, we were given drop scones, fresh butter, milk and eggs. Those months of hard training in Scotland were some of the happiest we had ever spent.

During the planning stage for the French operations, a crisis occurred in the history of the regiment. The Airborne Forces, under whose command we had fallen upon our return to U.K., rather resented the free-and-easy independence of a "private army" in their midst. There were many minor arguments which culminated in disagreement over the way in which we would be employed in Europe. The first plan was for our main parties to be dropped immediately behind the coastal area between the enemy infantry and his armoured reserve. Bill Stirling bitterly opposed this idea, saying that we were strategic troops who should be used against communications far from the main battle area. If we were dropped into the forested areas in Central France and Belgium, we would have a longer breathing space to organise on the ground. Eventually, the authorities compromised by allowing the major part of the Brigade to be dropped deep into France, while only a number of small parties operated in the coastal area.

There were many prolonged conferences and negotiations before this final plan was agreed upon. All of us were solidly behind Colonel Stirling. It was ridiculous to think that scattered parties of parachutists could do anything much to delay the arrival of the panzer divisions. Perhaps we might have caused some confusion for a day or two, but there was no way in which we could have been resupplied so close to the front and we would therefore have soon become ineffective. Far better to employ us further inland where we might operate for months.

These arguments proved such lack of understanding of our role that our confidence in the new command was severely shaken. Hitherto we had been ridden on a rather loose rein by Combined Operations H.Q., who had allowed us plenty of scope. Now it seemed that we would be closely harried by a staff which did not appreciate our value.

Bill Stirling, our Colonel (and with his brother David the pioneer of the S.A.S. idea), decided to send a letter saying that he had no confidence in our new command. I think that he made a tactical error in not fighting his case on the question of our employment. Instead, he delayed his letter until after our own plans had been accepted. He was asked to withdraw the letter.

Always alive to the final object, he realised that a firm stand would place his successor in an infinitely stronger position. It was time for a sacrifice. He refused to apologise and left the regiment. Now this was a serious situation for a volunteer unit, since our main allegiance was to our Colonel, in whom we had the greatest confidence. I knew the full facts and contemplated resigning, since I fully supported Bill Stirling's views over our proper role. If I had decided to go, almost all the regiment would have gone with me. As it was, Bill Stirling took the broad view and asked me to stay under Brian Franks, whose behaviour I had so much admired during the Battle of Termoli. I was very keen to fight with the S.A.S. in France, and as far as I am concerned, what Bill Stirling says goes. I agreed to stay. I have never regretted it since, for Brian Franks proved to be one of the best commanding officers one could wish for, and at least we knew that we were to be finally employed in exactly the way Bill Stirling had visualised.

Just before the D-Day operations began, an outstanding event occurred in my life. The strong Irish flavour of the regiment had given us a large Roman Catholic element. "Loopy" Cameron in "C" Squadron had been very interested in our religion, and had been taken to the R.C. Church in Troon on several occasions. Monsignor the Canon Hayes, the parish priest, was a grand old Irish character who frequently entertained us in his house. Loopy had been detailed to go to an aerodrome in the South of England the next morning, whence he would be conveyed to France. He came to me at about midnight and said, "Roy, I want to become a Roman Catholic before I go to France. What shall I do?"

I got out a jeep and drove him into Troon to see Father Hayes. It was past one o'clock before we awakened the old man. He seemed to take the strange request with incredible equanimity. After talking to Loopy for about four hours, he led us into the solemn silence of the church, where the new recruit received the Holy Sacrament. I have never been so moved in all my life. I felt the Holy Spirit everywhere. Loopy did not say a word as I drove him back in the jeep through the soft twilight of the dawn.

When my squadron moved down to Hampshire for the last stages before their operation in France, I was in hospital in Auchinleck with a bad knee. One of the wounds in my leg had gone wrong, causing a large cist on the kneecap. I agitated so much that I was eventually transferred to a hospital in Tidworth. It was humiliating that I should have missed the first landings before D-Day, and I champed at the bit the whole of the time I was in hospital. Grant Hibbert, who had become my second-in-command, had been dropped into the Dijon area to reconnoitre a base for our jeeps. At the moment when his first favourable messages began to come through, I succumbed to another attack of malaria. It was too much. Whatever happened, the squadron was not going into action without me. The base medical authorities, in their limited experience, took a much more serious view of malaria than we ever did. It looked as though I would be transferred to Salisbury Hospital, where I might remain for weeks, although Peter Milne, our own doctor, could cure me with quinine in forty-eight hours. The wound on my knee was almost healed, so I decided to quit the hospital.

A pretty F.A.N.Y. driver was in command of the ambulance which was to take me to Salisbury. I inveigled her into calling at our mess for a drink on the way, and the poor girl had to leave without me. It was a dirty trick in some ways, and I probably deserved the reprimand from the Brigadier, but at least I got to France.

Grant Hibbert was well established in the Forest of Chatillon, and had had four jeeps dropped by parachute. We decided to build his party up by dropping in another troop. As yet, he had not been allowed to operate against the enemy.

The main part of the squadron, consisting of twenty jeeps mounting twin Vickers machine-guns, each with a crew of four men, would be dropped in conjunction with a large airborne operation south of Paris. We hastened to load our jeeps into gliders, pushing and tugging all night to get them in through the narrow doors. The glider pilots were as keen to get to grips with the enemy as we were, and they helped with the sweating manual labour required to get the jeeps loaded. After six hours' work all the gliders were ready, when news came through that the operation was cancelled. The glider pilots were even more depressed than us, since they had taken part in numerous abortive airborne operations before.

Then the signal came through that the S.A.S. party was to transfer its jeeps to another airfield as soon as possible. There they would be loaded into Dakotas and transported to France.

The situation was that the Americans had broken through at Avranches, making the Paris operation unnecessary. They had captured Rennes airfield, on which there was one serviceable airstrip. Our party was to land there, and to attempt to infiltrate through the now fluid front towards the east, there to join up with Hibbert in the Forest of Chatillon.

CHAPTER EIGHT

FRANCE, 1944

I SUPPOSE that of all the operations carried out by the 2nd Special Air Service Regiment, the jeep operation "Wallace" was the one in which the greatest distance behind the enemy lines was covered. Of course, great distances were traversed in the desert operations under David Stirling and a certain amount of penetration was achieved in the first skirmishes after the landing at Taranto, but until August, 1944, people still doubted that we would ever again have a fluid situation which would allow us to drive vehicles about behind the enemy front. Until D-Day there was a strong school of thought which still imagined that only the most clandestine sabotage would be possible in enemy territory in Europe. In Italy we had still been pioneering in a new form of warfare. We had been trained to operate with an unfriendly local population and all our attacks were so cautious that they could not be regarded as much more than pinprick raids. They could be compared to the behaviour of a naughty boy who knocks on perhaps two doors in a street and then runs away. There was no organised form of re-supply from the air, and after our first load of explosive was finished we had no alternative but to return somehow to the right side of the lines. In France things were different. We were supported by the whole weight of Transport Command, and although we had not yet put our theories into practice, Italy had convinced us that we had been far too conservative in our approach.

We began by building up large bases in the forested areas in Central France. These areas were chosen at random off the map without local knowledge, but proved in every instance to have been well selected by Bill Stirling. From D-Day onwards parties were dropped in to reconnoitre the areas and to receive stores with a view to active operations after our landings in Normandy. Sometimes these parties were built up to operational strength in conjunction with the Maquis, but quite often they operated completely separately. Soon after D-Day, the Special Air Service Brigade (consisting of British, French and Belgian components) had bases in Brittany, the Forest of Orleans, the Grand Massif, the Forest of Chatillon, the area around Poitieres and the Vosges.

My own squadron built up its base in the Forest of Chatillon north of Dijon. Grant Hibbert, the Advance Party Commander, therefore had one troop with sufficient stores astride a direct line from Normandy to Belfort and roughly in the centre of France.

When the Americans broke through at Avranches we were presented once more with a fluid front through which it would be possible to infiltrate small vehicles. With a base already established halfway across France and with ensured air supply for our columns, we were in a position to cause great chaos behind the Germans who were withdrawing in front of the American Third Army. The operation could not have been better timed.

On 19th August, twenty jeeps containing the remainder of my squadron were loaded into Dakotas piloted by the British 46th Group. Each aircraft carried a jeep lashed into its fuselage, plus a crew of three men—sixty men in all. We landed on the only serviceable strip on Rennes Airfield, pockmarked from many heavy bomber raids. Within twenty-four hours the column of jeeps was winding through the forest paths north of Orleans, winkling its way round pockets of Germans to the open country in the enemy rear.

We drove down muddy, deserted rides through the trees until we met the main road at Les Bordes on the banks of the Loire. The village was full of excited Maquisards, to whom we were the first Allied troops. They told us that there were large German columns in Gien, Montargis and Sully, the three villages round about. I was most impressed by the bellicose air of the French partisans, who to this day I believe to have been the best guerrillas in Europe. The local Commandant readily lent me a young guide, who was unfortunately wounded and captured a few days later. I believe he was shot by a firing squad in Semur.

Before moving further east, I sent a jeep patrol up to the village of Les Choux on the Montargis road, while we celebrated the liberation with our new-found Maquis friends in the village street. When the patrol had reported the village to be clear, we moved off again in column by minor roads. So long as we kept to the tangle of country lanes we were fairly safe, for the Germans kept mostly to the metalled highways.

There was a mishap in crossing the main Montargis road when one of the jeeps became separated from the main column. Our system was to choose a point where the road was crossed by a track and to drive across in column at top speed when it was reported clear by a forward patrol. Unfortunately, the front jeep misunderstood its role and, instead of joining on to the tail when we were all across, it stayed in its position until first light the next day. After losing contact with the rest of the squadron, Sergeant Forster led it alone across France to join us in the Forest of Chatillon. He had many exciting adventures on the way, including a collision with a German staff car when he shot four high-ranking enemy officers.

We spent the night in the Forest of Dracy behind the cabbage patch at the back of a farm. I had to use force to convince the landlord that we were British for he had barricaded his door against intruders. I knocked hard and shouted for a long time at the front door, but had no more luck than Walter de la Mare's traveller. Eventually I burst in through the back and found a tiny little Frenchman cringing in the corner with his wife. When at last he discovered that we were indeed British, he was torn between a desire to shower on us presents of bread, butter and eggs, and a fear that the Germans would discover that he had harboured us.

Most of the 22nd August was spent in gathering information about enemy movements in the area, and Ramon Lee was invaluable at this stage. The local villagers soon smelled us out. Clustering around the jeeps as we sat cleaning our guns under the trees, they poured masses of misleading information into our ears. They were all terribly excited at the appearance of British troops. Amongst them was a young English girl, who had married a French farmer, and she was so thrilled by it all that she could only speak in short gasps.

We were all very satisfied that we had covered fifty miles behind the enemy front without a single serious brush with the enemy. I did not want to begin operations until we had reached Grant Hibbert's base near Chatillon, and to have covered a third of the journey in one day was a most encouraging start. I had decided to move just before dark when I reckoned that most of the German troops would be settling down for the night. Later experience proved this to be unwise since Allied aircraft had forced the Germans to move mainly under the cover of darkness, and we discovered that the best time for our own movement was around midday. For the next leg, I split the squadron into three parts—five jeeps under Ramon, eight under me and the remainder under Lieutenant David Leigh, an officer with considerable experience of jeep operations in the desert. Each party was to move at thirty-minute intervals on the same route, although they were not bound to keep to it if they ran into trouble. I was careful to instruct both Party Commanders that the present aim was to by-pass all opposition.

The Latin temperament is a most incalculable factor, especially in war, for it always does things at a rush, either forwards or backwards, and it was typical of Ramon that he should charge through the first opposition he encountered on the east side of the River Yonne. The fourth jeep in his column was destroyed by machine-gun fire, although the crew escaped with minor injuries.

When I arrived at a village called Mailly-le-Château a very excited Frenchman jumped on to the bonnet of my jeep, shouting that he was the man to lead the liberators into battle. I eventually had to quieten him by sticking a pistol in his ribs. It was a long time before I could get any sense out of the crowd, but it did appear that although there were Germans on the other side of the river, Ramon had passed through. This was difficult to understand in view of my orders, but it was clear that if his hot-headedness had led him into trouble, we would have to do what we could to get him out.

The Frenchman, now more subdued, led us down a hill to a place where the road wound under a steep cliff. He dismounted here and expressed a desire to return to the village, from which I gathered that the Germans were close. I walked round the corner alone and was immediately greeted by a burst of Spandau. From what I could see from my rather cramped position in the ditch, there were about a hundred enemy with some horse-drawn vehicles under the trees. Even if Ramon had been able to crash through in his first fine rush, I did not see how we could follow now that the element of surprise was gone. We fired a few tracers from the top of the cliff before we left and succeeded in setting a cart on fire.

The Frenchmen in the village looked rather dismayed when we retraced our steps to hook round to the south. I left a message for Lieutenant Leigh to conform to my movements and drove

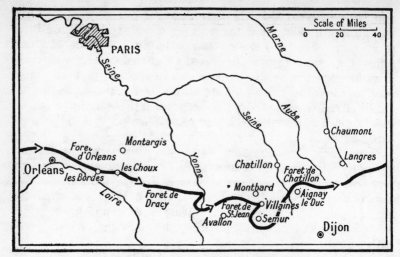

OPERATION WALLACE, FRANCE, 1944.

through the moonlight, for dusk had now fallen, to see if we could get across the bridge at Merry-sur-Yonne. Fortunately it was unguarded, although I had certain misgivings when we encountered a hay wagon, flying the white flag and containing three Germans wounded by our Bren.

We all joined up that night in the Forest of St. Jean, over a hundred miles behind the front. We leaguered near a Priory converted into a farm, where civilians from the village of Château Gerard found us the next morning. They brought presents of flowers, wine, butter and eggs, heaping them high on the jeeps. I was not too happy about the farmer, who was a shifty-eyed rogue and looked as though he would sell his own grandmother for two sous.

I was so angry with Ramon for his rash behaviour that I reduced his command to two jeeps, although I still allowed him to lead since his knowledge of French made him so much more useful at extracting information from the peasants. We started at five o'clock and within ten miles of the forest Ramon again ran into trouble. An unreliable civilian told him that a village called Villaines was clear of the enemy. He ran into a number of Afrika Corps troops in the streets and both his jeeps were destroyed. Ramon, as always, fought bravely and succeeded in escaping on foot to the hills, but three of our best

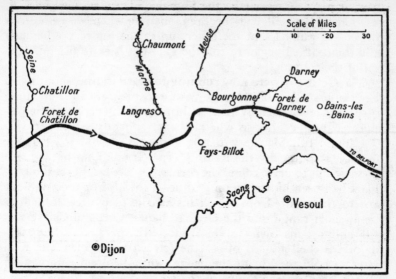

OPERATION WALLACE, FRANCE, 1944.

men were left behind. Worse still, there was no way of warning me.

I was breaking all the rules by motoring along quite happily at about thirty miles an hour at the head of my column, confident that Ramon would give notice of any opposition ahead. Only the very slowest speed is wise in enemy country since it is essential that you see the enemy before he sees you. As it was, we turned a corner to come face to face with a 75-millimetre gun blocking the entire road. Even as I told Corporal Clarke, my driver, to swing into the ditch, two Germans in Afrika Corps hats fired a shell at less than ten yards' range. Perhaps it was because we were so close to the muzzle of the gun that the shell whistled over our heads to burst in the road behind.

And then we were crawling out of the wrecked jeep into the ditch with bullets spattering all round. The little Maquis guide we had picked up at Les Bordes was shot in the knee. As I huddled under the bank, I could see the spare wheel from the front of the jeep rolling down the middle of the road. There were lots of Germans practically on top of us, shouting loudly and spraying the jeep with machine-gun fire. We had crawled about five yards from the vehicle when I remembered the codes and my marked map. Carpendale, the Signals Officer, crawled back to get them. We still had the Bren, so that when we came to a convenient gully I sent the others up to the top of the bank to hold them off. I began to run the gauntlet back to organise the rest of the column.

The Germans were now running forward in line, shooting as they came. A big blond brute with a schmeisser called upon me to surrender so I wildly fired at him with my carbine. He disappeared, but I cannot say whether he was shot or just taking cover.

I found Jim Mackie with the good old, bewildered look on his face, standing by the leading jeep. Thank God he had had the sense not to drive round the corner. In fact he at first thought that I had been blown up on a mine. I led him up a convenient lane to the right, from which his two jeeps poured enfilading fire at short range into the German flank. Corporal Clarke was still holding his own out in front with the Bren. Sergeant-Major Mitchell moved off to the left with ten men and four Brens to hold the line of the hedge, while I myself commanded the two jeeps in the centre of the road.

By now the enemy fire had become very heavy, including shells and mortar bombs. The Germans made a foolish charge along both sides of the road, giving us a magnificent shoot at less than fifty yards' range. Their casualties were very heavy and Jim Mackie's troop alone accounted for a whole platoon in a field. Instead of abandoning the attack, the idiots came on until they were so far into our rough semi-circle that we were cutting them down from three sides. I even shot a German with my own carbine—my only definite personal bag of the war.

Corporal Clarke's Bren was silent by now and I feared that he had been captured or worse. (In fact, he joined up with Ramon Lee some days later.) After we had been fighting for about an hour, a mortar and a machine-gun opened up behind us. I had been holding on in the hope that David Leigh would come along with the other jeeps, but it was now quite clearly time to break off the action. In any case his arrival had been so long delayed that I assumed that the sound of the firing had made him veer off on another tack. The trailer containing our wireless set was on fire in the middle of the road and I nearly got myself killed in a vain attempt to rescue it.

Under the cover of Jim Mackie's guns, we withdrew down a small lane which unfortunately proved to be a dead-end leading into a mill. We succeeded, however, in making our way over a stream and across country through many hedges to strike a country lane near Jeux. There we met a farm labourer who warned us that a whole Panzer Division (without its armour) was strung out in the villages between Semur and Montbard.

We drove on into the night, making a wide detour to the south of Semur. Once we lost our way in a maze of cart-tracks to the east of the main road, and the jeeps were driving about a ploughed field looking for an opening, when we noticed the head-lights of a large convoy on the road below. We switched off our engines and sat in complete silence until the last lorry had passed.

Meanwhile, David Leigh had run into the same opposition at Villaines after our withdrawal. He himself was killed, and the whole party only escaped with heavy casualties. Ramon Lee found the remnants of the column and, after several more brushes with the enemy, led them back to Paris. Some of the crews were dropped in to me by parachute a few weeks later.

I was very depressed to find myself with only seven of my original twenty jeeps the next morning. We had driven all night and were very tired, but I was determined not to stop until we had reached the cover of the forest. The country was typical of the Cote d'Or in the summer: tiny green fields, white red-roofed cottages, hedges and gently undulating slopes. The roads were very dry and we had to drive very slowly to avoid putting up a tell-tale dust cloud behind.

Dawn was still touching the grass with pink when we found ourselves halted by a closed level-crossing at the foot of a sharp decline. Before there was time to withdraw the jeeps under cover, I noticed the smoke of a train coming round the shoulder of the hill. The chugging gradually became louder until we were able to see that it was a goods train of about twenty trucks. When the engine was level with the gates I gave the order to fire, and all the Vickers poured in mixed incendiaries, tracers and armour-piercing bullets at fifteen yards' range. She did not stop at once, but rolled on for about two hundred yards with her boiler enveloped in a cloud of steam. As in a *Punch* cartoon, vapour was escaping in spouts from all sorts of strange places. Two German sentries in the last truck were killed, but when at last she came to a halt, a French driver dismounted from the engine cab and looked up at the flames now licking the woodwork as much as to say, "What is the use? This must be the sixth I have lost this week. If it is not aeroplanes, something else happens."

It must have been about the middle of the morning when we were just approaching the southern limits of the Forest of Chatillon. Jim Mackie stopped in the leading jeep and I ran up to discover the cause of the delay. He was still explaining that he had noticed a radar station in a clearing beyond the trees, when a number of machine guns opened fire on our jeeps. Although we sprayed the undergrowth with our guns, I could not see from where the fire was coming and therefore thought it wiser to withdraw. We learned later that the Germans in Beaulieu Radar Station had taken us for the advance guard of the American Third Army. At one o'clock that day they blew up the control tower and withdrew along the road to Langres. By that time I had sent off Jim Mackie to try to make contact with Grant Hibbert and he was lucky enough to meet a patrol commanded by Lieutenant James Robertson (who had been dropped in by parachute a fortnight before). Together they attacked the Germans, who were evacuating Beaulieu, and caused thirty-five enemy casualties.

The re-union with Grant was a great moment. He was quite astonished at the rate at which we had crossed France. Belittling my worry at our depleted numbers, he led me with his long strides into a cunningly concealed camp under the trees. Explaining it all in a dry voice, he showed me the dumps of stores, the tents made from khaki parachutes draped between the branches, and the brushwood barriers which protected the main exits. He certainly had not wasted his month in enemy territory. The rude shelters were impossible to detect except at the shortest range, and inside they were furnished comfortably with bits of parachute equippage. Most of the men wore beards and their red berets were beginning to fade, but their morale was high.

Grant had obeyed his orders to concentrate upon the building of dumps in the forest. He had secured an old civilian lorry which he used to convey the stores from the dropping field to various caches around Chatillon, and he had amassed considerable quantities of food, petrol and ammunition. He told me that he was in close contact with a large Maquis at Aigny-le-Duc, about fifteen miles to the south. Although these partisans were quite energetic, he had found that the difference between our respective methods made close co-operation difficult, and it was better just to maintain a loose liaison.

During the last few days Grant had begun his first offensive moves against the enemy. His patrols had destroyed a number of vehicles, had attacked a small post on the main road, had blown the Dijon railway line and had demolished several electric pylons the night before our re-union.

These activities had led to a number of counter moves by the Germans. They had picketed the road between Auberive and Aubepierre, and were said to be beating the forest north of the S.A.S. Base. After a long discussion, we agreed to move to a new combined base in the southern part of the forest so that the German interest in our activities would have to be reorientated.

The new hideout was in thick undergrowth so that the tents would be invisible from the air, although Grant was a little afraid that the absence of good paths might cause the new jeep tracks to be noticed. Actually, I think he preferred his old base, but that area was becoming too hot to be safe. Our combined strength was now ten jeeps, one civilian lorry and sixty men.

I had my first experience of re-supply during the night. Grant was so much more experienced in this sort of thing that I merely attended as an observer. We moved down to the field after dark and Grant distributed the vehicles under the trees around the edges of the zone. Ten minutes before the expected time of arrival, the operator on the Eureka said that he thought that he could hear a plane. Grant ordered three petrol flares to be lit at one-hundred-yard intervals, and I could see the men's faces reflected in the flames. This first attempt proved to be a false alarm and the flares had to be kept alight for another hour before the leading plane appeared. Many of our nights in France were spent like this—waiting on a lonely field in the darkness, shivering in the cold, half apprehensive that the Germans might discover us—and often with no result.

When at last the black shape of our Halifax appeared over the trees, our first fears were that it might be an enemy plane. Then, when it circled round for the run-in to drop, everyone whispered excitedly that it was indeed ours. Grant flashed the recognition signal on his torch and bawled at some men to stir up the flares. The first stick of containers was released and we could see the parachutes against the moon—too high, drifting with the wind over the field into the trees. If any containers landed in the forest, our work was always increased a hundredfold for every trace of the drop had to be removed before dawn. It was not always easy to get the chutes down from the branches and sometimes we could not even find them in the undergrowth.

The second plane made a perfect run-in half an hour later. The jeeps motored backwards and forwards over the dropping zone until all the containers had been loaded on the civilian lorry. As we drove back to the base, the conversation centred around what we had received in the stores. The first queries were always about the mail, but supplies of cigarettes caused almost as much anxiety.

On 27th August we commenced serious operations against the enemy. Patrols were sent on to all the main roads around the forest, where they succeeded in ambushing a number of vehicles, including a large petrol trailer on the outskirts of Chatillon.

I motored down with Grant to visit Colonel Claude, the Commander of the Maquis in Aigny-le-Duc. In spite of serious political rifts, the Maquis in this part of the world was very active against the Germans. They were well organised and even operated a stretch of railway line through their territory. We were stopped on the outskirts of the village by several French patrols who all waved us on with cheery " thumbs ups," which the "V" sign never quite replaced. Colonel Claude was an impressive young man and I soon realised that his national pride would never allow him to submit to my command. Grant's appreciation was in every way correct. It would be better to maintain a loose liaison, only combining together for certain joint operations.

After several glasses of vermouth with which we toasted every figure from the King to General de Gaulle, we agreed to meet for dinner in two days' time. I was very amused to meet Lieutenant Wiseman, who had come up on a similar mission from the 1st S.A.S. Base north of Dijon, for he is a witty little man and never ceases to pull my leg about my being too keen.

That evening we suffered one of those losses which are even more tragic because they are unnecessary. An extra plane was running-in to drop two more drivers—Corporal West and Kalkstein, a little Polish Jew who had been with me on several operations. It was a dark night and, although we could only see one parachute in the air, we were not particularly worried at first. I heard a loud thud on the ground and presumed that one of their leg bags had broken away. When West came up to report that Kalkstein had jumped before him, I became a little anxious. We shouted his name all over the field but there was no reply.

When dawn came they found his body under the trees. Acid had eaten through his static line in the Halifax and his parachute was not even pulled out of the envelope. His little figure was lying, almost undamaged, as if he were asleep on his arms under the trees. How we cursed the inefficient maintenance of some "penguin" in England who had committed murder by rank idleness.

Grant laid on a funeral in Recey-sur-Ource the next day. Kalkstein was buried with full military honours in the tiny churchyard, but I have since wondered whether the Jewish faith would be quite in agreement with the ceremony.

On the 28th August we knocked out a total of five trucks around the forest and Sergeant Vickers laid mines on the Langres-Dijon road. Grant had picked up a delightful American pilot called Glen Stirling, who operated as Jamie Robertson's gunner. His Texas drawl was beautiful to our alien ears and I shall never forget that he once reported having shot two Germans "way out in the cow pastures."

Although I will try to avoid monotony by not going into the details of each ambush carried out, the next two days deserve mention as highlights in the whole operation. Grant had received information that there was a German Headquarters in a farm called La Barotte, near Chatillon. I thought that it might be a good target for Dayrell Morris' three-inch mortar and so we decided to reconnoitre the area with a view to an attack the next day.

At a farm-house on the Recey road we stopped to inquire for further information, and the farmer, a lovely man with a round, red face, obligingly telephoned the Mayor of Chatillon. This dignitary reported that La Barotte was no longer occupied, but that the main garrison of Chatillon was in the process of being relieved by Panzer Grenadiers from Montbard. At that time there were only one hundred and fifty Germans with twenty trucks in the precincts of the Château, although more were expected the next day. I have never heard of a more farcical way of obtaining accurate information, but it was the sort of comedy which was always being played in guerrilla warfare.

Grant, Dayrell and I in one jeep motored slowly across country to the aerodrome, which was quite deserted. We entered the town by a side road to the amazement of the population. Sometimes reconnoitring on foot and then driving slowly along when we found the way clear, we passed startled townsfolk until we came to a dry river bed. I drove the jeep along under cover until we were at the foot of the high hill on which the Château stood. In Rupert of Hentzau fashion, Grant swarmed up the slope, scaled a wall and carefully inspected the German trucks in the courtyard. As there was much shouting from the Germans and many Frenchmen were watching from the top windows of their houses, I decided to withdraw.

Passing through an unguarded road block, we motored along the Dijon road. Soon after we had turned off along a track leading back into the forest, we noticed a convoy of four trucks proceeding towards Chatillon on a parallel bearing to our own. Turning the jeep around, we drove back at top speed in the hope that we would catch them at the junction.

We were too late, but the sound of firing told us that they had been stopped by the Maquis near Aisey-sur-Seine. Both sides were too engrossed to notice our stealthy approach from the rear. The Frenchmen were shooting down from cover on the side of the hill, but the Germans were giving as good as they were taking from the ditches along the road. It must have been a great shock when our deadly Vickers suddenly opened up at short range from their rear. Three trucks were destroyed and many Germans were killed. Dayrell Morris walked forward to call upon them to surrender in German, but those who responded were soon dispersed again by wild fire from the Maquis. The leading truck managed to run the gauntlet round the corner to safety. It had been a good day's work and I was amused at the extra delight the troops took in the fact that they had been feldgendarmerie or military policemen.

Several more vehicles had been knocked out by the other patrols during the day, and Grant and I went to dine with Colonel Claude in a victorious mood. It was a wonderful dinner, and in spite of our beards and dirty clothes the French treated us with as much courtesy as if we had been important plenipotentiaries. Many toasts were drunk and I partly blame the actions of the next day on the quantity of red wine consumed. I feel now that Colonel Claude considered that we were only bellicose in the aura of Dutch courage, and did not take our wild plans seriously. We suggested that we should all attack Chatillon at dawn the next morning, while the German relief was still going on. The Maquis agreed to supply five hundred men if we would give them enough petrol to move their trucks. This was arranged through Sergeant Linton back at the base.

The combined squadron attacked Chatillon at first light. My plan was to seize the important junction of the Montbard and Dijon roads. From there we would send a foot party with Brens, carried as far as possible by jeep, to attack the north of the Château. The signal for the attack to begin would be the firing of the three-inch mortar on the Château from the south.

Jim Mackie crossed the aerodrome and occupied the cross-roads without incident. I then moved the remaining nine jeeps containing forty men through him into the town. We occupied all the main junctions leading into the market square, while Jaimie Robertson took the foot party round the back. I placed Sergeant-Major Mitchell with two jeeps on the Troyes-Chaumont cross-roads and Sergeant Young cut all the military telephone wires.

Dayrell began to mortar the Château at about seven o'clock. He placed forty-eight bombs on the target in all. Fifteen minutes later a long column of about thirty German trucks, presumably containing the relief, arrived at the river bridge near Mackie's position on the Montbard-Dijon cross-roads. The battle was on. Sergeant Vickers, whose jeep was in the middle of the road, allowed them to approach to within twenty yards before he opened fire. The first five trucks, two of which were loaded with ammunition, were brewed up and we were treated to a glorious display of fireworks. A motor-cycle combination skidded off the bridge into the river. I thought I noticed a woman in the cab of the leading vehicle, but it was too late to worry. All the sounds of war echoed in the streets—the rattle of the Brens, the rasp of the Vickers, the whine of bullets bouncing off the walls, and in the background the stonk-stonk of the mortars. I got a Bren myself and, balancing it on a wall, hosepiped the German column with red tracers. The Germans had baled out from the back of the convoy and were firing a lot of mortar bombs. Bullets were whistling everywhere and it was good to see our tracers pumping into them. Parachutist Holland was killed by a bullet in the head and a brave French civilian dragged him into a doorway.

I could hear other shooting from the centre of the town as well as firing from behind the Château, so it seemed that Mitchell was also engaged, although by far the greatest weight of fire was around our position on the Montbard-Dijon cross-roads.

A pretty girl with long black hair and wearing a bright red frock put her head out of a top window to give me the "V" sign. Her smile ridiculed the bullets.

A runner came up from Mitchell to say that a number of Germans were fighting their way down the street from the Château. The situation was so confused that the enemy was mortaring his own side. I sent Dayrell Morris up to reinforce the position in the centre of the town which was now hard pressed. Jaimie Robertson's Brens were firing briskly from the back of the woods to the north.

At nine o'clock, three hours after the action had begun, I felt that since Mitchell was being subjected to such strong pressure from the houses, although only one jeep had been hit, I had better give the signal for a withdrawal. The Montbard column was becoming more organised and there was still no sign of the promised Maquis reinforcements. I walked into the middle of the road, waving to the girl in the red frock, and fired two Verey lights into the air.

Grant brought out Lieutenant Robertson's troop, while I led the remainder back along the Dijon road for breakfast. On his way back with the foot party, Grant met sixty of the promised five hundred Maquis waiting on the aerodrome. He undertook to lead them into the town with a party of seven men, at the same time sending a message to ask me to co-operate in a second attack. He became involved in a street fight in which he knocked out an armoured car, but was beaten into a tight corner from which the party only narrowly escaped. A bicycle patrol of thirty Germans trapped them in a garden and, while they were fighting their way out, Corporal Brownlee was hit in the most precious part of his body. When I arrived with the main party I posted jeep ambushes on all the main roads leading out of the town, which destroyed eight German vehicles loaded high with troops. Supported by Jim Mackie in a jeep, I led a foot patrol round the east of Chatillon. It was all very quiet except for occasional firing from the direction of Grant Hibbert. With our heads bowed, we stalked round some Germans on a crest amongst some beech trees, crossed a canal by a lock and walked along the sides of the tow-path. There were several Germans around the hospital on the other side, but they did not see us.

After walking for about an hour we found ourselves in a narrow lane leading down to the Troyes road. Looking around the corner, I was astonished to see a German machine-gun post on each side, facing outwards. They were all in great-coats and had their backs to us. I could not think what to do, so we sat in a garden and waited. Lieutenant Pinci begged a bottle of wine, bread and cheese from a French cottage, so we had lunch.

I tossed up which German we should shoot in the back and it turned out to be the left-hand one. Sergeant Young took careful aim through his carbine, and when I gave the word he pulled the trigger. At the same moment, Pinci, excitable as ever, shot a German on a bicycle to the right. All hell was then let loose. I do not know from where they were coming, but our little lane was soon singing with schmeisser bullets. It was so high-banked and so open on each side as to make it a death-trap. With angry bullets buzzing round our heads, we burst into the front door of a French house. Running straight through, we scrambled down the bank to the canal.

After we had run along the tow-path to the lock, I led the party across country to the east. We had just reached the cover of a thin hedge on a skyline when two machine guns picked us out. I had not realised that we could be seen. We wriggled on our bellies along the furrows in a ploughed field with the bullets kicking up great clots of earth all round. I have never felt so tired. I knew that if we remained on that crest we would be killed and yet I could not force myself to move any faster. Sergeant Robinson, behind me, was hit in the leg and still he moved faster than I. When we had reached a little dead ground I tried to help him, but I was too exhausted. Never have I been so frightened and so incapable of helping myself.

Jim Mackie appeared and we loaded Robinson into his jeep. At the friendly farm-house, from which we had telephoned the mayor the day before, I dressed his wounds on the kitchen table, while all the women clucked and fussed around with kettles of hot water. After we had despatched him to the Maquis hospital at Aigny-le-Duc, we motored back slowly through the forest glades to our base. **The Battle of Chatillon was over.** They say that we killed a hundred Germans, wounded many more and destroyed nine trucks, four cars and a motor-cycle.

During the next afternoon, fearing new reprisals for our Chatillon attack, I led the squadron into a new base south of Auberive. We had a big re-supply that night in which seven more jeeps were dropped, making our total strength up to eighteen. Grant and I decided to reorganise the squadron into three parties. The argument that a lack of trained leaders forced me to concentrate the whole squadron did not apply when such a capable person as Grant was available. He was just as experienced as I and there was no sound reason for running the risk of detection by operating in a large body. Accordingly, Grant and I each took sufficient personnel to man nine jeeps, leaving the remaining twenty-three all ranks to operate under Pinci in the Chaumont area. My plan was for our two columns to advance on parallel lines towards the Belfort Gap, where all the Germans retreating in front of the Third and Seventh American Armies were converging. There we hoped to link up with another S.A.S. Base in Alsace-Lorraine. I intended to advance via the Forest of Darney and Grant planned to move through the area north of Bourbonne. Grant's experiences were very similar to mine except that he destroyed a large petrol dump as well as many trucks. Pinci was killed by our own aircraft, but the foot party continued to do good work under Walker-Brown.

My column began to move east on the evening of the 2nd September. With the sun setting behind us, we wound round the narrow country lanes, across the Langres-Dijon road to the highway between Langres and Epinal. We failed to cross the highway that night when four separate patrols bumped into German posts. After talking the situation over with Big Jim by the light of a candle in a charming little cottage, where fried eggs and wine had been laid before us, I decided to lie up in the woods until we could make a proper reconnaissance the next day. There were loud explosions all night which pointed to German demolitions preparatory to a general withdrawal. I encountered the Commander of the 1st Regiment of France at an early hour the next morning. He had been under Vichy control, but had now gone over to the Maquis with his entire battalion. It was good to see smart, properly dressed soldiers again. While I was talking to this gentleman a Maquisard rushed up to tell me that six German deserters awaited collection in the next village. Unfortunately, when Mitchell went up to collect them, he found that over a hundred other Germans strongly objected to his casual visit. Then the other Frenchmen accused this informer of being a traitor. I did not believe that he was any more than stupid, but to make sure I took him for a ride in one of the jeeps and dropped him off in a lonely part of the country, far from a telephone.

Farther on, the 1st Regiment of France neatly felled a tree in front of my jeep, much to my alarm. However, after a few moments of anxious shouting, the obstacle was removed. That evening Sergeant Vickers found a way across the highway near Bize. I leaguered for the night on a thick wooded hill called Bois d'Anrosey, above Fays-Billot.

Carpendale and Young both carried out successful ambushes on the main highway in the morning. Sergeant Young thought that the quick retaliation to his attack on two staff cars was due to his having been given away by a man collecting mushrooms. I did not credit this at the time, but later experience taught me that this is a favourite French disguise for a look-out man.

All the boys and girls from the village came out in their Sunday clothes to look at the strange Englishmen in the wood. They brought presents of fruit, cheese and butter which were most welcome. An old man on two sticks kept whispering "Les sales Boches" in my ear and spitting on the ground.

We moved on in the afternoon past pleasant wooded hills, through tiny picturesque villages and along dusty lanes to the Forest of Darney. The enthusiasm of the locals at our unexpected arrival (I had attached little silk Union Jacks to the bonnets) was most embarrassing for the church bells began to ring with joy behind us, marking our trail to less friendly ears.

I chose a leaguer near a farm called Thomas, deep in the heart of the forest. There was information of considerable enemy movement on the roads and of mixed units re-forming around Bains-les-Bains. In view of these reports, our movement along roads by day had been made with astonishing ease.

Perhaps the worst thing about life behind the lines was the awful feeling of nervousness when hiding in forests. I think I felt it more in the Forest of Darney than anywhere. Perhaps it was the strain of the last five years beginning to tell on me after all this time. I think that it was more the tallness of the trees and the fact that we never saw the sun from one day to another. Every time the leaves rustled or we heard the wild pig running at night, I thought that the Germans were creeping up on us. As far as I was concerned, even as Leader of the Squadron, I felt that a mere trip to the clearing of Thomas for rations was an adventure, and yet I was prepared to send patrols out of the forest to attack Germans upon the main roads. I felt often that I was getting windy and my conscience pricked at always taking a back seat. I hoped and prayed that the others would not think that I was scared, for by now they regarded me as something akin to a lucky genius.

I sent Big Jim Mackie to patrol the roads leading to Darney. He dismounted and sent a foot party, which discovered that the road from Darney to Bains-les-Bains was barricaded so as to lead the traffic on to the road to Epinal. Later, he laid an ambush on the main road and, after half an hour, destroyed a motor-cycle combination, containing seven Germans, at under fifty yards' range. Only one man escaped. He then came back to me to report that the stories of a large German garrison at Darney were untrue. At last light, indefatigable as ever, he made another patrol with Sergeant Vickers to the road west of Attigny and brewed up an anti-aircraft truck.

Big Jim Mackie was my right hand in all my S.A.S. operations except the one near Pescara and the last one in Italy. I knew that I could trust him implicitly to obey every principle of my teaching in jeeping and was therefore merciless about always putting him in front at the trickiest moments. He never complained, but I have never known whether to attribute his continued life to skill or to Divine providence. Possibly it was a mixture of both. The fact remains that there were occasions, especially in France, when I felt such remorse at constantly doing an "Uriah the Hittite" on him that I foolishly went out of my way to lead myself. A Squadron Leader can never effectively command his squadron if he becomes involved in troop actions and (as I did when we bumped the 10th Panzer Division at Villaines) by so doing he might endanger his whole command.

On 6th September I sent Chips Carpendale off on a long reconnaissance of the Epinal area with a view to finding out the chances of crossing the Moselle. I told him that he could shoot up easy targets, but the primary object was to find a way across the river to the Belfort Gap and to find out if the Germans intended to stick on that line for any length of time.

Pricked by my foolish conscience, I led a patrol myself to ambush the main road between Darney and Epinal. We had motored slowly into a village by a side lane, after ascertaining from a ploughman that it was clear. The usual scenes of liberation soon surrounded the jeeps—pretty girls kissing our cheeks, bereaved mothers shaking our hands and everybody dancing around us with joy. Even through the fuss, I learned that large convoys passed along the road the whole time. It was only to be expected that at the moment that the first two German staff cars approached, women and children should be in the way of our guns. By the time we had cleared them, bolting with shrieks into the houses, we had only time to get in two bursts of Vickers at the rear one. We stopped it, but the occupants opened fire with a Spandau from the roof and I withdrew at top speed. The first liberation of Lerrain was short-lived.

While I was trying vainly to catch another fish on the Bains-les-Bains road, two Frenchmen appeared in a luxurious staff car. They asked me if the Allies were in Darney, which as Frenchmen they should have been perfectly aware was far from being the case. They were two odd-looking types, much too flashy to be members of the Maquis, but I was so engrossed in my ambush that I merely sent them back to report to the nearest Maquis Headquarters at Granrupt. If only I had known at the time that they had asked one of my men if he had heard of an "S.A.S. Mission to the Maquis," I would have dealt with them very differently. As it was, they of course never reported to the Maquis, since they were clearly Vichy agents working for the Germans.

I have neglected to say that on the 5th September I paid a visit to a fantastic Maquis in the forest near Granrupt-les-Bains. It was founded on a scout troop and all the members were very young, although the leaders were old enough. They were quartered in bell-tents near a mountain stream on the far side of the Bains-les-Bains Road and the whole set-up savoured of a youth club in peace-time. Their spirit was magnificent, although they had not yet operated against the enemy. I am sorry to say that they were cleared up by a German drive before they ever became effective. I gave them a speech in my comic-opera French and was nearly carried shoulder-high to my jeep. It is sad to think that they will be bound to consider that we behaved badly when they were eventually attacked, although I am sure that our actions were justified. I only pray that their dispersal was not a direct result of my soft treatment of those two strange French-men in their lovely black limousine.

I arranged to have my re-supply on the dropping zone of the Granrupt Maquis to give the boys some training in a "lancée" (as they called it). It was a large open field surrounded by trees, and what with the wind and the ineffective French signal lights, I did not really expect success. However, at two o'clock in the morning, when we were all shivering with cold and had almost given up hope, we heard the familiar drone of a Halifax to the south. Two planes came in, dropping their cargoes too high so that they drifted into the trees. Lieutenant Gurney, Lance-Corporal Challenor and Parachutist Fyffe (who had all gone astray with Ramon Lee) were dropped in with a jeep to rejoin us. Fyffe landed in a tall pine tree and it was several hours before we got him down. The wind had so dispersed the containers that we had not recovered all the chutes from the trees when dawn came. I took my party off to a shooting-lodge for breakfast and left it to the Maquis.

At six-thirty an excited boy of about nineteen ran into the house to warn me that six hundred Germans, four armoured cars, six troop-carriers and twenty staff cars had approached the field from the direction of Granrupt. The S.S. troops in Bains-les-Bains had obviously heard about the parachutage and were out to clean us up.

The field was completely enclosed by woods and the only exit was a lane which led towards the Germans in Granrupt. I knew that it would be useless to try to form a defensive position with the Maquis, who would be much better advised to with-draw into the woods. In any case, I had to think of my jeeps and the rest of my command in the Forest of Darney.

By this time, small-arms fire had broken out in the woods on the eastern perimeter of the dropping zone, so well marked by white parachutes still sitting in the upper branches of the trees. The Maquis were running back in disorder into the forest. Escape to the east and the north was impossible, and although I drove the jeeps around like a string of ponies, I could not find a route to the south or west. A deep stream ran through the woods on the north, which our jeeps could not hope to negotiate. In something like despair, I placed the jeeps in a hull-down position behind a small crest in the middle of the field. Suddenly, when we were about to do the Old Guard act, I noticed a gap in the south-west corner. We cut the wire and crashed through a spinney of young saplings, bursting through them like fear-crazed elephants in a jungle. Fire was still rattling away behind us to the east. On the other side of a small field we found a good track which led us down to the main road. In all, we had covered about four miles across country on a straight line.

Now that we had reached safety, my thoughts were for the Boy Scout Maquis and their first battle. I sent Lieutenant Gurney with two jeeps to attack the enemy's immediate rear along the Granrupt Road. He machine-gunned some German infantry, especially a group of officers standing on a mound, and knocked out what appeared to be their headquarters truck. I placed Sergeant Vickers in ambush on the road near Hennezel, hoping to catch the Boches on their way out. He was fortunate enough to catch two staff cars moving towards the battle and it was later reliably reported that amongst the dead were the Colonel and Second-in-Command of the attacking force. From the subsequent German reaction I do not think they were pleased with our day's work.

I decided that it was better to lie low for a while, so we remained under the dark shadow of the trees all day. On 8th September the patron at Thomas, who had been most helpful in arranging for a cartload of fresh bread from Passavant (where Carpendale had an aunt), excelled himself by arranging for two French mechanics to come out from the German workshops in Bains-les-Bains to repair a burnt-out clutch. These two characters arrived on a motor cycle, roaring with laughter at the thought that they were repairing a British jeep with German spare parts. Only this sort of comedy made life in Occupied Europe worth while.

During the night I sent out three separate parties to lay mines on the roads around Darney. It had suddenly occurred to me that mining was an inexpensive, if inglorious, way of annoying the enemy. It was subsequently reported that each nest had accounted for a truck.

I was overjoyed to welcome back Chips Carpendale, who had carried out the best patrol of the operation. In his three days away he had driven into a stores depot at Pouxeux, where he had destroyed a large lorry. On the 8th September, acting on information from a maquisard, he had attacked German billets west of Remiremont. Twenty Germans were killed while shaving in a farm-yard, and, strangest coup of all, he had knocked over a small anti-tank gun with small-arms fire. His news concerning the defences of the Moselle Line was not so bright. The Epinal Forts, which had previously been demilitarised, were rapidly being strengthened by the Todt Organisation. Over two thousand troops were encamped to the south-west of the town, so the chances were that General Patton was about to receive a check. He also reported that there was much traffic between Remiremont and Epinal, and that the villagers were being forced to build defences at Le Thillot and Rupt-sur-Moselle.

The jeep which towed the trailer of mortar bombs had again broken down with a burnt-out clutch, but the farmer of Thomas once more arranged for the two Alsatians to come out from Bains-les-Bains on a motor cycle.

When the repairs to the vehicle were completed I decided to move our base to another part of the forest. I guessed that the Germans would seek us out, but unfortunately I chose to move in the wrong direction. We had barely dispersed the jeeps in the trees when a loud female scream came from about five hundred yards away. It might have been farther for it is difficult to estimate distance in the quietness of the woods, but it could only have had one cause. The Germans were beating the forest. I could not risk starting up the engines again to withdraw farther south. All I could do was to send out a foot patrol to see if they could discover the exact whereabouts of the searchers. They came back just before dark to say that the village of Hennezel was burning and that there were many Germans along the line of the road running through the forest. This gave me more encouragement for I guessed that they would stop on that line for the night. As soon as it had got well dark, we moved in column down to the southern part of the forest. I had arranged a re-supply drop at eleven o'clock, the last before we moved on to the Belfort Gap, and if it was humanly possible I wanted to receive it. Our petrol was running low and there might not be another opportunity.

To accept a drop with the enemy within three miles of the zone was a great risk but I felt it worth taking. Six planes came in all and dropped an enormous number of containers which we only just got clear before dawn. It was like Christmas Day. We all had clean clothes, cigarettes, papers, mail and even a bottle of whisky. There was a special gift pannier from our beloved Quartermaster, Tom Burt, which required no receipt signatures. It was all a great fillip to our morale.

As soon as the jeeps had been reloaded, we moved on in column across the Saone to the south-east. The Germans were much thicker on the ground now for we were approaching the point of convergence of the two lines of retreat. As we crossed each road we left a nest of Hawkins mines on the tarmac. One had a bite so quickly that I thought Sergeant Hughes had blown himself up and started calling for the doctor. I was assured, however, that the only casualties from the explosion were some German officers in their staff car in a ditch.

We must have been somewhere between Vesoul and Luxeuilles-Baines when I first felt that the Germans were getting so concentrated that we looked like running into serious trouble. There were no convenient forests about and the only wood we could find for the night was not more than two miles square. I sent Hugh Gurney, who had been dropped in again at Granrupt, to see what there was to the west of us. Although I had clearly told him not to shoot up anything on the edges of our wood, he had not been gone much more than five minutes before I heard the rattle of the Vickers. He had shot up a convoy on the very entrance to the leaguer. Corporal Cunningham had just set up the wireless set for the evening schedule to London when Spandau bullets began to cut the branches over our heads. The Germans had discovered our presence and were coming into the trees to get us. A pitched battle would far from suit my plans, but I had no idea in which direction to withdraw. While I was screaming at the jeeps to start up, and while those on the edge of the leaguer were firing back at the Germans, I noticed Corporal Cunningham slowly rolling up the aerial with a faint contemptuous grin on his face. His sang-froid was like a douche of cold water on my excitement.

I led the column out on to the main ride through the trees and turned down to the south. On the far side of the wood I turned right again down a cart-track running into some thick bushes. The tail of the column was just under cover when the front three jeeps stuck in soft mud. The only answer was to lie low; if they found us we would fight; but there was no hope of moving. Frantically we threw bushes over the vehicles and those at the end of the column erased our tracks with spades. We heard the Germans crashing about in the trees but they did not find us. We were even afraid to cough. During the night it rained heavily and we sat shivering in the mud, listening to a large German column rolling down the road less than a hundred yards away. We could hear a military policeman shouting to all the drivers to beware of " terrorists."

In the morning we dug the jeeps out and pushed them by hand back down the track, not daring to start the engines. In this fashion we escaped from this wood to another thicker forest north of Luxeuil-les-Bains. There we met a small Maquis—one of the most gallant of our acquaintance—commanded by a doctor called Topsent. They agreed to provide us with guides for several operations I wanted to carry out that night. Amongst their prisoners was an Indian from the German Free India Battalion. He was a miserable man and I was amazed at the forbearance of the French, who had suffered much at the hands of these traitors. I advised them to house him with the pigs.

Although the operations of the night were successful, we suffered heavy casualties for the first time since our bad luck at Semur. Hugh Gurney took on a column at under ten yards' range in the village of Velorcey. It was a cruel jest of fate that his first bullets should cut into a truck full of explosive, which blew both sides to pieces. Hugh almost escaped from his wrecked jeep but was shot down by a Spandau in the street. Lieutenant Burtwhistle, another reinforcement, led a raid on a German horse-drawn column in Fontaines-les-Bains. He shot a number of Germans and fired five carts, but one of our jeeps was knocked out and three of our men wounded. Jim Mackie had better luck nearer Luxeuil.

By now I could hear the American artillery to the south. There were so many Germans on the roads that there was no question of our moving. Instead I decided to shrink back deeper into the woods. Soon after we had reached our new position and had camouflaged the jeeps, Germans began to dig in on the edges of the trees. Less than a hundred yards away a battery of 88-millimetre guns set up a position. For three days we sat there, listening to the gunners talking and afraid to give away our hideout by attacking them. I sent out one or two foot patrols to try to make contact with the Americans, but they only succeeded in mining the roads before they were compelled to come back to admit failure. I led a patrol up to mine the railway which the Germans were still using. Apart from these dismounted patrols we sat inactive, hardly daring to whisper, waiting for fate to play another card. Once a tin of bacon exploded and sent us all diving for our weapons.

The climax came when the American artillery started counter-battery fire against the German guns. Most of the shells landed around us in the woods, although there were no casualties for by then we had dug deep funk-holes. That evening the Germans withdrew.

The next morning our Maquis friends led in the crew of an American armoured car. We were so overjoyed to see their grinning Yankee faces that we danced a Highland reel on the spot. The operation was over and none too soon, for we were all suffering from great nervous strain. I was amazed to discover that our saviours were from the 7th Army and not from the 3rd as I had expected. Our total bag of trucks in France was ninety-five and we spent almost exactly a month behind the enemy lines.

We took our time in recrossing France, looking with pride at the skeletons of all the trucks we had destroyed. I allowed the squadron a week's leave in Paris, although it was supposed to be out of bounds to British troops at that time. Grant, whose adventures had ended in roughly the same way as ours, joined us at Arromanches and the whole squadron arrived in Southampton together.

CHAPTER NINE

GREECE, 1944

WITHIN a few days of my return from the jeep operation in France, certain events occurred in the Mediterranean which made me agitate to go abroad once more.

The Allies had landed in the Peloponnesus and the Germans were rapidly evacuating Greece. I felt that I owed such a debt to the Greeks for their hospitality in 1941 that the least I could do was to take steps to ensure that I took part in the liberation. If there was to be any fighting in Greece, I wanted to be in it. With my knowledge of the language, it should not be too difficult to persuade someone in the War Office to give me a job there.

The difficulty was that although I was technically second-in-command of the 2nd S.A.S. Regiment, command of the base in England had been left to a Major John Bingham by the Colonel when he parachuted into the Vosges. I could not ask the Colonel's permission to be away for a few months, so that strictly speaking I was within my rights to give myself leave as far as the regiment was concerned. Major Bingham, however, strongly objected to my going. We had a heated argument over the telephone and in the end I defied him by catching an aeroplane the next day. It has since occurred to me that Major Bingham was quite correct in his stand, and that it was very wrong of me to go tearing off to the other side of the world without the Colonel's sanction.

I had persuaded the Director of Military Intelligence at the War Office to attach me to Land Forces Adriatic as an S.A.S. observer, who could act as an interpreter. It was fortunate from my point of view that Land Forces Adriatic should be commanded by Brigadier George Davy, D.S.O., of my own regiment. However, when I arrived in Bari, I had the feeling that although we were on common ground as far as the 3rd Hussars were concerned, my connections with the Stirling family and my abortive mission to try to raise recruits in the Middle East in 1943 had made the Brigadier rather suspicious of my motives. Perhaps he feared that the S.A.S. were about to pull a fast one to poach on his preserves.

Whatever it was, although I had the run of the Brigadier's own mess in Bari, it was over a fortnight before I managed to get anywhere near the theatre of operations. My first visit was something in the nature of a joy ride. A Commando Brigade had landed on the Albanian coast north of Sarande with a view to cutting off the withdrawal of the German forces from Corfu. Land Forces Adriatic were grossly under-supplied with the equipment needed to maintain a prolonged seaborne operation, and when torrential rain converted the operation from a simple clean-cut attack to a long battle in the mountains, the supply of the Brigade became very precarious.

I went in one of the few landing craft, carrying supplies to the Brigade. I saw nothing of the fighting and can only, therefore, describe the scene at the beach-head and a second-hand account of the battle.

Sugar Beach was a small cove surrounded by bare, precipitous mountains. It rains in Albania as it rains in few countries in the world. Water was simply pouring down in torrents on the deck of our craft, so that we were even reluctant to stretch our legs on the shore in the way that one usually does after a rough sea passage. The cargo had to be lifted out by British Pioneers and dumped high up the beach, for there was a great danger that the floods would wash it back into the sea. The whole beach-head was under about two inches of water.

Ragged Albanian partisans were hovering on the outskirts of the dump, watching carefully for a chance to pilfer some of the stores. I have seldom seen such miserable poverty-stricken peasants; they seemed to be a sort of hybrid mixture of the East and the West. Occasionally the guards would fire shots over their heads when they approached too near for safety.

The Commandos must have had no protection at all from the elements on those bare, rocky slopes. They had been dressed in gym. shoes and light kit as for a quick scramble landing, and were in no condition to withstand the rigours of mountain warfare in such a climate. I believe that there were about three hundred casualties from trench feet and pneumonia in the first week.

Mules could only carry the supplies part of the way up the hill. The major part of the journey had to be covered by Commando porters, carrying the heavy rations on their backs.

When eventually the Commandos took Sarande, most of the Germans had made good their escape. I have often wondered why our troops preferred to sit on the tops of the mountains, shivering in the rain, rather than push inland to cut the main road to the north. However, it must have been a most miserable operation, and I am glad that my visit was such a short one.

We called in at Corfu on the way back. In contrast to Albania, the sun was shining over this beautiful Greek island. I walked through the port, practising my Greek, and was appalled by the damage bombing had caused on the island. Corfu was bombed by the Germans, the Italians, the British and the Americans, so that the peasants had had a fair taste of the various national techniques. The coast of the island is one of the most beautiful in the world, and I stood for a long time watching the blue sea break in clouds of white spray on the rugged inlets. It was difficult to lose oneself for long in the beauties of Nature, when all around the people were suffering so much. Many streets were still blocked with rubble; food was terribly scarce, and most of the women would have sold their souls for a tin of bully beef. Already I was beginning to feel a sense of fury and frustration at the way this great little nation had been rewarded for its bravery.

After our return to Bari, I persuaded Brigadier Davy to be good enough to allow me to fly to Athens in order to renew my acquaintance with the people who had sheltered me three years before. Athens had been first occupied by S.A.S. troops (the S.B.S) under Lord Jellicoe, and soon afterwards British parachutists had landed on Megara airfield.

I landed on Phaleron Aerodrome, from which I obtained a lift into the town. Already, others told me, the E.L.A.S. partisans were causing trouble. I still could not believe that a people which had achieved such unity of purpose at one period of the war should now be torn apart by internal strife. My first experience of Athens confirmed that it was only too terribly true.

My way was blocked by a huge parade of Communist partisans. I stood on the steps of a large hotel, watching the fantastic display, unable to force my way through the crowd. Hundreds of men, women and children were marching through the streets behind a huge banner depicting Stalin, all chanting slogans and singing a stirring partisan tune. Greek flags were in evidence everywhere. I could not understand and felt a little afraid of the mood of the crowd. It was like the roaring of a herd of wild beasts. And then, after one of the many brass bands had passed, the tension broke. A little man in clerical attire brought his umbrella down with a resounding crack on the head of one of the uniformed E.L.A.S. soldiers. The mob picked him up and tore him apart, tossing him about like a football. Eventually, some E.L.A.S. officials rescued his bleeding remains from the pavement. I felt a certain sickness in the pit of my stomach.

Before the incident, I had noticed a pretty Athenian girl standing on the edge of the crowd. She had that blonde beauty peculiar to some of the women in Athens. Her face was trembling and I could see that she was very alarmed by it all. Now, at the height of the brawl, I could see her being buffeted about between the fury-crazed mob. I pushed my way through the struggling bodies, seized her by the arm and fought a passage for her to the steps of the hotel. I pushed her through the swing-doors, into the safety of the building. It was a long time before she had regained her breath enough to speak. I remember that she had a very deep resonant voice and that she expressed her gratitude very sweetly. When the streets had quietened, I conducted her as far as the tram stop, but she would not allow me to go any farther. I have often wished that I could see her again.

The next morning I went down to Piraeus to see if I could find my old friends. It was only when I reached the harbour that I realised with a shock that I had no notion of the addresses. I walked up and down the streets for a long time in the hope that some object or face would excite my memory. It was of no use.

I decided to try in Kokinia and hopped a lift there in a Greek truck. I wandered through the streets for hours, inquiring in all the cafés for a dentist called Tino, until at last someone guided me to the home of my old friend. He had reduced his girth in the years of famine and now he had a new wife, Maria having run away with a sailor. He was overjoyed to see me, and while we were talking about old times over a cup of coffee, he sent off a boy to fetch Elias and Sortires. For the next four days I went around with Elias to meet all my old friends. Elias had spent two years in gaol on account of his having helped British prisoners, and most of the others had spent a period in the Averoff Prison.

Perhaps the most amusing interlude was my reacquaintance with Elpice, my erstwhile girl friend. I knocked on the door of the tiny house, and suddenly there she was, resplendent in a red kimono. She clasped her arms around my neck and kissed me

255

on both cheeks. As she dragged me inside the house, she called for Kathia to come quickly. Then came the big surprise. She introduced a blond young man as her husband, George, who was another dentist. Apparently she had been arrested by the Gestapo in 1942, and had fallen in love with the interpreter at the Military Tribunal. Before I left, George demonstrated his prowess and his hospitality by whipping out one of my teeth before I had time to work up a proper defence.

They were happy days, although most of my friends were out of work. We went to an E.L.A.S. propaganda play, which was all about the ill-treatment meted out to the Communists in the Concentration Camp at Hymettis. I was relieved to see that most of them secretly disapproved of the new party, although I cannot say that they were exactly strong supporters of the King.

Once Sortires took me to a cabaret with a man I had only known slightly, who had become one of the notorious "black caps" or veteran members of E.L.A.S. After closing time, the proprietor quite properly objected to serving more drink. Our partisan friend, who was leaning back with his jackboots on a chair, beat upon the table with his crop and threatened to do all sorts of things to the proprietor for being so insolent. Fright reduced the poor little man to a quivering jelly and drinks were produced before we could say "knife." I was appalled by this high-handed, dictatorial attitude, and silently prayed that Greece might be saved from the awful tyranny of E.L.A.S.

Almost the only man I met with a balanced political outlook was our old patron, Valisarki, who was commanding the battle-ship *Averoff*, then at anchor in Piraeus Harbour. His democratic attitude led him to entertain Sortires and Elias—my two coster friends—and me in the wardroom of the Greek flagship. I have a tremendous admiration for this man Valisarki, who is one of the nicest men I have ever met.

I heard a rumour the next day that the Commando Brigade was in the process of loading into landing craft for an operation against Salonika. Ronnie Todd, the new Commando Brigadier, was an old friend, who would be certain to take me if I asked him. I was lucky enough to meet Frank McGasky, the British liaison officer with Archbishop Damaskinos, who had been in prison with me in Kokinia. He kindly agreed to run me down to the docks in his car.

I was just in time to board one of the landing craft before the convoy sailed. Sortires and Elias waved good-bye to me from the docks. We sailed through calm seas to the island of Skythos, which had already been occupied by the S.B.S., and was to be the base for this operation. Typical of the rocky little islets in the Ægean, it had one pretty village and a harbour for fishing boats. It had been shelled once by a German gunboat when two German officers were killed during a tour of inspection. The people were woefully poor and most of the children had sores on their bare legs. I strolled up to the top of the hill one evening to take a glass of "oozo" with one of the peasants. It was gratifying to hear how much he was opposed to E.L.A.S., for I had begun to fear that all the poor people were supporting the Communists. On the contrary, it appeared that the partisans were worse brigands than Greeks had ever known before. I did gather, however, that the King was still identified with the tyrannical Metaxas regime, which had been so much hated before the war.

We lived in rather restricted quarters in the local school, while we waited for the navy to clear the vast minefield in Salonika Bay. The delay was irksome, especially since the Colonel had no idea of the situation in Salonika. We bathed daily in the warm sea below the school, basking afterwards in the sunshine until we were burnt to the colour of fresh almonds. There was another wanderer on the island called Xan Fielding, who had about as much right to be there as I, and who had carried out several operations behind the German lines in the Ægean. Xan Fielding speaks Greek fluently and is the modern version of a soldier of fortune. We became close friends and I often wonder where he is fighting a war now.

After we had been on Skythos about a week, the Colonel agreed to allow me to make my way to Salonika to discover what exactly was happening. I travelled up in a fishing boat as far as the isthmus to the east of Salonika Bay. There I hired a car to carry me over the unmetalled cart-tracks to the town. The Greeks in Macedonia are very different from the Athenians, being more slow and less light-hearted in their manner. They are equally embroiled in politics—perhaps even more so since Macedonia has been overrun by so many various races. In their slow shy way, they were glad enough to see me since they had suffered considerably under the Bulgars.

The car was about a 1922 model tourer and spurted mixed steam and water from its radiator cap. It might have made the distance if the driver had not insisted upon picking up a peasant complete with chickens in every village through which we passed. As it was, we were compelled to finish the journey in a bus. I perched on the top amongst turkeys and chickens, baskets of fruit and lots of children.

It was clear by now that the Germans had withdrawn. Partisans armed to the teeth, wearing German helmets at crazy angles, were standing about in the villages. I stuck up my thumb at every person we passed and they joyfully whooped when they saw my British uniform. We were two hours behind the German rearguards when we arrived in Salonika. A tremendous E.L.A.S. victory parade was in progress with hundreds of partisans giving the clenched-fist salute and chanting "Kapa Kapa Epsilon." When they saw my British uniform on the top of the bus and saw me giving the "thumbs-up" sign, they broke ranks to carry me shoulder-high through the town. It was fun to be able to break up a Communist parade, even if most of these Greeks did not really understand the meaning of the word. E.L.A.S. had so well organised their propaganda machine that neon lights were flashing their slogans the same night.

I was carted off to one party after another, until the haze of alcohol closed down over my memory. I can vaguely remember dancing in the streets, dancing with a blonde who claimed that she had broken many hearts, including a German officer's, and singing "Tipperary" until my voice was hoarse.

Andy Lassen, who was to get a posthumous V.C. at Commachio and who was a Danish squadron leader in Jellicoe's S.B.S., had entered the other side of the town on a fire engine. We met in Salonika the next morning, when I witnessed the requisitioning of the Hotel Mediterranean, in itself an amusing adventure, for neither of us was exactly the type to be Military Commander of a large city.

The next day I was summoned back to Skythos. One of the Greek Sacred Regiment's caiques gave me a lift, firing a fine *feu de joie* of tracer bullets over the harbour before they left. I am rather sorry now that I persuaded them not to shoot out the red-lighted "K.K.E." slogan over a tall building on the front.

There was an urgent signal at Skythos demanding my return to Italy. A "Walrus" seaplane flew me to Athens, a Hudson to Italy, and thence, after a wait of a few days, I flew back to the United Kingdom by B.O.A.C.

Book III

S.A.S. OPERATION IN ITALY, 1945

CHAPTER ONE

PRELIMINARIES TO TOMBOLA

THIS OPERATION differed from all others in the S.A.S. in that heavy weapons and large forces were used more than ever before. It can be regarded as the culmination of S.A.S. experience in the last war. The beginnings were cautious until, in this last operation, the power of the gun was realised. It has, therefore, been treated in more detail.

We had always looked upon Italy as an ideal country for S.A.S. operations, especially since our brief taste of success in 1943. We looked back on the opportunities presented by the original landings at Salerno with great regret, since all ranks believed that if at that time we had been allowed to drop the whole regiment across the railways leading into the leg of Italy, we would have achieved decisive results, which might have saved thousands of lives in the subsequent fighting. Unfortunately, the prevailing shortage of transport aircraft at that time had made it impossible.

After our operations in France, I had paid a brief visit to Greece, where Brigadier George Davy, commanding Land Forces Adriatic, had again drawn my attention to the unique opportunities presented by the situation in Northern Italy.

It was therefore a pleasant shock indeed when Ian Collins, our Chief Staff Officer at the Army Air Corps Headquarters, informed me that a project was in train for me to take a squadron to Italy. He had himself returned from a visit to the various headquarters in that part of the world, and he was very optimistic of our chances of success. He had been received well by both Allied Force Headquarters and Fifteenth Army Group, which General Mark Clark had just taken over from General Alexander.

It was not long before the plan was confirmed by Army Air Corps Headquarters. We were to fly to Italy on December 15th, the heavier equipment following by sea. During the period immediately after our arrival in Italy, we would be looked after by S.O.E. in Bari as far as administration was concerned. S.O.E.

261

was the organisation responsible for the supply of partisans in South-East Europe, and it was fortunate from our point of view that we should start with such excellent opportunities for liaison.

The squadron selected for the task was not my own squadron, with which I had operated in Sicily, Italy and France for the last two years, but was a fresh unit raised since our return to the United Kingdom. It was mainly composed of volunteers from the airborne divisions. The men had been trained rigorously for a year by their Squadron Leader, Major Michael Rooney, who had unfortunately broken his back while parachuting into France. I attribute a large share of the credit for our subsequent successes to the efficiency of Major Rooney's training methods. Some of the squadron had operated in France, but had been unlucky enough to be overrun by General Patton's Third Army soon after landing, so that they had had little opportunity for excitement. The remainder were entirely fresh, and in many cases had not been into action before. Consequently, the whole squadron was simply rearing to go—desperately anxious to prove their worth to the other members of the regiment. They were an excellent lot, varying in age between twenty and thirty-five, many of them being regular soldiers. If anything, their discipline was better than that of the two other squadrons, and during the whole of these operations we did not discover a single passenger.

Since my object is not to give a complete record of the achievements of No. 3 Squadron, 2nd S.A.S. Regiment, but is to give an account of Operation Tombola in particular, I will not go into the details of other operations carried out by the squadron. In any case, the fact that they were all concurrent with my own operation caused my knowledge of their events to be more scanty than my acquaintance with the story of Operation Gallia, which in a way was the forerunner of them all. Walker-Brown was dropped into the area north of Spezia, where he fought outstanding guerrilla actions for three months, in spite of the severe Arctic conditions, lack of supplies, and the fact that the enemy swept the area with over six thousand troops.

It is enough to say that three other operations were carried out between December, 1944, and the end of the war, in addition to Gallia and Tombola. The first was a gallant attempt by Ross Littlejohn and his troop to block the Brenner Pass by causing a landslide. It failed, mainly because the weather was so terrible that it precluded re-supply except at infrequent intervals. In a country which reminded me in a brief view from the air of a film called *Northwest Passage*, his hungry men fought against exposure and snow without fulfilling their main object of blocking the pass. Ross Littlejohn and Corporal Crowley were captured by a German ski patrol and executed by a firing-squad at Bolzano. The two Germans responsible have since paid an equivalent penalty for their crime.

The two other operations were a good one in the Turin area by a Canadian called Captain Buck Macdonald, whose expert handling of a 75-millimetre howitzer spurred the Italian partisans on to the capture of Alba, and secondly, a moderate operation in Walker-Brown's old area under much more favourable weather conditions.

Our inability to score another conspicuous success after Walker-Brown's withdrawal led me to consider dropping in myself with the remaining troop. I suppose I partly felt guilty of an error of judgment in committing Ross Littlejohn to an attack on the Brenner in such appalling weather. When he was reported missing, the feeling became worse. The trouble was that we were so woefully short of experienced leaders. Towards the end of February I decided to lead the next operation, regardless of clear orders from U.K. to remain in command in Florence, and notwithstanding objections which would certainly be raised by Colonel Riepe at Fifteenth Army Group. If I could not go officially, I would have to fake an accidental fall from an aircraft, making sure, of course, that I had a parachute.

I had long toyed with the idea of a really large operation behind the centre of the front, close enough to be able to bring a direct effect to bear on the main tactical battle. In my dreams I visualised myself as a G. A. Henty figure at the head of a whole army of partisans. Fortunately we did not reach such proportions.

Emilia, the province between the Gothic Line and the Po, was divided into departments based on the ancient Emilian cities. Three of these departments seemed suitable for my purpose—namely, Parma, Reggio and Modena, although Parma was perhaps a little too far west. They each had one or two valleys occupied by partisans between the main highways running north and south through the mountains. These partisan formations varied considerably, but on the whole were not very active against the enemy at that time. If the Germans made a drive through their mountain strongholds, they simply parted like a flock of startled birds, eventually returning when the danger had passed.

Each department had its own Partisan Headquarters or Commando Unico, which paid nominal allegiance to the Central Headquarters in Milan. Each Commando Unico controlled a number of brigades, about two-thirds of which were Communist and one-third was Right Wing or Christian Democrat. A partisan brigade was really a battalion of about three to four hundred armed men.

Political feeling ran high and relations were often strained between the Left and Right Wing groups, especially over questions concerning the distribution of arms dropped by the Allies. A British or an American officer was attached to each Commando Unico, and his job was to arm the partisans and to persuade them to fight, the latter not always being easy.

My first move was to ask Charles Mackintosh, commanding Special Forces in Florence, to circulate the British liaison officers in Parma, Reggio and Modena areas, with a view to finding out what their reactions would be to my proposal to drop in about fifty men.

This he did. The answers from Parma and Modena were not encouraging. The British officers concerned feared that the arrival of fifty British parachutists would call down retribution from the Germans, which would destroy all the partisan organisation before the main Allied attack. Michael Lees of Reggio Province was an officer of sterner calibre, however, and replied that he would welcome British troops with enthusiasm. He had been waiting for such an opportunity for months and felt sure that they would have a good effect on partisan morale in the whole area. He could offer several good targets including a corps headquarters, and would carry out an immediate reconnaissance.

I heard that Lees had a wild reputation, but I felt from the tone of his message that if his deeds were as good as his words he was certainly the man for me. I later learned to admire him as the best partisan L.O. in the whole of Italy.

Reggio fitted in well with my plans. The partisans were not quite so scattered as those in the Modena mountains, who were a little closer to the front. The nearest point of the Allied line was at Mount Belvedere, some twelve miles away. This suited our purpose splendidly since we should, with any luck, have time to organise on the ground, unmolested by the Germans.

The next move was to select my team. The squadron had arrived from England under strength, so that I had permission to recruit a few officers and men from the Infantry Depot. I paid this establishment a visit and, after interviewing hundreds of volunteers, chose two officers and ten men on trial. The two officers, Lieut. Tysoe and Lieut. Eyton-Jones, did not have time to complete a parachute course before the operation, and did their first jump behind the enemy lines. As my second-in-command I chose Captain Jock Eyston, a tough old Scot with a heart of gold. He had only just returned from two years in a prison camp and was supposed to be resting in a safe liaison job in Florence. With typical gallantry, he was only too ready to agree when I suggested an operation. My chief difficulty with Jock was that he spoke such broad Scots that I could hardly understand a word he said. To hear him giving orders to a partisan in pidgin Italian with a Falkirk accent was as good as the star turn at the Gaiety in Ayr. Perhaps the most outstanding officer of the troop was Lieut. Riccomini, who had escaped from prison with Eyston. He had only just completed Operation Gallia, but I required him again for his knowledge of Italian, good interpreters being rare. He received the news with something akin to delight. Ken Harvey, a new Rhodesian recruit, was my other officer. He was a nice, clean-faced boy of nineteen.

As for sergeants, I selected Sergeant Godwin, Sergeant Hughes and Sergeant Guscott, who was still with his wireless set in the Spezia area. I decided to order the latter to march across the mountains to join me. Godwin and Hughes were both veterans at the game and thoroughly reliable. I should say that the men in the troop were a good cross section of the whole regiment. They included Ramos and Bruce, two Spaniards who could both speak Italian, an Austrian interpreter called Stevens, and a dear old Italian sailor called Louis, whom Walker-Brown had brought back through the lines. Louis' English was an incredible mixture of Bronx and Whitechapel, even more difficult to understand than Jock Eyston's, but his smile was of greater value than all the interpreters in the world.

It was an odd collection of toughs. I loved every one of their cracked, leathery faces. There was not a single passenger in the whole crew and they marched with the same cocky roll to the end of the operation. Up on Cisa, somebody wrote a song and I can still hear the words rolling down to Febbio.

"We're reckless parachutists, at least that's what we're told,
But when action station's sounded, we don't feel quite so bold,
We're the boys who ride the slipstream, we're the heroes of the
    sky,
But we all know deep inside us, it's an awful way to die !

    "Up off the floor, Up off the floor !
      And I'm seeing scores of gremlins,
    Stand to the door, Stand to the door !
      And me poor old knees are trembling,
    Green light on ! Red light on !
        Out through the door we go,
        Fighting for breath, battered near to death,
        And drifting down to earth below.

"There are some who jump for glory, and some who jump for
    fame,
But if your parachute don't open then you get there just the same,
There's a big court of inquiry and the packer gets the sack,
But all the juries in creation can't fetch the poor chap back ! "

I put the scheme up to Colonel Riepe, who agreed in principle provided that we did not begin to operate until ordered by Fifteenth Army Group. He categorically refused my application to be allowed to command the party. I pretended to accept with good grace, knowing well that it would not be long before a slender thread would hang between me and a court-martial.

I went down to our new billet near Leghorn to check up on the administrative organisation for the first drop. Officially an advance party of Captain Jock Eyston and four men would jump on March 4th, having been despatched from the plane by me. In fact, I intended to lead the stick in front of Eyston and my kit would be pushed out on a separate parachute by an R.A.S.C. packer. The air crew was briefed to tell a sad tale of mishap on their return. They did this so successfully that I was reported as a casualty until my first wireless message came through.

On the 1st March I took the whole squadron for a fifty-mile

march across the mountains. They returned weary and footsore, but with a better idea of what to expect. Many non-essential items of kit were jettisoned when they got back to the billet, and methylated spirits could be smelled everywhere as frantic attempts were made to harden the soles of blistered feet. A great air of excitement ran through the corridors as rucksacks were packed for the last time.

CHAPTER TWO

ARRIVAL IN TOMBOLA VALLEY

IT WAS cold standing in the door of the Dakota, although we could see the sun shining on the snow beneath. We had flown high over Spezia Harbour, but now we were low enough to see little black figures outlined against the tracks in the valleys. All the others had shuffled up behind, staggering under the weights of their sixty-pound leg-bags, as we bounced in the sudden upcurrents of cold air. They were all glancing nervously at the bare, white mountains below; their fumbling fingers were testing their kitbags for tightness. Two Thunderbolts were flying level with our port-side wing. I could plainly see the heads of their pilots in the cockpits.

It had seemed very easy in Florence, but I thought of the future with anything but confidence in that cold slip-stream, away above the Apennines. Apart from the immediate business of getting out of the aircraft, which in any case made it difficult to concentrate on anything else, there was the uncertainty of that which lay before us on the ground. It was different from being dropped as part of a large airborne formation. Then one knows that at least there are lots of others in the same circumstances round about, and that the duration of the operation before a link-up with the main forces is limited. Here we were being dropped behind the front with no prospect of relief for perhaps two, three or even four months. It might have been worse, because at least we were dropping to reception by partisans, but our last wireless contact was three days before, and many things might have happened since then.

Then I began to doubt if we would be dropped at all that day. Even if the pilots, who were by no means infallible, found the dropping zone, it was quite on the cards that the people on the ground would not have the markers out. If this should prove to be the case, should we drop blind? It was important to make it to-day, because the weather was certain to break soon.

I had been shivering in the door for about ten minutes when the aircraft began to lose height. My heart thumped like a bilge pump when I glimpsed a circle of red and yellow parachutes laid

268

out on the snow beneath. There were little black dots moving round it like water spiders on a pond. We circled round slowly for the run-in to drop.

It was a long, narrow valley, and the dropping zone seemed to be in a basin at the southern end. I recognised the largest and whitest mountain as Cusna. It looked very different from the ring of contours on the map. And that long shoulder running towards the plain must be Prampa. Smoke was coming from three or four tiny villages in the valley. I peered at them closely to see if they had been burnt out, the usual sign of a rastrallamento.

The red light went on, which meant that we had ten seconds to go. The dispatcher put his hand over the box, but I told him to take it away, preferring to watch for the light myself. I turned round to look at the rest of the stick. They were pale and nervous, but had enough confidence to raise a smile. Kershaw cocked his thumb up with a grin and shouted something, which was blown away in the slip-stream. It was his first parachute jump. Orthodoxy had never been our strong point.

The ground seemed very low and we could see white, up-turned faces against the snow. I was just contemplating the advisability of another run in, when the green light came on. This was no time to argue, having keyed myself up to the pitch of getting out. Then I was in mid-air. My 'chute opened with a crack, tugging at my shoulders. I heard somebody shout "Woa, Mahomed" as I recovered my breath. Kershaw, I suppose. Fortunately the dropping zone, which was only as big as a suburban back garden, was on a steep slope, and the wind was strong enough to make us drift down the valley. I had barely paid out my leg-bag, when I hit the snow with tremendous force and rolled over twice down the hill. While I was still flat on my back, trying to collapse my parachute, a boy in battledress ran towards me.

He smiled into my hot, uncomfortable face, and shouted, "Buon Giorno. I am Bruno." Before I could recover my breath, he had slung my heavy kitbag over one shoulder and had begun to walk away.

I struggled to my feet, shouted, "Come here, you little brute," and promptly slipped on to my back again. The boy came back, put my kitbag down, and gravely helped me to my feet. With his assistance I rolled up my silk parachute, intending to have at least one souvenir at the end of this operation.

By now the aircraft were running in again with the containers. Clouds of coloured parachutes burst in puffs above us. Many containers were dropped wide and some came whistling down like bombs as they broke away from their chutes.

Seeing no signs of the other members of the stick, I started off up the hill, with my parachute under my arm and the boy following with the kitbag. I climbed, slipped and crawled over ditches and banks up to where I could see several Italians on a track. The surface of the snow had been melted by the sun and had then frozen, making the whole area as slippery as an ice-rink.

On the track, I dumped my kit and took off my airborne smock. It was quite hot in the sun. A tall Italian with a grey beard and a feathered Alpini hat seemed to be in charge. He introduced himself as "Scalabrino," and saluted very smartly, from a proper position of attention. His green jacket, battledress trousers, white socks and long Italian carbine gave him a quaint Robinson Crusoe air, but at least he looked more of a soldier than the motley collection of long-haired youths around him. They were wearing all sorts of bits of uniform—German, Italian, British and American. Round their necks were tied pieces of coloured parachute silk, and they were armed to the teeth with knives, pistols, tommy-guns and rifles. Many had beards and they all had great cascades of black, greasy hair, tumbling over their shoulders. They did not seem very robust and I noticed that several of them had only one eye.

I asked Scalabrino in pidgin Italian and broken English if he had seen the other five members of the stick. He saluted smartly and said, "Yessir," which gave me false encouragement, because I soon learned that this was the sum total of his English vocabulary. I tried again and he pointed towards a village, about a quarter of a mile down the track. I made him understand that I wanted them all to rendezvous with me on the track, and he sent off a partisan boy to find them. The torrent of words and the kick in the bottom with which he accomplished this gave me new respect for his powers of command.

I explained to him that I wanted all the containers dragged in to a central point. With many more kicks and heated words, he soon had the long-haired boys running in all directions. I could see teams of oxen towing sledges, winding up the slope from the village towards the containers. Six mules also appeared and I was duly impressed by the Scalabrino efficiency. He after-

270

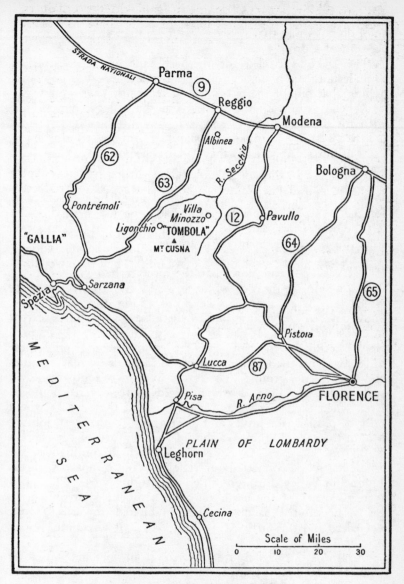

GALLIA AND TOMBOLA AREAS.

wards became my dropping zone king and handled all supply drops. His honesty was far superior to normal valley standards, and I do not think that we ever lost more than about twenty-five per cent of a drop.

The Dakotas circled for the last time and the escort of Thunderbolts did a victory roll in the valley. I waved good-bye, hoping that one of the pilots would report that we were O.K.

Kershaw came up the track from the village, hatless, but with his bronzed face cracked wide in a huge smile. He told me that Eyston had broken his shoulder, but was coming up in a few minutes. Apparently they had dropped on top of the village and their parachutes had barely opened before they struck the ground. Kershaw, himself, had slid off the roof on to the shoulders of an Italian woman. It had given him an anecdote for the rest of the operation and had probably saved his life. All the others were safe, although one kitbag had broken away, smashing Bruce the Spaniard's carbine.

I sat on my parachute and looked round the valley. It all looked very peaceful now that the aircraft had gone. Mount Cusna, a shining mass of white, towered over the whole basin, which ran in the shape of a key, into a long, forge-like valley. Snow covered everything, but nowhere was it very thick, except in occasional drifts. It had already begun to thaw. Over to the west I could see the tiny, grey hovels of Febbio ; only three miles away on the map, but separated from us by many gullies and folds in the ground. The tracks were mere footpaths down steep slopes, and up and over hundreds of ice-covered boulders. Even when the snow went, I could see that these tracks would only be possible for mules and ox-sledges. To the west, joining Mount Cusna and Prampa, a shoulder which formed our western wall, was Cisa Pass. Cisa was a saddle which commanded the whole basin and connected our valley of Villa Minozzo with the Ligonchio Valley, through which ran Highway 63. The south-eastern corner of the basin ran into a much lower and more easily negotiated saddle, which undulated towards Mount Belvedere and the Fifth Army front. In that direction lay our principal danger.

A familiar bronzed figure in an American shirt and battledress trousers came up the track towards me. It was Smith, the Junior Liaison Officer of the Mission, whom I had met in Florence two months before. He looked fit and was in exceptional high spirits.

He had not expected such a luxurious supply drop and five more British soldiers in the valley was a welcome addition, even if it did rouse vague fears of a German drive. He talked excitedly of the formations in the valley and how surprised he was to see me. Had we brought any mail and how was Florence? It was obviously a pleasure to talk English and well it might be, after two months with only one other British officer as a companion in a remote valley in the Apennines. Scalabrino was apparently his pet partisan, and he soon had this faithful old greybeard organised on towing containers into a central store in the village. Scotland was Smith's home, and he was in his natural element in the mountains. He could outwalk and outtalk any man in the valley. I think the partisans had a special soft spot for his Gaelic Italian. Occasionally he would wrinkle his brow in a puzzled frown, which others might have taken for a lack of understanding, but which I soon discovered to be the herald of coming embarrassment. Smith was intensely shy and alternated between fits of bubbling high spirits and acute depression. It was not always easy to be second-in-command to a liaison officer like Mike Lees—the best and yet the wildest, the most difficult to tame, the most domineering mission commander in Northern Italy. I can understand Smith's feelings. He felt that he was being thrust into the background and he so wanted to play a leading role. His private command in the event of trouble was the power station at Ligonchio in the next valley, six hours' march from the mission base at Secchio. This power station was one of those extraordinary neutral islands one so often comes across in guerrilla warfare. It supplied electricity for both the partisan villages in Villa Minozzo and for the German posts along Highway 63. If we cut off the power to the German positions, they would undoubtedly attack and take Ligonchio, which would probably end in neither side having electricity. It was not likely, therefore, that the power station would be destroyed by the Germans, except in the event of a withdrawal when it might well be blown up as part of a scorched-earth plan. Smith's role was one of anti-scorch. He would hold Ligonchio until the last moment and would then demolish the power station in such a way as to only temporarily disable the machinery.

Eyston came staggering up the track, looking very ill. His face was blanched and he held his arm as if in great pain. After being sick twice, he fainted in the snow. We brought him round and carried him to the village, where we put him in the cleanest bed we could find. It looked more like a dislocation to me than a break, but whatever it was there was no doubt about his need of urgent medical attention. Smith sent the boy Bruno off for a doctor, who lived some twelve miles away.

The rest of us had a meal of fried eggs, bread and red wine, all organised by Smith in the village café. It was a picturesque little place, this Casa Balocchi, busy now with mules and bullocks, bringing in loads of containers and parachutes. Peasant girls in bright scarves were leading the oxen and working as hard as the men. Scalabrino had a white horse tied up outside the café. He told me that he had captured it from the Germans last year, during a raid near Barga. The partisans wore red stars in their caps and gay squares of parachute round their necks. In all there were about a dozen houses in the village, joined together by a five-pointed star of steep, cobbled paths, slippery with ice. These cottages looked like hovels from the outside, but the interiors were spotless. A great open charcoal fire with a spit burned in most of them, and they were lit by tiny, naked oil lamps. Peasant dwellings are much the same the world over, and I was reminded vividly of those neat little white farms at home, which one finds every two miles or so all over South Down and County Tyrone.

Mike Lees arrived on a big-boned, brown mare. He was a huge man, with excited, urgent eyes, who pumped my hand until I began to think my parachuting days were over. In all the time I knew him, he was never one to waste a minute.

"Delighted to see you. Had no idea you were coming. What! You jumped without permission. Good show! Have lots of targets for you. Now we can get cracking. These farts are bloody useless. You ought to shake 'em up. Farts is our name for the Itis. You know, corruption of parts, abbreviation of partisan. I've arranged for Monti to come over to-night. He is supposed to be the C.O. around here. Let's get cracking. My base is at Secchio, three hours from here. Sorry I was not here to see you drop. Sent Smith instead. Was everything laid on all right?"

I drew a deep breath, and said:

"But isn't that Secchio on the hill over there?"

He roared with laughter, and replied:

"Yes, that's Secchio all right, but it's not as near as you

274

think. Track's covered with ice. It'll take us about three hours' walking. I'll leave my horse here."

I cannot with truth say that my morale was not slightly shaken by the thought of a three-hour march, but it was not easy not to be infected by Lees' high spirits. We trudged off towards Secchio, my clumsy feet slipping and stumbling over the boulders, as I tried to keep up with the long stride of this dynamic, mountainous man.

CHAPTER THREE

THE ORGANISATION OF THE BATTALION

LEES HAD his own bodyguard of picked partisans, great strapping fellows, who called themselves the "Goufa Nera" or "Black Bats." One of them was playing a guitar in the kitchen and singing "Bandiera Rossa," in a full, unashamed baritone.

The room was lit by a bright, uncovered electric bulb and a large iron stove gave out tremendous heat from one corner. An untidy bookcase full of bottles, paper and glasses covered one wall. The other walls were decorated with postcards of the Holy Lady and a big, gilt-framed picture of Garibaldi at the gates of Rome.

Lees, Monti and I sat round a bottle of Sassuolino on a polished table, with our chairs pushed back and German cigars in our mouths. We were discussing the startling proposal that a new partisan formation with a nucleus of British parachutists should be formed under my command. At least I think it was startling as far as Monti was concerned.

He looked like a soldier, this Monti. A clipped black moustache, a fine upright carriage, a thin handsome face, tightly drawn over his cheek bones, and a slick, dapper appearance gave him the sort of look one associates with a Guards Sergeant-Major in civilian clothes.

It was obvious from the start that the most important thing was Monti's personal prestige. Officially, he was Military Commander of all the partisans in the province—Communists, Christian Democrats, Garibaldini, Green Flames and all the rest of them. He was what they called apolitical, (which is a word meaning apathetic to politics,) and was interested in only strictly military matters. In point of fact, he was something of a puppet king, tolerated by both main parties, but especially by the Communists, of whom he was afraid. If anything his own inclinations were towards the right, although he was so weak that he made more concessions to the Communists than to the Christian Democrats.

All partisan bands in the valley paid lip service to the

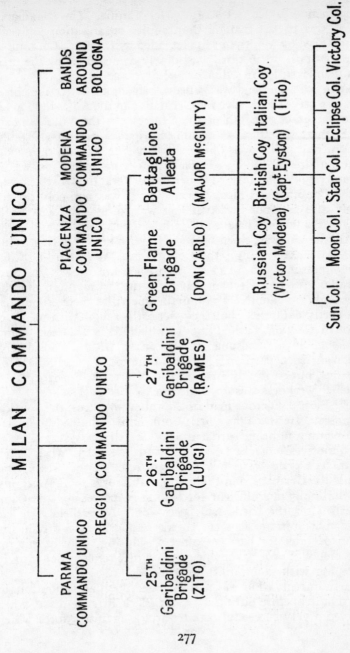

ORGANISATION OF PARTISANS IN APENNINES.

MILAN COMMANDO UNICO

PARMA COMMANDO UNICO — PIACENZA COMMANDO UNICO — MODENA COMMANDO UNICO — BANDS AROUND BOLOGNA

REGGIO COMMANDO UNICO

25TH Garibaldini Brigade (ZITO)

26TH Garibaldini Brigade (LUIGI)

27TH Garibaldini Brigade (RAMES)

Green Flame Brigade (DON CARLO)

Battaglione Alleata (MAJOR McGINTY)

Russian Coy (Victor Modena) — British Coy (Capt Eyston) — Italian Coy (Tito)

Sun Col. Moon Col. Star Col. Eclipse Col. Victory Col.

"Commando Unico" of Reggio Nel 'Emilia. The Commando Unico was in the main a Communist organisation, officially commanded by Monti, but in fact ruled by Nero, his Communist Chief-of-Staff. It, in turn, was loosely commanded by the main Commando Unico in Milan.

Each partisan band was called a brigade to flatter the chiefs. This also served to deceive the Germans and the Allies in Florence as to the exact strength of their forces. In the Villa Minozzo Valley there were three Communist Brigades, called Garibaldini, and one Green Flame or Christian Democrat Brigade, each about three hundred strong. A second right-wing formation was in the process of being formed under Barba Nera, the Quartermaster of the Commando Unico. Ostensibly it was non-political and purely military, but in actual fact was to be a counter-weight to even the adverse balance of numbers between left and right.

All the partisan chiefs were of a very high fighting value. Zito, Rames and Luigi, the Communists, were hard-fighting, honest peasants who had distinguished themselves in three rastrallamentos (or German drives) in the last eighteen months. After eighteen months as mountain guerrillas their ardour had been partly dampened, but they were still tough with plenty of personality. Don Carlo, who commanded the Green Flame Brigade, was a handsome young priest with a considerable reputation as a partisan. I found him to be very gallant on occasions, but so highly strung as to be erratic in performance. His chief weakness was an addiction to intrigue.

The most dangerous man in the valley was Eros, the political commissar. He was a fiery little Communist who had graduated from being a fighting partisan. He was extremely suspicious of Allied motives and yet effused a great surface charm when he felt like it. His plans were only partly directed at the present war against the Germans, and I felt sure that he was more concerned with building up sufficient force to seize power for the Communists after the battle had been won. Nevertheless he had considerable military acumen. He was responsible for introducing badges of rank for partisan officers, saluting, punishment for disobedience of orders, and one or two other reforms not entirely in keeping with Communist doctrine.

Partisan reputation was mainly based upon an action fought nine months before during a Fascist Black Brigade drive, when Nero led a very successful counter-attack against a force which had surrounded Luigi, Eros and fifteen others. All the old Communist partisans of any standing had won their reputations in this battle. Since then, three large rastrallamentos by German and Italian troops had taken a lot of the punch out of both Communists and Green Flames. Although they had dispersed and reassembled with few casualties, they showed great reluctance to make enough nuisance of themselves to warrant further German counter measures. The burning of the mountain villages did not directly affect them, because the majority came from the towns on the plains. What they hated, and we also learned to hate, was the sense of insecurity. Not more than about one small raid a month was therefore carried out. These were usually done by the same intrepid sections of veteran partisans, perhaps twenty men in each brigade. Generally there was some material motive behind the raid, such as the theft of horses from the Pelegosso Front.

Monti's attitude to our proposal was therefore very mixed. He feared that the arrival of British parachutists might cause a fresh German drive. He was afraid that he would be eclipsed by a British officer in his post as Commander of the Commando Unico, although he was secretly relieved that there might be an additional curb on Communist influence. If this British force would only pay lip service to him, he would increase in glory. Also he guessed that there would be increased support in the way of air supply for his valley. The Reggio Nel 'Emilia Province would appear to have been honoured before all others by Allied recognition.

He sat back in his chair, fingering his glass of grappa and agreeing to this big proposition in a way which was most encouraging to me. Actually, Monti was no fool as far as military affairs were concerned, and in the Battaglione Alleato, as it was agreed it should be called, he saw an excellent strategic reserve. Lees explained to him through an interpreter, that as far as actual operations were concerned, we would accept responsibility for no particular zone in the valley, and would receive our orders direct from Florence. We would only come under Monti for administration, although we would naturally co-operate to the best of our ability if the valley were attacked. This was a bitter pill for him to swallow, but he agreed, provided that as far as the other partisans knew, we were a part of the Reggio Commando Unico.

The next thing to be discussed was the composition of the

force. It was agreed that I should absorb the whole of Barba Nera's non-Political Formation. Also, we would have Modena's Russians, who at that time numbered about sixty and were serving with Zito's Garibaldini, on the other side of Highway 67. They were for the most part Russian deserters from the Wehrmacht, who had been conscripted by the Germans, after having been taken prisoner on the Eastern Front. They were highly disciplined and considered by Lees to be the best fighters in the area. Some had actually escaped from German prison camps and had never served in the German Army. I promised that a minimum of fifty British parachutists would be dropped in, and made many rash promises of the stores I expected to receive, all of which I am glad to say were fulfilled. At that time I was, of course, still gambling upon Colonel Riepe's approval of my plans. He might easily have ordered me to return to Florence immediately, and I have always admired him for not having taken the narrow view.

To balance the ostensibly non-political, but in reality rightwing, force of Barba Nera, I asked as a favour from Monti that a detachment of twenty Garibaldini should be attached from each of the brigades of Rames and Luigi, intending to keep them to make my British company up to strength, but pretending to offer to train them in the use of heavy machine-guns. This proved to be a sound move, and during the whole of this operation we had very little political trouble from either side.

As far as basic rations were concerned, Monti agreed that we should draw certain items of meat and flour from Commando Unico resources. He promised to try to obtain for me at least six mules, notwithstanding the fact that the total number in the valley for all purposes was only thirty.

I knew that our administrative side would be well looked after by Barba Nera if I gave him enough money, since he had all the knowledge acquired by a year as Chief Quartermaster of the valley. All the arrangements seemed highly satisfactory.

Having exchanged handshakes to seal the bargain, we opened another bottle of grappa. Lees, who had been the force behind all the negotiations, clapped his hands for one of the Goufa Nera. A huge partisan with a piano accordion entered, and sat on a chair in the corner of the room. He tossed back his shiny black locks, loosened an orange kerchief round his neck, and began to sing in a rich, melodious voice :

"Avanti, avanti, Brigata Garibaldi !
Patrioti, patrioti, Brigata Garibaldi !
Far niente, far niente, avanti patria,
Insieme, partigani, noi siamo in guerra."

Some hours later, after Lees had sung his own special marching song, which was something about "the cow kicking Nelly in the belly in the barn," we steered Monti to his big brown mare and waved him off down the track on his long ride back to Febbio.

CHAPTER FOUR

FORMATION OF THE BATTAGLIONE ALLEATO

EARLY the next morning Victor Modena arrived. Purely by chance he had been passing through the area, and had decided to come to Secchio to plead for more arms from Lees. I was overjoyed. A staffeta or messenger would have taken two days to reach Zito's brigade, and I had not hoped to put my plan to the Russians for at least a week.

Modena was a big, blond Russian from Smolensk, with a charming smile on his face and a very captivating swashbuckler's air. He had a great reputation as a partisan and had been one of the first twenty to come to the valley. He was universally respected for his bravery. His Russians were highly disciplined compared to the Italians, and were very proud of their superiority. As far as politics were concerned, I think that Modena and his Russians were absolutely neutral and were certainly less fervent Communists than the Italian Garibaldini.

I put Modena's age at about twenty-seven. He wore a blue peaked sailor's cap and German jack-boots—exactly the costume I would have expected a Russian to wear. Round his neck he had wound a strip of Cambridge blue parachute silk. His horse, which he had captured on the Pelegosso Front, was the best in the valley. Its chief assets lay in its sure-footedness and enormous strength—two astride being a common spectacle amongst partisans.

Modena did not attempt to conceal his delight at being so honoured. At last he would fight with proper soldiers, and his priority for arms and equipment would be the highest in the valley. He said that he would immediately increase the size of his force to a hundred Russians, by gathering in any odd deserters who had attached themselves to other partisan formations. Actually, Russian deserters were coming in every day from the 162 Turkoman Division, so that his plan was quite feasible. I agreed, but placed the limit at a hundred, not wishing to be embarrassed by too large a force, with an overwhelming preponderance of Russians. He undertook to start out for his band immediately, and to concentrate them in Governara, a village near the dropping zone at Casa Balocchi. When I explained the transport difficulties, he winked and said that he would steal twelve mules from Zito, who, being on the other side of Highway 63, was better off for animals.

In the afternoon Barba Nera called from Quara. He was quite a fine-looking Italian, who had been a sergeant in the Air Force. He wore a very smart battledress and a black beard. His reputation as a militarist was not an outstanding one, but his experience in partisan administration was invaluable. I officially appointed him as Vice-Commandant of the New Battalion and told him to raise an Intendance Staff of fifteen good men, who would be responsible for rationing and equipping the companies. He would receive 45,000 lira a week for purchasing extra rations, and I would personally give each Company Commander 30,000 lira each week for the purchase of extra cigarettes, tobacco and vino. Partisans did not receive any pay.

These sums of money seem large, but the Apennines are very poor and excursions would have to be made to the plains for purchase from the black market. In addition, there was the problem of finding fodder for the mules and paying for the hire of the numerous bullock-carts we would need for big supply drops. I pointed out that any extra money required could be found from the surplus parachutes and containers there would be certain to be after the supply drops.

Eyston had recovered a little from his hard landing and had begun to organise a billet for the British in an old disused church at Tapignola. Two local doctors had given him a terrible gruelling, but had managed to get his shoulder back into position. His spirit in bearing up so well with the pain was beyond all praise.

Furthermore, he had commandeered one of the only two non-partisan horses in the valley as a mount for me. The owner, a voluble widow from the village of Corignano, complained bitterly, but I am afraid we had to be ruthless in such matters. It was a beautiful little black pony, which was probably a bit young for work in the mountains, but nevertheless did good service under me for the next two months. Jock constructed a bit out of the handle of a kitbag, a saddle from a piece of felt, and all the rest of the equipment from parachute harness. He also got one of the village girls to sew some pretty cockades of blue silk, which made us look as though we had won the first prize for dressage in the coster pony class at Lambeth Fair.

On 6th March I rode down to Quara with Mike Lees to address the Italian Company. We dismounted and tied our horses up to a tree in the main street. The houses round about began to disgorge Italians. It was obvious that Barba Nera was making a great effort to impress. The officers, who were the only ones in battledress, were shouting and waving their arms. Eventually the company formed up in two woebegone ranks. Barba Nera saluted smartly and the inspection began.

I was very shaken indeed by the raw material. It looked like a tableau of Wat Tyler's Rebellion. The men were all young, but nearly all of them had some physical defect. Many had only one eye. Some had one shoulder higher than the other, and they all looked as though they were in the grips of some horrible disease.

It appeared that Mike Lees' forebodings were correct. They were the worst partisans in the valley and had only arrived recently from the plains to avoid conscription for labour by the Todt Organisation. They were dressed in all sorts of bits of uniform. About half were armed with rusty old rifles, which I should have hated to have had to fire. The others had nothing. Some had not even shoes on their feet.

I began the address. I told them what wonderful chaps they were, but that soon we would make them into something better. Where my words were not sufficiently flowery, the interpreter added his own poetry to the translation. I said that Italy was glorious and would live again; that they would get shoes and battledress and good food and arms; and that they must realise now that they were Italian soldiers about to fight for their motherland. At the word fight, I suspected that several faces dropped. I said that they were to follow me and Tito, their new commander, just as they had followed Barba Nera. I called for a cheer for Italy. A small cheer floated back.

We then adjourned to quite a fine house for lunch with the officers. Barba Nera had laid on a splendid meal with excellent wine. I liked the look of Tito, in spite of the rumour that he had run away to Civago in the last German drive. Pompeio, his second-in-command, was a long-haired, garrulous boy, who was eventually transferred to Barba Nera's Headquarters Staff. They were all worried about the limitation I had imposed on their numbers, because their ulterior aim had been a right-wing force to balance the Communists, although they stoutly protested that this was far from the truth. Another thing that secretly worried them was a suspicion that they were to be a shock force to carry out actual operations, instead of sitting in military splendour in the mountains like the majority of the partisans. They were prepared to go ahead with the plan, but were apprehensive about the future. The move of making Barba Nera Vice Commandant of the battalion had really won the day and they had very little option but to accept.

The next day we received confirmation of a night drop to bring in three officers, one instructor and an Italian interpreter. I had demanded these officers ahead of the main force with a view to training the Russians and the Italians. They were not old, experienced members of the regiment, but were the recruits I had obtained from the Infantry Depot three weeks before, to make up the casualties we had sustained in France. In two cases there was not time to give them a parachute course, but working on the principle that parachuting must not be considered a bogey and is only a means of getting to the objective, I insisted on their doing their first jump on the operation. The interpreter was the old guide whom Major Walker-Brown had found during his brilliant operation north of Spezia in January, the old sailor with a lion's heart called Louis, who was now to make his first jump.

We built bonfires in the form of a letter X and lit them at about eleven o'clock. When the deep throb of aircraft engines could be heard behind Cusna, we also lit green, phosphorescent flares, which reflected against the snow to give the whole scene a green glow of phantom twilight. The light struck the silver belly of the Halifax as limelight picks out a tinselled dancer on a darkened stage. Then one, two, three—a space where someone had hesitated at the door—four, five, we counted, as a perfect stick of huddled figures was strung out across the sky, long, squeezed grapes of billowing silk behind them. Poor Louis made a perfect landing, as he had been told in Leghorn, but a gust of wind caught him before he could release his chute. He was dragged some twenty yards across the ice, until he was anchored by a deep gully, breaking his shoulder in much the same way as Eyston. The others all made soft landings in the snow.

A large quantity of stores and weapons was dropped, which

made certain of my success from the start. It was obvious to them all that I had the full support of the Allies, since I had conjured up the biggest drop ever seen in the valley within three days of my arrival. A night drop, even if more dangerous, was a spectacular business, and I am sure that every eye in Febbio was watching the flares and fires. This demonstration of power was the prime cause of the success of the operation, since it engendered immediate confidence in both Russians and Italians. Having been at the Florence end myself, I appreciated how much work Walker-Brown must have put into laying it all on. Scalabrino was delighted at his new importance as O.C. Dropping Zone. I do not think that we lost more than a dozen pairs of boots from the whole drop.

The next fortnight was spent in equipping and training the companies. On 9th March, an advance party of twenty-four British officers and men was dropped in safely by day on the same dropping zone. One officer and four British other ranks were attached to the Russian and Italian companies: both as a stiffening and for instructional purposes. Each company was concentrated in a village on Mount Prampa, the British, who finally numbered forty, being quartered in the church at Tapignola. The Russians created quite a stir when they first arrived, marching past the British billet in step followed by their mules. In the half-light they were nearly mistaken for Germans, since no other partisans marched with any semblance of discipline. They proved to be exceptionally keen students. In fact, the Russians were so mechanically minded that they mastered the stripping and firing of a three-inch mortar in one day. Machine-gun classes could be seen every day on the village greens of Governara and Corignano. I frequently rode over on my horse from Secchio to inspect progress and occasionally to show them off to Mike Lees.

During the period from the 8th to the 23rd March I received orders from Fifteenth Army Group not to operate against the enemy, but to concentrate on training and equipping my battalion until the time was ripe.

In view of the obvious difference a stiffening of British personnel had made to partisan morale in the area, I decided to send out detachments with heavy machine-guns under the command of British other ranks, with the object of forming a first line of defence to protect our base in the Villa Minozzo

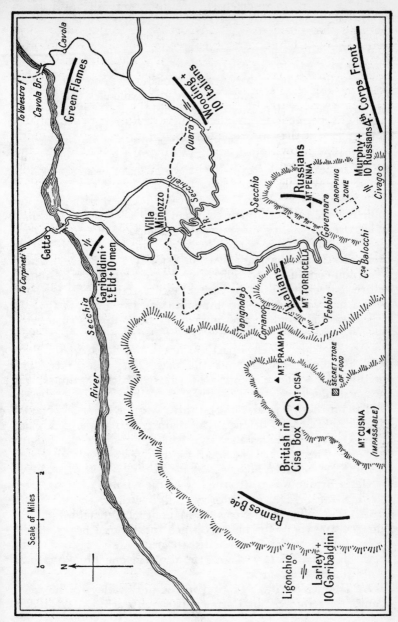

TOMBOLA VALLEY.

Valley. Some of these defensive positions were already held by partisans, but in view of Lees' opinion that they would run away if pressed, I reinforced them with these detachments. I expected that these outpost positions would delay the enemy sufficiently long to give us time to organise ourselves in the main positions in the valley. The whole idea of offering firm resistance to a German drive was contrary to accepted principles of guerrilla warfare, but my view was that we could not afford to give up our base, when the army offensive was so imminent. I might say that I had never thought on these lines in a previous operation, but considered that this time a successful drive by the enemy would so scatter my force that it would have been impossible to re-form in time.

It was extraordinary how successful the British common soldiers were as detachment commanders. They reacted to their sudden responsibility magnificently. I suppose the inborn contempt a Briton feels for all foreigners made them go out of their way to demonstrate their superiority. Very few of them were non-commissioned officers or had ever had responsibility before. Parachutist Murphy commanded a section of ten Russians with a heavy Browning machine-gun and two Brens at Civago, which was the remotest and most dangerous outpost. He became the benevolent despot of this little village within three days. On one occasion, when a partisan drank too much in the local café, Murphy promptly put the place out of bounds. The intelligence about the enemy, which he sent back by runner, was most valuable.

The northern boundary of our area was the River Secchia, an excellent obstacle to defend. The main crossing was at a place called Gatta, which was already defended by Luigi's Garibaldini Brigade. There was also a small footbridge at Cavola, defended by Don Carlo's Green Flames.

Gatta Bridge was really the key to the whole valley, so, after blowing the bridge, I reinforced Luigi with a section of ten British (including one Norwegian) under Lieutenant Eld. He dug good positions for his three-inch mortar and heavy water-cooled Vickers machine-gun, sited to bring fire to bear on both the bridge and Gatta village. He also had one Bren for local protection of the mortar.

At Ligonchio Power Station in the next valley to the west, Rames was reinforced by Corporal Larley, Parachutist Whittaker and ten of my Garibaldini, with a thirty-seven millimetre cannon. To bolster up the Green Flame Brigade at Quara, I sent Parachutist Wooding with ten members of the Italian Company and a heavy Browning machine-gun.

By now the battalion was beginning to take shape. Each company was about a hundred strong. Every man was equipped with battledress, a khaki beret, good boots and a weapon of some description. The Italian Company wore green and yellow feathers in their hats and an embroidered badge on their pockets with our motto—" Who dares wins " or " Chi osera vincera." I regret to say that the British often parodied this motto to read "Who cares who wins," but I am sure that nobody would believe that they meant it—much. The Intendance Staff under Barba Nera was functioning well and for one drop we requisitioned as many as a hundred bullock carts. Each company had six mules, in various stages of debilitation.

Everything we asked for from base was dropped. I asked for a piper to stir the romantic Italian mind and to gratify my own vanity. Within three days, Piper Kirkpatrick of the Highland Light Infantry dropped by day, kilt and all, with his pipes under his arm. To the excitement of the partisans, he piped retreat each evening across the valley from Tapignola. I signalled back with a torch, if I had heard it plainly and was satisfied. One of the greatest moments was when the British Company gave a demonstration of the eightsome to the Garibaldini, who, I am sure, thought them completely mad.

Jock Eyston raised a squad of runners from the fittest members of the Italian Company. Apart from their normal duties of carrying despatches, they provided orderlies for the company commanders and myself. Jock had my pseudonym, " McGinty," embroidered on their pockets, and invented a badge consisting of a bow and arrow, with the word "speed" underneath.

About once a week I sent one of these " staffetas" through the lines with despatches for Florence. They were never caught, although two were badly wounded on mines.

Perhaps the most colourful section of all was the Intelligence Squad raised by an Italian called " Keess." This consisted of fifteen strong-legged partisan girls. Their functions were numerous. Apart from cooking and sewing and mending, they were excellent for reconnoitring German-held villages. It was a trick I had learned in France. Where a man could never venture without faultless identity papers, an attractive girl could pedal a bicycle through a German-held village with impunity. They could also carry messages with greater safety than a man. Keess sent them on numerous long expeditions to the plains for information and they never failed. Oh, how a woman can loosen a soldier's tongue ! These girls could march better than any man in the company, and their morale was always high, in spite of the fact that they lived in the same filthy conditions as the men. Later on they cared for the wounded, loaded machine-guns, carried despatches, and were always a good influence on morale. When the Germans attacked at Gatta, one of our blondes was the only Italian to stay behind with the British.

One girl in particular will always remain in my memory. Her name was Noris and she was a tall, raven-haired girl with Irish blue eyes. She was as brave and dangerous as a tigress, and was completely devoted to the British Company. When she was not dressed in her finery for a reconnaissance, she wore a red beret, a battledress blouse and a thick grey skirt made from an army blanket. The pistol in her waist-band was a sign that she was more than capable of taking care of herself. John Stott, the Liaison Officer from Modena Valley, used to say that she had all the devils of the world in those eyes. Noris was worth ten male partisans.

On the hills round the basin at the southern end of the valley we conscripted civilian labour to build deep earthworks. These main defensive positions were permanently garrisoned by the various companies. The Russians were on Mount Penna, facing east towards the front at Mount Belvedere, ten miles away. They were equipped with one three-inch mortar, one heavy Browning, an Italian 45-millimetre cannon and ten Bren guns. I considered that Mount Cusna, which ran from east to west along the south of the basin, was not necessary to defend, since the thick, melting snow would make it impassable for another month. Between Cusna and Prampa lay the high Cisa Pass. Here the British Company constructed an all-round defensive position known as the Cisa Box. Enough food was buried for seven days on all positions, and another seven days' supply was hidden in the thick snow behind Mount Cusna, which would be our last retreat if all other positions collapsed. The Italians were similarly dug in on Mount Torricella, covering both the valley and the basin with a forty-seven millimetre cannon, a three-inch mortar and ten Bren guns. On Cisa Pass we mounted our strong piece—a 75-millimetre howitzer, which Walker-Brown had contrived to drop by parachute for the first time in history. It was christened "Molto Stanco," after the sweat and tears expended in dragging it up to the top of the pass. The British Company also had a mortar, a Vickers machine-gun and ten Brens.

My plan of defence was in three phases. In the first instance I ordered the detachments on the outposts to hold on as long as possible, after the partisans had fled. They would then withdraw slowly into the main positions. After a week, the Russians on Penna and the Italians on Torricella would withdraw into the Cisa Box.

During this first defensive period, the only contact with the enemy was at Quara, when a German patrol penetrated the Green Flame position at Ceredelo and crossed the River Secchia. On encountering opposition from Wooding's Browning they withdrew.

On about the 20th March, Mike Lees suggested over a bottle of grappa that the battalion was now ready to go into action. We agreed that the most tempting target was the German Corps Headquarters at Albinea, where the foothills ran into the valley of the Po. Lees had obtained considerable information on the layout of the headquarters, and it looked as though we would be able to get within five miles of the place under cover of the foothills.

Maria and Argentina, two of the female staffetas, were sent down to the plain to confirm that the positions of the sentries had not changed since our first information. They returned with a glowing report of the possibilities of the target.

Accordingly, it was proposed to Fifteenth Army Group that we should be allowed to carry out this attack before the time set for our other activities. Fifteenth Army Group agreed and dropped in air photographs. Later they revoked their decision. It was too late. We were already on our way to the plains.

CHAPTER FIVE

THE ATTACK ON THE CORPS HEADQUARTERS

IT WAS unfortunate that the Germans should have chosen this moment for a drive. It appeared that they were advancing with about one battalion strung out in line from the Po Valley at Scandiano straight towards the River Secchia. Wild rumours were flying about as to their exact intentions and position. The ill-organised partisans of the foothills had fallen back before them without firing a shot. It was certain that they were in Baiso, the next village, because we could see them through binoculars from the high hill above our position at Vallestra. What we were not sure of, however, was where in the valley they had billeted their sections and when they intended to advance again.

Lees and I were both convinced that if we did not carry through the attack, having got so far as the start-line, we never would. Security in the valley was so bad that rumours of the impending raid would soon reach German ears and we would never have the same opportunity again.

I looked around the farm at the tired figures sprawling on the grass. We had to go through with it. What would the Communists think if the loud-sung Battaglione Alleato was so easily discouraged on its first operation? If the Germans did not attack us before the next night we would march. I cursed the Russians for being so exhausted that they could not go on that night. What was Modena thinking of to have allowed them to come up the hills at such a pace? To-morrow night was the night. If I could not infiltrate a hundred men through a widely dispersed battalion at night, it was time I went on the staff. At that moment a runner arrived from the wireless set at Secchia, bearing a signal from Fifteenth Army Group, which ordered me not to attack. The moment, they said, was inopportune. That decided me. We would march at dusk on the morrow. Did those pen-pushing map-boys in Florence understand that if I did not attack now I would never attack at all? Did they understand that my prestige with the partisans would be *nil*? In my foolish, blind rage at having my movements ordered from so far away,

I failed to understand that I was attacking the right headquarters at the wrong time. How could I understand that the main Allied thrust was to be against this corps in ten days' time, and that my attack might put them on the qui vive? It is so easy to be wise after the event, and after all, little harm was done; but when I returned to Florence and heard the true story, I thanked God for Riepe's mercy in not having me court-martialled and resolved never to question a staff decision again.

They were a motley crowd of ruffians. In all there were thirty Russians, forty mixed Italians and twenty-four British, including Lees and myself. Most of them were asleep in the ox-sheds or in the hay, but a small knot of Garibaldini with silk scarves round their heads were singing softly a partisan song. Their boots were cracked and they looked half-starved, but their morale was good. I had borrowed twenty veterans from Luigi's Communist Brigade, not yet trusting my own company. I could hear Kirkpatrick tuning up his pipes. Most of the British were on lookout, watching towards the Germans in Baiso, but one or two were cleaning their tommy-guns by the wall, listening to the Garibaldini. Swarms of frightened peasants were hurrying down the track towards the mountains away from the Germans. Most of them seemed to be men. I suppose they were afraid of being conscripted for labour by the Todt Organisation. Noris and Valda were sitting amongst the singers, occasionally casting provocative glances at the English. A typical Cockney wisecrack in broken Italian would be answered by peals of laughter, and Valda would whisper some sly retort in Noris' ear. It was hard to believe that great danger lay only five miles away and that by to-morrow we would be in the thick of it.

I called for Yani of the Garibaldini and Modena, the Russian, to collect their men. They gathered round me in a loose, ill-assorted crowd. Even the British looked unkempt. You cannot live in ox stables and on the tops of mountains for weeks and still look like a guardsman.

There was plenty of colour in the crowd, however. Here and there, amongst the dirty khaki, were red berets, bits of parachute silk, green and yellow plumes, a few red stars and the summer frocks of the girls. Everyone seemed to be armed to the teeth, with knives, pistols, sub-machine guns and bullets.

I explained the plan for the attack over the air photographs we had received from Florence. Each sentence was translated first into Italian and then into Russian. We would infiltrate through the enemy positions as soon as it became dark, marching quietly in three tightly-packed columns led by me with two local guides and two British scouts. On the left, Lieutenant Harvey, the Rhodesian, would lead a column of ten British and twenty Garibaldini. In the centre, Lieutenant Riccomini would lead ten British, the Goufa Nera and Lees bringing up the rear with the girls. Modena and the Russians would form the right-hand column. We would march all night until we reached our lying-up position in a farm called Casa del Lupo, ten miles from the objective. If we encountered any opposition during the march, everybody would lie still in their tracks until orders were received from the front. On no account would fire be returned unless ordered. The danger signal would be the leading files going flat, at which everyone would follow suit immediately. At Casa del Lupo we would confine all civilians to the farm.

We would remain under cover during the day until it again became dark, when we would advance in the same three columns towards the German Headquarters. The difficult point would be at the crossing of the main road, one mile before the objective, when it was very important that we should not be spotted.

The Headquarters consisted of two main buildings, separated from the foothills by a large number of small houses in which the troops were billeted. Of the two main buildings, one was the Chief of Staff's villa and operations room, and the other was the residence of the Corps Commander. Between these villas, ran the main road, and each was guarded by four sentries. In addition, there were six machine-gun positions sited tactically round the camp.

I had decided to concentrate on the two important villas and to place the Russians in a semi-circle to the south to isolate these targets from assistance from the remainder of the headquarters. Ten British would force an entry into each villa, after killing the sentries. They would be immediately reinforced by twenty Italians at each building.

After I had explained the plan, I gave a few words of encourage-to the Italians. There was a small mutiny when they demanded that we should stay where we were to help the partisans of the foothills to repel the German drive. It was plain that this was sheer bravado, and it was soon made clear through Yani that the attack on this German Headquarters would have a much greater bearing on the war. Even if they had stayed, they would have done very little to stop the Germans. A few gallant rounds might have been fired in the air at long range, which would have served only to anger the enemy, not to stop him.

Kirkpatrick in his kilt then gave them "Blue Bonnets Over the Border" as a grand finale. They stood around in their ragged, colourful circle and clapped their hands with delight. The pibroch echoed between the hills, while crowds of refugees, hurrying towards safety in the mountains, looked at the scene with mouths agape. One of the boys broke into a fling on the lawn and then started to give Noris elementary instruction in the pousette. After the strains of the pipes had died away, they broke into the soft, defiant lilt of a partisan song.

As I walked up to the look-out on the high ground above Vallestra, their voices followed me up the track. Let me get them in that mood for the attack and nothing in the world could stop us.

From the machine-gun post, we could see through glasses that the files of Germans in blue-grey uniform were marching in step up the hill towards Baiso. I released a satisfied sigh. That surely was a sign that they were 'going into billets for the night, and did not intend to drive any farther before the morning.

Even so, it was an uncomfortable night, with every sound starting me up from my bed. There were so many restless nights like that behind the lines. I think the strain on the nerves caused by constant watchfulness was the most tiring thing of all.

At first light the next day we were up by the look-out on Vallestra, gazing anxiously towards Baiso. All day there were excited rumours of further German advances. The partisans round about were very jumpy and all threatened to withdraw headlong over the Secchia into the mountains. Most of these rumours proved to be false. Odd shots, the unmistakable tack-pung of a Mauser, were occasionally heard from the valleys, but it seemed that the enemy was only advancing slowly towards Carpineti.

Evening arrived and we were still safe. As the sun was going down behind Carpineti Castle, I gave the order to begin. Hans, a German deserter, had captured a large German Diesel lorry on the Sassuolo road, and Lees had arranged for it to be towed across the Secchia by sixteen bullocks. I never quite got the story of

295

the capture of this lorry clear in my mind, but I believe Hans had stood out in the road, dressed in German uniform, and had just ordered it to stop. He had then shot the driver with a Sten gun. How he had managed to get it up to the hills I will never understand. Anyway, it was ideal for carrying us on the first two miles of our twenty-mile trek, since the road was clear as far as the blown bridge at Riccomente. Hans ferried the force down as far as this in three lifts, past odd amazed partisans, who presumably thought that we were about to launch the first counter-attack in the history of the valley.

We began marching down the hill, along narrow tracks, by-passing Baiso to the west. The long column trudged along in complete silence. Sometimes a pebble would go tumbling down the cliff and an angry, muttered word would rebuke the offender. As we came to odd farms and hamlets, the leading files would lie flat and everybody behind would follow suit. The two British scouts would creep forward with an Italian guide and, finding all clear, would whistle us on. We seemed to march up and down those hills for hours. Sometimes we would stop for a drink at a stream or interrogate an Italian peasant in some lonely farm as to the whereabouts of the Germans. One cottager, at the bottom of a valley below Baiso, told us that a German section had left at six o'clock. The dogs were a nuisance. At every house they seemed to bark, and dogs all over the hills would take up the cry.

We had to cross Highway 63 at Casa del Pazzi, which we knew to be occupied by German Security Police. It was unfortunate that just as we were coming up to it we should lose our way. One of the Garibaldini came up from the back of the column and claimed that his home was not far from where we were, and that the guide had taken us out of our way. After a long whispered argument he took over the navigation, and we passed so close to the village that we could have thrown stones at the houses. Our hearts were beating wildly, and I found that I was biting my lip when the dogs began to bark. The moon had risen and it seemed that a sentry would be certain to observe our long, straggling column. Nothing happened, and we reached the top of a steep hill above the main road with relief.

It was apparent that we were all tired, except the girls, who were not burdened with heavy weapons. I called a halt for thirty minutes. A fresh egg was mysteriously produced by Noris, and wonderful clear, cool water was brought in buckets from a tiny cowshed known to the partisans.

We lay on our backs, faces turned to the stars, wishing that the march was over. It is at such moments as these that one regrets turning down a soft staff job in Cairo. I was worried about Mike, who had suddenly developed malaria. He was in pretty poor shape, but refused to go back. Ricky, who commanded the centre column, said that some of the Italians were labouring under their loads. I refused permission to throw away a few grenades, but promised to moderate the pace. The thirty minutes passed all too quickly, and it was soon time to move on again. Andiamo! Andiamo! The word was whispered down the files, and we heaved ourselves to our feet.

The going was easier now. The worst bit was over and we were getting into the lower foothills. Not a soul was seen, as we straggled on through woods, over streams, around villages and farms, up and down the hills towards the plain.

It was nearly dawn when Casa del Lupo appeared on the top of a hill. Ken Harvey swiftly reconnoitred the buildings to find all clear. No Germans had been in the area for two days. Our luck was in, and when daybreak brought a thick Scotch mist, we thanked God for kind weather.

The farm was big enough to house the whole band, and soon everyone was fast asleep in the lofts and ox-sheds. Two sentries manned Bren guns in the upper windows, while the remainder made the most of the opportunity to rest. The old farmer was very frightened, but his natural joviality soon reasserted itself. He produced bottles of wine, slices of bread and rich salami sausage in the kitchen for Lees and me. His son, it seemed, was still serving in a Blackshirt division, but his politics were so hazy that he thought we were on the same side. Poking our ribs with a stubby finger, he roared with laughter as he told us the family joke about his child being the son of the priest. Poor old Mike was in no mood for humour. The fever had really taken hold of him, and the only solution we could think of was another bottle of grappa. I suggested that he should go back or stay in the farm, but he would not hear of it. His face was flushed and he was running a high temperature. Only a man with a giant frame like Lees could have carried on so far. I was worried.

At midday I sent off the girls to look at the target. They

came back at about five o'clock with good news. Everything seemed normal in Albinea.

The mist was still thick in the evening. We could not have wished for better weather. A guide from the farm agreed to take us down to the main road.

The three columns wound down the last few slopes, knee-deep in thick, wet grass. Only the girls remained behind in the farm, and I had to be very rude to ensure that they stayed. Looking back up the hill, the black figures seemed like tall trees as they moved cautiously towards the road. The slightest strange sound made us go flat as one man. Suddenly we were overlooking the valley of the Po. Clusters of lights showed us where the big towns lay, and we could see the silver streak of the river winding between them. Everything seemed so near. We felt that we could see to the Alps and that everyone in Italy could see us. And then down into the mist once more.

We were startled when we reached the road so soon. Fortunately it was deserted in both directions, and we were across in a flash. I gritted my teeth at the terrible noise as, one after another, the hundred tired bodies wriggled under the hedge on the far side. An unsuspected dyke brought several of us to our knees. Then we were making the last sweep round to come in from the north. Farms lay close together, and the ground was level now. Occasional dogs barked, but nobody stirred in the houses. We tiptoed on with our hearts in our mouths.

Across a big field, and I was just wondering if we had lost our way, when the moon clearly shone on Villa Calvi, straight ahead. It was easy to recognise it from the air photographs. Perched on a small hill, it was a large white mansion, surrounded by trees. No lights were showing, and I began to wonder if the Germans were really there. Farther back and slightly to the right was Villa Rossi, the residence of the Corps Commander. Everything was in the right place. There was the guard-room, and there was the telephone exchange, where there were reported to be two machine-guns. Even farther to the right were the troops' billets and the prison. It seemed so peaceful. The quietness of it all alarmed me.

We moved on to the dispersal point behind the wood near Villa Calvi. I began to get that old excited feeling. Over and over again I repeated the "Hail Mary." Fear, nerves, excitement,

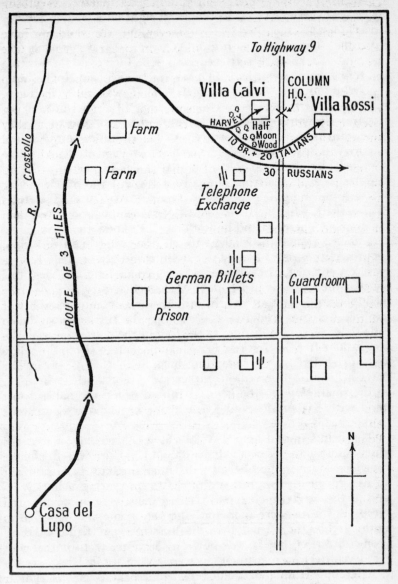

ATTACK ON GERMAN CORPS HEADQUARTERS.

apprehension, worry, plans—all jumbled up together to make me start at every noise. It would be all right once we got going. I tried to say something to Ken Harvey, but the words would not come. Then I tripped into a slit trench. I lost my pistol in the mud. Kirkpatrick retrieved it. I sent him over for Ricky, and found my voice at last. In a whisper which came in gushes, I pointed out the various targets. That was the telephone exchange, where there were two Spandaus. Modena would look after it. He was to be careful crossing the road, and to watch in the direction of the guard-room. After twenty minutes he was to withdraw, whether he saw the red Verey light or not. I wished him luck and told him that I would give him three minutes to make the front door. Poor Ricky, I was never again to see him, and Mike too, who is crippled for life. The ten British, with Mike and the Goufa Nera behind, moved off at the double. There was no hesitation. They knew their job.

I looked around for Modena to tell him to move off to form his protective screen. I could not see him and got excited. Kirkpatrick went to look, but after a few seconds he came back to say that the Russians had gone. I guessed that they had left for their positions without orders, which was fair enough. Three minutes were up, and it was Ken Harvey's turn to approach Villa Calvi. I guided him up to the foot of the house and wished him luck. After the first few British had begun to climb the hill, we noticed that we were standing on a minefield. Who cared? The Garibaldini followed on, rather more reluctantly, winding up the small slope to the lawn. I moved round the half-moon wood with Kirkpatrick and Keess to my headquarters position on the road.

The firing started first at Villa Calvi. A tremendous burst, which must have been a whole Bren magazine, was fired by someone. Tracer bullets began to fly in all directions. Although we had reason to congratulate ourselves on getting a hundred men to the target unobserved, the Germans were by no means asleep. Spandaus were soon spraying the whole area from the south. I thought at first that the Russians were firing in the wrong direction, but it was not long before I realised that at least seven German machine-guns were awake. I told Kirkpatrick to strike up "Highland Laddie," just to let the Germans know that they had the British to contend with. He had only played a few bars, when the phut-phut of a Spandau picked us out. I pushed him into a slit trench and he continued to play from his cramped position.

At Villa Calvi Ken Harvey killed two sentries on the lawn before they realised that they were being attacked. The front door was locked, but was soon burst with a bazooka bomb. Four Germans were killed on the ground floor, but others fought back valiantly down the spiral staircase. In one room, Harvey was confronted by a German with a Schmeisser. He ducked, but neglected to extinguish his torch. Fortunately, Sergeant Godwin was quick with his tommy-gun, and shot over Harvey's shoulder. Several attempts were made to get up the stairs, but the Germans kept up a concentrated fire from the first floor, which made it impossible. Corporal Layburn was wounded by a grenade rolled down from above. Another British parachutist called Mulvey was hit in the knee by a bullet.

From the lawn outside an equally furious battle raged against the top windows. Several Germans were killed by bazooka and tommy-gun fire. Harvey realised that it was impossible to take the house in the twenty minutes allowed. He therefore decided to start a fire on the ground floor. Working frantically against time, the British heaped up maps, chairs, files and curtains in a great pyre in the middle of the operations room. With the aid of a few pounds of explosive and a bottle of petrol, the trail was laid and ignited. The wounded were carried out to safety, while the Germans were kept inside by tommy-gun fire until the whole house was ablaze.

At Villa Rossi things had not gone so well. I had not allowed Riccomini sufficient time to cross the road, and Ken Harvey had opened fire on Calvi too soon. A siren gave the alarm from the roof of Villa Rossi, and all the lights were turned on. Ricky killed four sentries through the iron railing with his tommy-gun and then rushed the door. It was open, but a hail of fire greeted them at the foot of the stairs. Somebody, I think Taylor, shot out the lights. Four Germans were killed and two surrendered on the ground floor. I believe the Goufa Nera dealt with the prisoners. Two attempts were made to carry the stairs by assault, but were repulsed with heavy losses. Sergeant Guscott was shot in the head and Mike Lees was seriously wounded as he tried to rally the attackers on the first landing. Ricky was killed in one of the rooms on the ground floor. The Germans made an attempt to come down, but withdrew when three were killed on the landing. It is believed that one of these was the General. Two of the Goufa Nera were also wounded in this sortie. Kershaw, Green, and some others then started a fire in the kitchen, while Ramos and Sergeant Hughes carried the wounded outside.

Bullets were flying everywhere, and over it all, the defiant skirl of the pipes. The Russians were brusquely returning the German fire, but I knew that our ammunition must be nearly finished. Star shells were being fired from Bologna, Modena and Reggio, and the Germans had even opened fire on Villa Calvi with the anti-aircraft guns from Pianello. Rossi was beginning to burn and Villa Calvi was like an inferno. I pointed my pistol at the sky and fired a red Verey light—the signal to withdraw.

There was little hope of collecting the whole party, so we moved off in twos and threes on the line of retreat due west to the River Crostollo. Somehow, the various companies collected together on the far side of the river. I found myself with almost all the British and a few Garibaldini. Between us we carried Corporal Layburn and Mulvey, staggering under their weight, until we reached temporary sanctuary on the south side of the main road. Burke and Ramos, the Spaniard, refused to leave Mike Lees, who was in great pain. They hoisted his fifteen-stone body on to a ladder and wandered with him through the plains, now alive with angry Germans, until after four days they reached a safe hiding-place. Having assured themselves that he would be well cared for, they returned to our base in the mountains. Some time later I arranged for a Fieseler-Storch to pick him up from an improvised landing ground in the foothills and to convey him back to Florence. Burke and Ramos were awarded the Military Medal for this action.

Yani and his Garibaldini also got the badly-hit leader of the Goufa Nera to a place of safety, and he also was evacuated by air to Florence. Our only permanent losses were three British killed and six Russians captured. Included amongst the dead was Ricky, one of the bravest chaps who ever lived. It was his second operation in three months, and by rights he should have been resting in safety on the other side of the lines. Another grave loss was Sergeant Guscott, who marched across the mountains from Spezia to join me. It is strange how the best men are always the first to die. Perhaps we others are not good enough.

We walked westward as fast as we were able, taking our turn

at carrying the wounded, with the flames from Calvi lighting up the sky. German transport was moving up and down the main road to the south. After wading across the River Crostollo, we struck south again towards the road. An error of navigation nearly led us into the anti-aircraft battery at Pianello, but the sharp eyes of Green spotted a German signpost in time. When at last we had got across the road, we left Mulvey in a friendly farm, after having made arrangements for him to be smuggled up to the mountains in a bullock cart. At Casa del Lupo, where the padrone was very frightened, a horse was requisitioned for Corporal Layburn. We tied him tightly to the saddle with his wounded legs hanging limply by the horse's side. The horse was blind and frequently stumbled. Poor Layburn must have been in great pain, but he never once complained.

There were no halts this time. The whole countryside seemed to be buzzing with Germans, and it was often necessary to make a detour to avoid them. The mist was still thick, which was in our favour, but rain had made the mountain tracks slippery under foot. We were all exhausted and benzedrine tablets were swallowed freely. Even so, most of the boys were in high spirits and ceaselessly recounted their experiences at the back of the column. The loss of Ricky and Guscott depressed us all, but there was some elation at the success of the operation. Twice the horse slipped in the mud to bring Layburn's battered old body tumbling to the ground. Finally, we abandoned the beast, and constructed a litter from saplings and an army blanket.

Carrying him up those hills was a heavy job even for four men, but although he volunteered to stay behind, the others would not hear of it.

After marching non-stop for twenty-two hours, we crossed the Secchia. No Germans were encountered, and we successfully passed through their lines near Carpineti without contact. For pure show, we marched in step through the village of Vallestra, in column of threes behind the pipes, with Layburn on his stretcher leading the way. I hoped that the Germans would hear the pipes from Baiso and wonder if they were dreaming. There were only excited women and children in the village, who waved as we passed. The Secchia was in flood, so that we could only cross at Cavola foot-bridge, which compelled us to march another ten miles along the banks. The old wounds in my legs gave out just before the end, forcing me to the indignity of finishing the march on horseback. I felt very foolish.

It was a great home-coming. The Green Flames turned out into the streets and gave us a tremendous ovation, cheering over and over again for McGinty and the Battaglione Alleato. Fried eggs, bread, and vino by the gallon, was produced all over the village, but I think most of them were too tired for merry making. I was soon fast asleep in the schoolmistress's bed and did not wake up for fourteen hours.

CHAPTER SIX

DEFENSIVE ACTIONS IN TOMBOLA VALLEY

OUR NEXT FEARS were for a German drive or "rastrallamento" against our mountains. We had not long to wait. On 28th March, a battalion of mixed Russians and Germans with two field guns formed up opposite our position at Gatta on the other side of the Secchia.

Our outpost at this point overlooked the junction of the River Secchiello with the River Secchia. It was held by Luigi's Communist Brigade, supported by Lieutenant Eld with ten British in the centre. Eld had a mortar and a water-cooled Vickers, dug into strong emplacements covering the blown bridge. Since the Secchia was in flood, there was little danger of an enemy crossing, provided that the partisans maintained their positions.

I ordered Mike Eld to hold on as long as possible, even after the partisans had withdrawn on his flanks. If hard pressed, he was to withdraw from ridge to ridge along Prampa to our main position in the Cisa Box.

On the afternoon of the 28th the three-inch mortar shelled the enemy troops in Gatta Village. The Vickers also fired at long range at a column of horse-drawn transport in Osteria. Some casualties were obviously inflicted, but very few enemy shots came back across the river.

On the 29th March I rode down to Gatta to inspect the position. The British were quite happy, but the partisans were getting rather jumpy. Enemy snipers were quick to fire at an exposed head, making it dangerous to walk between the weapon pits. Through the glasses, I noticed an enemy company walking about in Ceriola village, making no attempt to conceal themselves, seemingly contemptuous of our fire. After moving the three-inch mortar, I directed twenty bombs into the village to teach them better manners. Our fire was not very accurate, but at least three bombs burst in the street. I regret to say that Mike Eld paid for this after I had left, when two enemy mortars registered some near misses around the Vickers position.

On the 30th and 31st March the enemy maintained an intense

fire against our positions with machine guns and mortars. The partisans became very restless on our flanks and threatened to withdraw. The British were magnificent and did not allow their weapons to be silenced. They went out of their way to show how much better they were than the Italians, by opening up a defiant stonk on Gatta in every lull in the enemy fire. Nevertheless, the position was becoming serious, and I was even more worried when I received reports of the arrival of enemy reinforcements from Felina.

At three o'clock on the morning of the 1st April a runner awakened me with the alarming news that two hundred enemy troops had crossed the Secchia at Cavola.

The Green Flames had withdrawn after a weak fight and were in a state of disorder in Quara. I issued orders that on no account was the 26th Garibaldini Brigade or the British detachment to abandon the Gatta position, taking the responsibility on myself without reference to the Commando Unico. However, I knew the partisan fear of encirclement and was not surprised to learn that many of them had already flown.

I ordered Captain Eyston to take the British Company and the whole of the Italian Company to Villa Minozzo to hold the switch-line of the Secchiello. I, myself, rode down to Quara with Morbin, my batman, to take a look at the enemy. In Quara, I found that Captain Lees (who had replaced Mike Lees) and Captain Oughtred of the British Mission had already arrived with the Goufa Nera. The Green Flames were hopelessly disorganised, and I found that the death of his brother, during the night, had reduced Don Carlo to a state verging upon nervous breakdown.

With Lees and the Goufa Nera, we moved cautiously forward to renew contact with the enemy. Two ridges from Quara, a whistle of bullets overhead told us that we had succeeded. We exchanged small arms fire for about an hour, until it was apparent that, for the moment at least, the two enemy companies had halted on the two hills in front. I had a narrow escape when, rolling over to talk to Lees, I missed a burst of Spandau, which passed between me and Morbin.

Lees and I adjourned to a cottage to discuss the situation. It seemed probable that the Germans would outflank Gatta after dark, so that there was no time to be lost. I did not think that they would dare to advance farther up the valley until Gatta

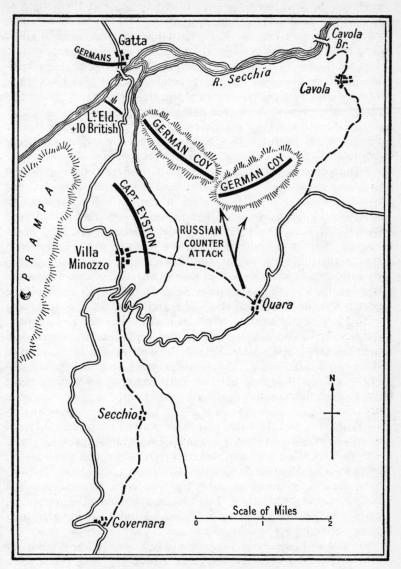

COUNTER-ATTACK ON EASTER SUNDAY.

307

had been subdued. The only hope was an immediate counter-attack by the Russian company. If Modena arrived, we might even get the Green Flames moving again.

I sent off a staffeta to Governara to tell Modena to march down with all speed. We would launch a counter-attack at dusk.

The Russians arrived at about four o'clock, but Modena was not entirely in favour of the counter-attack idea. A lot of bullying and persuasion was necessary to secure his consent. The Green Flames were drifting back, and before long, we had two hundred men on the ridge facing the Germans.

After a lot of twiddling, Modena opened up with his preliminary barrage. His three-inch mortar put down bombs all over the four square miles between us and the Secchia. One bomb went sideways and killed two of the Green Flames. An intense barrage of every sort of small arms was fired anywhere towards the enemy, tracer bullets bouncing off the hills. After this wild barrage, I got up, waved my pistol and ran five paces down the hill. Not a soul moved. I ran back to the ridge with bullets whistling by my ears. I tried three times, once succeeding in getting them to their knees, before the whole mob followed me down the slope. It was all very exciting. Stevens and Taylor had got them moving on the right and, with loud cheers, we charged the German positions. It was too much for the enemy. One or two forlorn distress signals were fired into the air, then, throwing away their weapons, they bolted for the Secchia. We did not stop until we got to the river, where we had great fun picking off the Germans on their way across. The Vickers gun from Gatta did a lot of execution in the water. By nightfall, not a single German remained on our side of the river, except their twenty dead and twenty-five prisoners they had left behind. As one Green Flame said to me, it was an enjoyable Festa di Pasqua.

I met Monti on my way back to Secchio. He was astounded. Perhaps even a little mistrustful. He could not believe that it was really true that the partisans had repelled a German attack. It was an unheard of thing. I grinned and reassured him that it was true. With a wave of his whip, he galloped off to Quara to find out for himself.

We were always busy on "Tombola." On Easter Monday, the day after the counter-attack, we had a big supply drop at Casa Balocchi.

In all the airborne operations of the war, I have been most

impressed by the efficiency of the American Transport Command in Italy. Dakotas used to come in to us three or four times a week. It is not exactly the safest job in the world to fly an unarmed transport plane over the front in broad daylight with a load of containers. When one adds the difficulty of finding a ground signal in the mountains in bad weather, the task becomes a dangerous mission. It took very bad flying conditions indeed to persuade Hardt, their Commanding Officer, to cancel an operational trip.

After a drop the whole valley was like an ant-hill. Bullock carts and mules would be going in all directions after containers. There were fights to stop the peasants from pilfering boots and clothing. Old Scalabrino was quite unshakable. He would surround the dropping zone with his own men, who fired warning shots at any stranger who came too close. When everything had been gathered into the central store in Casa Balocchi, weapons had to be checked carefully against the load lists, and then split up fairly amongst the battalion. Anything which was not required was sent to Commando Unico, which had difficulty in meeting its manifold expenses. I think all Monti's staff wore silk pyjamas.

For days after a drop Barba Nera and I were constantly pestered by peasants demanding payment for their work. Many hard-luck stories were invented to get a larger share.

Normally, we tried to pay the owners of bullock carts with linen parachutes and bits of harness, all of far greater value than money. Walker-Brown marked special "comfort" containers with a red streamer, and there was always a race for one if it was spotted on the way down. They contained mail, bottles of whisky, extra food, operational money, newspapers and other special luxuries for the British Company. I remember one terrible day when we had an inquiry into the circumstances connected with the finding of one of these containers. Scalabrino was heart-broken. The culprit was found a few days later, and delivered to Scalabrino for punishment. I believe he was tied to a tree for three days.

The position at Gatta was much the same as before the counter-attack, except that the enemy return fire was weaker. We were only once shelled by field guns, presumably owing to lack of ammunition.

On the 4th April I had a conference with Major Jim Davies,

who was the Liaison Officer to the Modena partisans in the next province. His area was much closer to the main front and would be more important when the grand offensive began. Subject to approval from Florence, we agreed that I should move my battalion into the Modena province as soon as possible, and sever my connections with the Reggio Commando Unico. It would be another slap in the face for Monti, but I am sure it was justified by the overall situation. My chief worry was with regard to my leaving the partisans to defend Gatta, knowing full well that Eros, the political commissar, would accuse me of running away.

This new move was confirmed by Fifteenth Army Group, who sent a signal ordering me to attack Highway 12 by fire when the army offensive began. This route was the main supply channel to the 232 and the 114 German Divisions on the Fourth U.S. Corps Front.

Owing to the fact that they were living in such close proximity to the battle line, the partisans in the Modena Department were organised in small, highly mobile bands. They were in much more frequent contact with the enemy than the Reggio Commando Unico, and therefore had a greater percentage of men prepared to fight, although the proportion was still remarkably small. I cannot remember the name of their leader, but I think it was something like Mario. Whatever it was, he was a guerrilla of no mean ability.

After receiving these orders from Fifteenth Army Group, Barba Nera was instructed to raise at least one hundred bullock carts to move all our force to Quara. Owing to the fact that most of our weapons were dug in on the tops of mountains, and that the battalion would have to be reorganised on a more mobile basis, even working day and night we could not hope to be ready before the 7th April.

I chose Quara as the forming-up area, because it was the only feasible place to receive the jeeps which Walker-Brown had promised me. It was also in a salient of the Reggio Area, which projected into Modena Province and had fairly good roads. With typical treachery, I calculated that if I did not tell Monti that I was moving until the last possible moment, I could continue to draw rations from Reggio Commando Unico even after we were under way.

At one o'clock on the morning of the 5th April the first jeep was dropped. It was a great moment. I was sure that the Germans could see the fires and fluorescent flares from Gatta and I hoped that they would take it for a bombing raid. Half an hour before the allotted time, we picked up the aircraft's beam on Eureka (our homing equipment). Another aircraft flew overhead, but it was not ours, and we gazed at the sky with mixed feelings, half expecting a bomb. At last, with a throb-throb of heavily-laden engines, the Halifax appeared as a black sillouette above the mountains. We lit a flare, which illuminated the whole fuselage of the aircraft, showing us the outline of the jeep protruding from the bomb bays.

She was running in from the north when the jeep was released. It looked like a dinky toy, as it floated down with four large white parachutes billowing above it. It looked at first as though it had been dropped too high, and would drift off the dropping zone, but suddenly it came down with a crash right between the fires. We had had some doubts about the suitability of the field, since it was on the side of a hill, but luckily she landed square. The Halifax made two more runs-in with the driver and containers, all perfect drops. As she turned homeward towards Bari, a light winked farewell from her wing-tips. Silently we blessed her crew and wished them God-speed on their journey back.

Then began the business of clearing the area before dawn. This was not a secure dropping zone like Casa Balocchi, where mountains hid us from view. Here the reflection from the lights could probably be seen from half a dozen different German positions.

The heavy containers were pushed, rolled and dragged to bullock carts on the road. Twenty shoulders strained at the back of the jeep to push it off its crash-pans. When at last we got her free, she roared up the hill in triumphant low gear, with at least a dozen ragamuffins whooping on the back.

On the 5th April I received a signal from base saying that the Army offensive had begun. Staffetas were sent off post-haste to the companies to tell them to expedite the process of lugging their heavy weapons down from the mountains. Stripped to the waist, they worked twenty-four hours a day.

Corporal Larley, who commanded the 37-millimetre cannon at Ligonchio, fired twenty rounds into the German garrison at Busana on Highway 63 before he left for Quara. When I asked him why, he answered with a grin that he had to do something, after having had Busana in his sights for a fortnight.

On the night of the 5th April two more jeeps were dropped. After the convincing spectacle of the drop the night before, I had invited the local partisan chiefs to watch this demonstration of Allied power, so that it was most unfortunate that the first jeep should whistle down like a bomb, followed two minutes later by its parachutes. However, their confidence was somewhat restored when they witnessed the next one make a successful, copy-book landing. By this time, of course, they had learned that Allied demonstrations were better watched from a safe distance.

Walker-Brown arranged for the last two jeeps to be dropped in daylight on 6th April, since it was now urgent that we should move into our new area without further delay. This was another example of the flexibility of the Air Force when required, since to fly a slow, heavy bomber unescorted in daylight is contrary to all the accepted rules.

The next day the battalion moved off in four columns organised as follows:

Code Name.	Composition.	Weapons.	Commander.	Area of Operations.
SUNCOL	5 British 100 Russians 6 Mules	1 How. 75 mm. 1 Mor. 3 in. 1 Brown .5 in. 15 Brens 2 Mors. 60 mm.	V. Modena K. Nurk	Route 12 south of Pavullo.
MOONCOL	25 British 30 Garibaldini 6 Mules	2 Vickers 1 Mor. 3 in. 2 Mors. 60 mm. 10 Brens	Maj. Farran Capt. Eyston	Route 12 between Monfestino and Pavullo.
STARCOL	5 British 60 Italians 6 Mules	1 Brown .5 in. 1 Mor. 3 in. 2 Mors. 2 in. 15 Brens	Lt. Tysoe Tito	Route 12 north of Monfestino.
ECLIPSECOL	10 British 4 Jeeps (1 more Jeep was still expected)	4 Twin Vickers	Lt. Eyton-Jones	Plains in area Sassuolo to Modena.

We moved off at timed intervals from Quara. The Russians marched slowly in step, with their blue cloth caps and big boots distinguishing them from the rest. Modena rode in front on his brown mare, looking very debonair in his blue sailor's cap. Immediately behind him walked his camp followers—three young girls and a dark Italian with a piano accordion. His weakness for the fair sex provided substance for the gossips, who weaved fantastic stories around this gay, romantic character. The Italians were smart in their green and yellow plumes, but best of all were the British. Kirkpatrick played the pipes in front, and the great, swaggering toughs marched behind in sticks of five on either side of the road. Their red berets may have been faded. Perhaps their battledress was not exactly clean and may even have been lousy; perhaps their boots were cracked and the bits of parachute round their necks not quite the thing; but there was a confident smile on their bearded faces, wrinkled by the sun, as they laughed and sang and teased the Italians unmercifully. How I loved that cocky swing of theirs! There was not a weak link amongst them. I called from my horse to the leading file:

"How are you, boys? Contente? Mabsut?"

Fitzgerald answered, with a grin: "Sure, sir; I'm after thinking that if me heart were as tender as me feet, I'd be the kindest man in the world."

CHAPTER SEVEN

ATTACKS ON HIGHWAY TWELVE

ON THE 8th April we received a signal from base ordering us to attack Route 12 on the 10th. All columns, therefore, marched over appalling going, up and down gruelling hills, into positions from which they could base their attacks.

Before this operation, I had met an old friend called Karl Nurk in Florence, and had decided to try to buy him from S.O.E. for "Operation Tombola." He was a White Russian who had spent most of his life in Kenya hunting big game and whom I had met with George Jellicoe in the Ægean earlier in the war. He appeared to be just the man to act as my go-between with Modena and the Russian column, especially since I had experienced much difficulty in explaining my orders to Modena, our only common tongue being indifferent Italian. Accordingly, I sent signals to Florence agitating for his early despatch.

Karl arrived with the jeeps, just in time for our attacks on Highway 12. He immediately made great friends with Modena, and on the first night I heard them singing Russian songs together at a very late hour. Karl was especially delighted with the 75-millimetre howitzer, which he made his own special responsibility. I had attached it with a British gun crew to the Russian or Sun Column, and it became Modena's chief source of strength.

On the 9th April I moved up with Mooncol to a hamlet called Monteforco. It was a collection of small farms on the top of a ridge, just large enough to conceal the whole company. Our greatest fears were that some Germans might come into the farm for eggs and discover our presence before nightfall. If shooting started before we were ready, the whole element of surprise would have been lost. Half a mile to the north of us was a large German wireless station. In a farm, two hundred yards away down the hill, we watched a section of Germans doing arms drill. There was an anxious moment when one of the mules decided to take its three-inch mortar over to the enemy. Fortunately it was recaptured in time. On the other side of the valley, we could see the 232 Divisional Supply Centre, containing about fifty lorries. Just north of Pavullo, staff cars were going to and fro from the Divisional Headquarters. Along Route 12 itself we counted a convoy of ten ambulances.

All the plans had been made for an attack at nightfall when a wireless message was received ordering us not to attack until the offensive on the Fourth Corps Front had begun. Having already disobeyed orders over the attack on the Corps Head-quarters at Albinea, I did not feel justified in risking another Nelson act. Bitterly disappointed, we marched back all night from our exposed positions to a safer harbour in a village called Marinella. Nothing has such an adverse effect on morale as pointless marching and counter-marching with no battle at the end of it. I also ordered the Russians to withdraw from their position opposite Lama Mocogno to a hill south of Marinella, but linked to our feature by a low saddle. The Italians also withdrew to Ceredelo in the north. Meanwhile, the last jeep had been successfully dropped to Eclipse Column at Quara.

It was three o'clock in the morning before the mules had been unloaded and we were all asleep. It had been a hard, unsatisfactory day, what with being fired upon by a partisan sentry at the bottom of the valley and this Duke of York farce of marching up to the top of the hill and marching them back again. At about seven o'clock, having broken my rules by oversleeping for two hours, I was awakened by the crash of shells falling in the village. Everybody was shouting and running about. It seemed that for the first time the Germans had caught us unawares. I ordered the column to move at top speed to the top of the moun-tain, so that at least we should have the advantage of high ground. Shouting in the middle of the cobbled street, I tried to restore order. The mules were bucking and kicking, refusing to remain quiet while their loads were tied to their backs. Every few moments a shell would whistle overhead and crash against one of the houses, filling the street with dust. There was terrible confusion, but somehow we got moving at last, mainly, I think, through the efforts of Fitzgerald and Manners with the mules. By a miracle, there were no casualties, although I had no idea where the Germans were or where the shells were coming from.

The top of the mountain was quite thickly wooded and we were soon under cover of the trees. It was a steep slope, and we were panting hard when we got to the top. One of the mules, a sickly beast with which we had had trouble before, just lay

315

down and died from the effort. I still could not see where the Germans were or in what strength they had advanced, but I took the precaution of putting the company in fire positions all round the hill. The only indication was the sound of small arms fire from Monte Spino, which pointed to an attack on the Russians. I sent out Fitzgerald, who had taken Guscott's place as senior N.C.O. of the British company next to Godwin, with a patrol to see if he could discover what was happening. He came back with a few odd stragglers from one of the best partisan bands in the valley with the information that a whole Panzer-jaeger battalion had penetrated between us and the Russians. This news was substantiated by our Vickers gun suddenly opening fire.

I ran along, shoulders hunched, to its position looking towards Monte Spino. A few bursts of schmeisser were whistling round about, but nothing really to worry about. The Vickers was chattering away from behind an old monument on the crest of the hill. I wriggled across on my belly to where I could see it pumping round after round of Mark 7 tracer ammunition into a column of German infantry and mules caught on the saddle between us and Monte Spino. The poor devils were trapped in the open. There was not a scrap of cover round about, and they lost eighteen men and two mules within five minutes. Fire was returned for about an hour, but we eventually beat them back, capturing a mortar.

Fighting went on all day, but the fiercest attacks were launched against the Russians. Karl Nurk won the day when he opened fire with the 75-millimetre howitzer over open sights. Nicholai, Modena's lieutenant, counter-attacked under cover of the gun, and the Germans withdrew in disorder, leaving thirty-three dead behind. A lucky shell burst in a room in which the Germans had established their headquarters, killing their commanding officer. Six of Modena's men were killed and three were wounded.

They were transported to our hospital, which Captain Peter Milne, the doctor, had been dropped in to command. In all, including Layburn and Mulvey, it now had seven patients.

By nightfall, all enemy troops had withdrawn to Pianorso and, although we expected the attack to be renewed the next day, the Germans never again took the offensive against our columns. Prisoners afterwards told us that the object of the operation was to open up the road through our area as an additional supply route to 232 Division, since they feared that the Air Force might block Highway 12 altogether. The plan was abandoned owing to our strong opposition and, I suppose, there was too much for them to worry about at the front at that time. I must add that the partisans acquitted themselves well in this action.

On the 11th and 12th April, the whole battalion concentrated in Vitriola. It was a lovely little village with large villas and beautiful gardens. A picturesque little church was surrounded by privet hedges and a field of rich green grass. The tranquillity of the village was soon disturbed by the busy scene of a partisan band re-equipping for action. Long, greasy-haired pirates were sitting on the steps, cleaning their weapons in the street. Jeeps dashed everywhere with supplies. The night air was broken by the tap-tap-tap of Morse from our wireless sets and the Russians sang as they refilled their magazines. At night, one could hear Modena's tame accordionist and occasionally Kirkpatrick's pipes, which were now suffering from lack of treacle, an essential lubricant for the bag, I am told.

I was not quite satisfied with the performance of Tysoe as the commander of the Italian column, since he did not seem to hit it off with Tito. I therefore switched commands, giving Tysoe Eclipse and the jeeps, and appointing Eyton-Jones to Starcol.

Barba Nera had done a great job in moving all our stores of ammunition and petrol up to Vitriola from Quara. He had hired an enormous caravan of bullock carts which so blocked the streets that I had fears of our own aircraft.

On the 13th April, Fifteenth Army Group ordered us to commence a general attack on the Route 12 area. All columns accordingly moved off to their appointed places: the British in the northern sector, the Italians in the centre, and the Russians in the south. I decided to go myself with the jeeps to the plain. During the day, the Russians had clashes with German patrols on Monte Spino, but there were no casualties to either side That night, all columns set ambushes on the main road, but no transport was seen.

We, in Eclipse Column, ran the gauntlet past a German observation post on the main road to the plain, and reached Baiso without making contact with the enemy. The peasants turned out into the streets and gazed at the jeeps in amazement. Some of them thought that we were Germans and ran into the houses in terror. It is not surprising that German prisoners told us later that they had heard rumours that we had got tanks in the hills.

The four jeeps leaguered for the night in a lonely farmhouse, purposely chosen for its two exits in case of surprise. We hammered on the door until the padrone appeared. None of our protestations could convince him that we were not Germans, and his cringing servility did nothing to soften our hearts towards him. If he chose to believe we were Germans, well, it would serve him right if we behaved like them. I beat on the kitchen table with a stick and demanded eggs. He came back in five minutes with a basketful. The best vino in the house was produced, which belied the stories that the peasants usually fobbed off the Germans with the poorest wines. I intensely despised this man, who reminded me of some of the worst types of Italians we had captured in the Western Desert at the beginning of the war.

The main problem before us was how to cross the River Secchia on the plain to get back into the Modena department. There were rumours of a broken footbridge at Castellerano, which was the only alternative to bluffing our way across the main German bridge at Sassuolo. We decided to try it.

Castellerano proved to be unoccupied, although we were told that German vehicles often passed through it. It was quite a shock to find ourselves in a factory area on the plain and caution slowed down our speed. The bridge proved to be half-finished and unsuitable for jeeps. However, the river seemed to be fairly shallow where it crossed a pebble bed near the bridge, and I decided to try to ford it. All the jeeps got across except one, which stalled in midstream. We hitched up a yoke of oxen to it with a tow rope and, after much shouting and heaving, they pulled it up on to the far bank. In the village of Castellerano I believe the population thought that the main army had arrived. Italian flags were produced and there was much premature rejoicing in the streets. Bunches of grapes, bottles of wine and bouquets of flowers were tossed into the jeeps. There were so many women who insisted on demonstrating their patriotism by kissing us on the cheeks that I found it impossible to get any intelligent information out of the crowd. In fact, the jeeps were in danger if they stopped. The hitch at the river had delayed us just long enough to allow the girls to put on their party frocks, and I feared that if we waited any longer, not only would the vehicles be covered by pretty females, but there was a strong possibility that the crews would be carried bodily away. I never seemed to have any luck, and was only kissed by the oldest and most ugly women.

It was now extremely dangerous to throw up dust on the roads in daytime, since the skies were full of our own aircraft. We moved cautiously through a built-up area towards Sassuolo. Excited members of the local resistance, who had been very clandestine until our arrival, told us the locations of German billets in the factory area.

Since our object was to attack Route 12 and not Sassuolo, I turned right just before the town and cut back into the hills. Near a village called Montegibbio, we reached a high vantage point from which we could see the whole of the valley of the Po laid out like a map beneath us. We leaguered here for the night, after some judicious reconnaissance on the telephone by a resistance sympathiser. One of the most amazing features of the underground in France and in Italy was that the civilian telephone always worked, even to German-occupied villages.

The next day we discovered an extraordinary little band of partisans called the Battalion Stop. They had been equipped by the Americans and were unusually active. They could not have been more than about fifty strong, but I believe they carried out more operations than most of the partisans in Emilia put together. One of their leading characters wore battledress and a bowler hat, which had a bullet-hole through it before I said good-bye to him at the end of the operation. Almost every night they did something against the Germans on the plain. They were apprehensive about the effects of our arrival, since at the time they were in close contact with a German patrol in Rocca Santa Maria, two miles away. They had observed through glasses that the Germans were aware of our arrival, and feared that it would precipitate an attack. However, they agreed to provide a guide to take us through to the plain, where I hoped to reach a friendly area called Torre Maino.

I sent one jeep off to the south to attack a German garrison at Moncerato. After killing two sentries in the village and firing into the windows of the billets, it returned safely to base at Vitriola.

As soon as it became dark, the other three jeeps motored slowly down into the plain by a side road. A danger point early in the journey was a large German Field Hospital at a place called Urbisetto, on a cross-roads. It was unfortunate that the other two jeeps were not very experienced and began to lag behind. I did not realise that they were not in sight until we came to the cross-roads, where I was forced to stop for fear that they might take the wrong turning. There were two ambulances parked beside the hospital, and a German sentry audibly clicked the bolt of his rifle. For some reason he did not challenge us, and we drove on to cross Highway 12 at top speed. Crossing a main road is always an anxious moment when jeeping behind the enemy lines. The system we used was for one person to approach the junction on foot. If he saw that it was safe to cross, he would flash a torch, and the whole column would drive over in a bunch at top speed, the look-out jumping on to the last vehicle. Once in France, the crew of the last jeep went to sleep and thus missed the signal. After having been woken up by the look-out, they were so anxious to catch up the remainder of the column that they neglected the usual precautions with the result that they collided on the cross-roads with a German staff car.

We proceeded in column to a village called Columbara. Unfortunately, the two rear jeeps lost contact here, having taken the wrong turning. There were many German road-signs about and my guide was uncertain of his way. I told him to inquire at a quiet-looking house on a road junction. He knocked on the door, but in a few seconds was racing back to the jeep, screaming that the house was occupied by Germans. The alarm was given and several bursts were fired at us. We seemed to have disturbed the biggest hornets' nest in the entire area. White Verey lights were fired, and shooting went on long after we had left. Going back through Columbara, we noticed a German half-track parked in a side street, which had escaped our attention on the way through.

I now had the impression that the whole area was thick with Germans, and decided that the only thing to do was to ask a local inhabitant in some quiet farm exactly where we were. I walked up with the guide to a peaceful-looking little house and knocked on the door. Some guttural German curses answered my inquiry as to the whereabouts of the Boche. The alarm was given again, and we vanished in a cloud of dust. The Germans were alert everywhere by now, so that the only solution was to try to get back to the hills. I feared for the other two jeeps. Actually, they had done better than we had and had succeeded in reaching Torre Maino by a different route, after having travelled down the entire length of a stationary German transport column, scattering a lot of Germans in the middle of the road. Tysoe did some good work from here later in the operation.

At last we spotted a tiny hovel—so small that no self-respecting German could possibly be living in it. A number of small stones at the window aroused an old Italian in a nightcap, who did not seem in the least bit surprised when we told him that we were English. Holding an oil lamp high aloft in his left hand he led us into his kitchen. In a hoarse whisper he told me that there were Tedeschi everywhere. A large contingent of reinforcements was on the way to the front at Bologna. He moved my map nearer to the light and jabbed at the German positions with a stubby finger. I thanked him and moved towards the door. Oh, no, he would not hear of it. First we must have a glass of wine. Shuffling over to an alcove in the wall, he produced a musty old bottle and three glasses. With a great ceremonial flourish, he blew the dust out of the glasses and poured the wine, muttering the word "festa" under his breath. Then, standing rigidly to attention, a stern look on his face, he gave us the toast: " Down with the Duce." As we went out of the door, he pressed an onion and a piece of bread into each of our hands.

It seemed that the only way across Highway 12 was the point at which we had crossed it before. We motored up towards it, but the sound of voices in the darkness brought us to a sharp halt two hundred yards short of the crossing. I told my batman, Morbin, to crawl up carefully to investigate. He returned after a few minutes with the disquietening news that a machine-gun post had been placed on either side of the road. While we sat there, trying to work out a solution to this dilemma, what sounded like a large column of horse-drawn transport began to pass down the highway.

Silently, fearfully, we put the gears in neutral and began to push the jeep back down the road. We had pushed it perhaps two hundred yards, when we heard a truck turn off Route 12 towards us. There was only one answer. I started the engine and backed the jeep into an olive grove. We switched off and waited there, fingers trembling on the triggers of our guns, ready to shoot it out if necessary. When the truck went straight on, it seemed that we had pulled off the "Bulldog Drummond" trick successfully, but there was still the problem of crossing the road. I considered running the gauntlet or attacking the column, but rejected the idea as too desperate to be sensible. Jeep ambushes are all very well when one knows one's where-abouts and has planned an escape route. Here we were all alone with half the German Army on the alert behind, and what must have been a convoy of several hundred carts moving along the road in front. For three hours we sat shivering in silence, listening to this huge column rattling by, barely four hundred yards away. If only we had been on the other side of the road we might have been able to do something. The situation had its comic side. Captain Peter Milne, the doctor, had asked to come in my jeep, and now he was getting more than he had bargained for. We had been in an almost exactly similar fix together in a rain-soaked wood in France, and now he was looking at me with mute accusing eyes as much as to say: "Do you always do this?" The rumble of the carts, the click-clack of the horses' hoofs, and the cracks of the whips ceased at about four o'clock. I decided to take a chance on running the gauntlet before it got light.

At sixty miles an hour we rushed the cross-roads. Just as we were approaching Highway 12 the engine began to cut out, the certain herald of a petrol stoppage. We looked at each other in terror and decided in our hearts that this, at last, was it. Then the engine picked up again and we were across. Not a shot was fired at us. By the hospital we ran under the nose of an astonished German ammunition cart, but did not stop to argue. When at last we reached asylum in the hills, we each lit a cigarette and deeply inhaled the smoke as we congratulated each other on a deliverance which could have only been in answer to our prayers.

The other columns had also had very little success. The Russians with their British gun team had shelled Lama Mocogno and Cadignano, but had not done much else. I did not reckon that their shells would have done much damage, since it had been purely a shoot off the map, although the Germans had replied with mortars and machine-guns. A few German patrols had been beaten off Monte Mocogno by Russian machine-guns, but this still was not attacking Route 12, as we had been ordered.

The British ambush on Highway 12 had only succeeded in drawing a determined German effort to outflank them. They escaped the net by some gruelling marching, and withdrew to Vitriola for further orders. The Italians had seen nothing from their ambush near Monfestino. On their return journey the alarm was given and shots were exchanged with German sentries. There is nothing worse for morale in guerrilla warfare than an unsuccessful operation after a long approach march.

The trouble lay in the fact that Route 12 ran along a ridge on which there was no cover. It is easy to ambush a road which runs through a valley, because safe cover positions exist from which it is simple to withdraw. In this case it was necessary to get right up to the road to attack it. In addition, the Germans had billeted themselves in small farms along the road to avoid the bombing to which the Air Forces were subjecting all villages behind the front.

On the 16th April I called a conference of all column commanders in Vitriola. I issued a general reprimand for the position that since we had been ordered to attack Highway 12 on 13th April, no concrete results had been obtained. From the 17th April we would make an all-out endeavour to inflict casualties on the road. Most of the officers pointed out that they had been unlucky in not finding traffic on the road when they got there, which was true enough.

As a boost to morale, I decided to lead a sally into the plain myself with the object of shelling German positions around Sassuolo with the 75-millimetre howitzer, "Molto Stanco." I took fifteen British with the three jeeps, and motored down by the same route to Castellerano. The River Secchia was slightly more swollen at Ceredolo, but we crossed the ford without difficulty, although the barrel of the gun was almost below water in midstream. Similarly, the ford by the incompleted bridge at Castellerano was negotiated without the help of oxen.

We were greeted by the same demonstration of affection in the village, where they told us that one or two inhabitants had paid for the folly of exhibiting the Italian flag after our last visit. I cut the telephone wires outside the village, just in case a Fascist sympathiser should be so unkind as to pass the news of our approach to the Germans in Sassuolo. We were unlucky enough to miss catching a German captain on a bicycle, who, we were told, had pedalled at a phenomenal speed into the town when he had heard rumours that we were crossing the ford. This meant that the alarm had been given in any case.

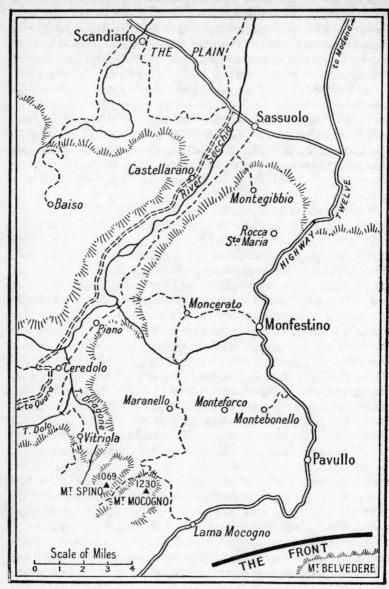

THE MODENA VALLEY.

I left Harvey with the Vickers gun and one jeep to cover the turning off the Sassuolo Road, while I led the remainder up to the top of the hill by Montegibbio. The climb was dangerous, since for several hundred yards we were in full view of the town, but we drove slowly to avoid throwing up dust, and passed into dead ground without trouble. I left Eyston with the third jeep to cover to the east, while we swung the seventy-five into action in a farmyard.

This quiet little farm called Casa San Marino was transformed by a busy scene of activity, as the gun crew dug in the trail and piled up the shells ready for action, oblivious to the squawking chickens, flapping their wings under the jeep. From the observation post we could see our targets laid out below us like a sand table model. In all there were six towns occupied by Germans within range of our gun, and I decided to give them each ten shells, with an extra ten on the bridge at Sassuolo for luck.

The factory chimneys of Sassuolo presented the most promising indication mark, and we could see several German vehicles in the street. I gave the order to fire. There was a loud report from the gun, enveloping the farmyard in smoke, and just before the burst of the shell came back to us on the breeze, I saw a puff of white smoke fall short of the flak position by the bridge. When we had bracketed a target, we fired five rounds rapid, which sounded like a stick of bombs as they burst on the ground. Occasionally, the only response to my order to fire was a clanging sound as the crew endeavoured to free a jammed case with a crowbar. Many shells had been damaged in their parachute descent, and their cases were so distorted that they jammed in the breech.

Seventy shells were fired in all. Hits were observed on the flak battery in Sassuolo, on the Hotel Italia, which was the headquarters of the Town Major, and on a factory occupied by the Germans. As soon as the shells had been fired, we hitched up the trail and drove home by the same route. There was no retaliation, but I was amused to see that the streets of Castellerano had become strangely deserted.

An informer told us that early the next morning a battalion of German security troops and Mongols occupied Montegibbio near the gun position, and stayed there until the army breakthrough. I could imagine the court of inquiry which would be held over the empty shell-cases. The enemy also put up many road-blocks in the area, and a stream of civilian refugees left Sassuolo for the mountains within an hour of the shelling.

This technique seemed so effective and so easy to carry out that on the 17th April I sent Lieutenant Eld off to mortar other targets on the plain. He plomped thirty three-inch mortar bombs on a village called Boglioni, where we had heard that there were two hundred and fifty enemy troops with a hundred horses. The girls found out later that he had obtained a hit on the enemy headquarters, killing one and wounding six. Many horses bolted and the enemy moved the same night. Only a few rifle-shots were fired haphazardly in Eld's direction.

On the 18th April four Dakotas carried out a brilliant re-supply drop on the parish field at Vitriola. A large quantity of valuable stores was dropped, including spares and shells for the gun and petrol for the jeeps. The whole village was busy with unpacking and storing containers. At last we had some cigarettes, which was a great relief, since I had noticed that one of my rogues had become so desperate that he was using the leaves of a prayer-book in lieu of cigarette papers.

Lieutenant Harvey left at midday with a reorganised British column, which excluded all Italians who were not fit enough to stand long route marches. I had had a small amount of trouble with the Communists, who complained to the Commissar that I was driving them too hard. A letter from Eros alleged that on one occasion, when a Garibaldini had lagged behind through sore feet, a British soldier had prodded him in the bottom with a fighting knife. I investigated this complaint and found it largely true. It was also revealed that one Italian had been given a gentle tap with the butt of a carbine when he fell out of the line of march to steal some eggs. I gave the British responsible a lecture on diplomacy and rebuked the Garibaldini for bad discipline, at the same time softening the blow with an extra ration of vino and cigarettes. It was too much to expect that all these willing, but undernourished, little Italians, who had been brought up on pasta asciuta and macaroni, should be able to keep up with selected parachutists who had been trained to march for years.

I had complete faith in Harvey's ability to command in spite of his years. He was only just nineteen and had joined the army from Rhodesia barely a year before, but the performance in the Corps Headquarters attack at Albinea had convinced me that he was worthy of a column command. He was later awarded the

Distinguished Service Order for this attack—no mean distinction for a subaltern.

Perhaps I was getting tired, but at this time I seemed to be finding fault with everything. I summoned Modena and Tito and gave them an ultimatum. If results were not produced within two days, Allied support would be withdrawn and the Battaglione Alleato disbanded. I suppose I was annoyed at our meagre efforts on Highway 12, our principal target. They both left looking very depressed, but the rocket was justified by the immediate results it produced.

CHAPTER EIGHT

VICTORY COLUMN

THE ITALIANS carried out a highly successful attack on Route 12 the next night. Two small parties under British N.C.O.s penetrated a thickly-populated German area near Selva. Corporal Ford's party, which had four tommy-guns and a Bren gun, attacked a column of ten armoured half-tracks and fifteen trucks, setting five trucks on fire. The operation was especially creditable in that they were compelled to fight their way back. Ford was later awarded the Military Medal for this action.

On the following night the Italians under Eyton-Jones attacked Montebonello by fire. This village on Highway 12 contained a very large number of Germans, including the Service Corps Unit of 232 Division and a Divisional Signals Unit. Nothing could have done it more good than a few thousand rounds of heavy Browning bullets. The enemy return fire went on until the morning of the 20th April, some time after the raiders had left.

There was some reason to believe that Harvey was running short of ammunition, since I had received second-hand reports that he had been engaged in a series of actions with the "Battalion Stop." I wanted to pay him a visit to see how he was getting on and decided to get the ammunition through to him in a jeep myself, accompanied by Sergeant Godwin on an airborne motor cycle. We found that it was impossible to get through by road, the only route being blocked by the battalion which had moved into Montegibbio after the shelling of Sassuolo. Godwin tried to get through on his motor cycle, but was chased by two German trucks, only avoiding capture by hiding in a farmyard. While I was waiting for him in Castellerano, where there were no Germans, we were bombed and machine-gunned twice by a Black Widow night fighter.

During the night Lieutenant Harvey attacked Route 12, but was ambushed in turn by the Germans. Two Germans were killed and our own casualties were nil.

Soon after this, the enemy placed machine-guns covering the road to Castellerano to deny the use of it to our jeeps. There were still other ways to the plain in the west, however, and this move did not restrict our activities in the least.

On 20th April Lieutenant Eld repeated his mortar trick on Scandiano, a large town to the west of Sassuolo. He fired thirty bombs into the town, which could not have been good for German nerves. As the Italians were placing an ambush near Montebonello on Route 12, they were attacked by a German patrol, but got the best of the exchange of fire which ensued.

That evening, Major Davies of the Mission came to see me. He had been working a twenty-four-hour-a-day wireless programme to base as opposed to my two-hour-a-day schedule. Although he had received no official notice, he guessed from the tone of his messages that the Army Offensive had succeeded. We had been worried by the absence of sounds of bombardment from the front for the last three days, and this was indeed welcome news. Actually, during the day, the female staffetas had picked up rumours that 232 Division was about to withdraw, which also accounted for the lack of activity against us. We had a glass of vermouth in the village to celebrate, and I told him that we would attack with our whole force immediately.

When Jim Davies had gone, I summoned Barba Nera, Modena, Karl Nurk, Eyton-Jones, Tito and Eyston. They sat round the table in the café, leaning on their elbows, some of them taking notes, as I gave the orders for a general attack. The Russians would launch an infantry attack against Lama Mocogno on Route 12 and would take it. The Italians were to attack Montebonello. As far as we knew, Harvey was still operating with a British column at the point where the highway ran into the plain. I would also endeavour to get a message through to Tysoe at Torre Maino to tell him to carry out raids on German transport on the plain around Modena. The remainder of the force would be grouped in a new mobile column under my command, henceforward to be known as Victory Column. It would consist of twelve British, thirty Italians (the residue of the Garibaldini), three jeeps, the seventy-five gun and twenty-three bullock carts. This force would move off, as soon as Barba Nera had arranged the transport, to attack targets in the plain between Reggio and Modena, which I anticipated would be the line of the German retreat from Bologna.

Barba Nera rushed about in a frenzy of organisation. It was his biggest day, and he even excelled his great feat of moving the battalion stores from Quara to Vitriola in one day. The cobbled streets of the village were jammed with oxen and carts, mules and Garibaldini, staggering under the weight of petrol cans, 75-millimetre shells and Vickers ammunition. All our weapons were stripped, bathed in olive oil and reassembled. From somewhere Barba Nera produced two ramshackle old lorries, which he loaded high with kit until their springs were nearly touching the ground. One of the wireless sets was dismantled ready to accompany me with Victory Column. Everywhere there was a hum of busy excitement and by evening we were ready to move.

Within five hundred yards of the start, both lorries groaned and gave up under the strain. It was clear that their excessive burden was too much for them. I told Jock Eyston to supervise the transfer of the kit to the bullock carts and to follow on to join us in Baiso as soon as he could. I pushed on ahead with the jeeps, the gun, and some of the carts.

At the first river we had some difficulty in persuading the oxen to enter the stream. Hurling stones at their heads, pushing and shouting waist deep in the water, it took several hours to cajole them across. Two of the jeeps crossed the ford without mishap, but the one towing the gun stuck in midstream with the barrel beneath the level of the water, and had to be towed out by three bullocks.

In the half-light the ford was a colourful picture of confusion. The jeep crew sat on the bonnet of their vehicle, silhouetted against the red setting sun and shouting encouragement at the Italians, while they waited for a rope to harness up the rescuing oxen ; two ox-carts stood stubbornly immobile in the water at each bank, with parachutists tugging at the animals' mouths; a queue of carts stood waiting on the track for their turn to cross, while their drivers threw stones into the river or shouted advice to those already in the water. While we were still trying to disentangle the muddle, an airborne motor cycle came spluttering down the track with a message from Major Davies, saying that he had received definite confirmation of the German withdrawal.

I decided to assault the Emilian city of Reggio without delay, since it would certainly be the German line of withdrawal to the Po. The most sensible course was to leave Eyston to usher on the carts, while I took the three jeeps and the gun into the attack. He was annoyed at being left behind and even more at

330

the prospect of a fifty-mile march with the bullock train, so I gave him permission to control the column from the back of my horse. This seemed to mollify poor old Jock to some extent, although I believe he loathed horses. Somehow, he always seemed to be given the most arduous and least exciting tasks from the construction of the Cisa defences to the issue of stores at Vitriola.

Leaving him to vent his anger on the Italians, we motored on with all speed towards the plain. There was a slight delay at the River Crostolo, when the gun again bogged down in midstream, but oxen were soon found to come once more to the rescue. Owing to the German machine-guns covering the road near Castellerano, it was necessary to make a wide detour to reach the plain unobserved. It was therefore daylight before we reached Baiso, where we had a large breakfast of fried eggs and red wine.

More cautiously, since from Baiso onwards the country was unknown, we crept into Vignola, having to by-pass a blown bridge. The peasants in the village had been in frequent contact with the Germans and were apprehensive about the possible results of the presence of parachutists and partisans in their village. A fat solicitor, who appeared to be the local squire, took us into his house and told us alarming reports of large numbers of Germans in Scandiano, the nearest town. I waved aside his fears and followed a route to by-pass Scandiano to the west. Soon we were on the good roads of the plain. The people were now regarding us with mixed feelings of astonishment and fear. Some thought we were Germans, others recognised us as British and gave the thumbs-up sign or waved, but the majority peeped from behind their windows with looks of terror.

Choosing the smallest lanes, we made our way slowly through the olive groves towards the city. Occasionally we halted in shadows as Allied aircraft passed overhead. I was concentrating so much on the trees at the side of the road, searching for signs of the enemy, that I failed to follow a bend and drove the jeep and the gun into the ditch, puncturing the reserve petrol tank on a sharp stone. Some of the petrol was saved in a bucket brought by a quick thinker from a cottage nearby. Enough was lost, however, to make it essential to return to Baiso by the most direct route after the attack. On the main road, only three miles from a village in which Germans were known to be billeted, we turned right, continuing along to a cross-roads only two miles from the city.

Quickly, the crew swung the gun into the action position, aligning the barrel on a bearing previously taken off the map. I climbed up to the top storey of a high farmhouse, from which it was possible to see the towers, the "Snow White" battlements and the domes of the city laid out like the scenery in a pantomime. There were many prominent buildings, including a hospital with a large Red Cross flag, but I calculated that the main square would probably be at the foot of the cathedral, an ornamental dome which stood out above all others in the centre of the town.

A runner carried down the order for the first shell to be fired. The crash of the gun shook the whole farmhouse, and I visualised the alarm being given in all the German occupied villages round about. A few seconds later, there was an answering thud from the town as the shell burst, and a column of brown smoke came up from the foot of the cathedral. I hoped that it had burst in a main square packed tight with fleeing German transport. In any case, it was near enough to the centre of the town to panic the enemy, which, after all, was our object. I told the runner to tell them to fire five rounds rapid. Five more thuds came from the direction of Reggio, and the cloud of smoke thickened in the centre of the town.

The shooting was not good, but we were not trained artillerymen and at least all the shells were bursting somewhere near the Germans, which was sufficient for our purpose at that stage. A siren sounded from the direction of the city. I imagined the surprise and confusion caused by those few shells landing near an enemy, safe in the thought that he was fifty miles behind the front. Afterwards we learned that the Fascists and the local German Headquarters abandoned Reggio within two hours of the raid. The panic spread quicker than we had anticipated, since they had already heard rumours of an Allied break-through near Bologna and took us to be the advance guard of the American Armoured Division. In all, we fired twenty-five shells at the town. After the twenty-fourth shell had been fired, there was a pause, so I ran down from my observation position to find out the cause of the delay. A damaged shell, slightly bent in its parachute descent, had jammed in the breach and had to be removed with a crow-bar.

When they had removed the damaged case, I ordered one last shell to be fired. There was a loud explosion and Sergeant Hughes, one of the gun crew, staggered back, hands to his eyes, blood streaming from his face. At first I thought that the enemy had scored a direct hit on the gun position, but then it was explained that our last shell had hit the branch of a tree overhead. The hard ground had precluded digging in the trail in the proper fashion and, I suppose, the gun had recoiled out of position with the shock of the last round. In addition to Hughes, several other people had received small wounds from pieces of shrapnel.

We laid Hughes across the seat of a jeep and the doctor applied a field dressing to an ugly wound beneath his right eye. A door was torn from a cowshed to make a rude stretcher, which was balanced across the back of one of the jeeps. It was time to withdraw. Already enough time had been lost, and by then the whole area must have been alerted by the alarm. We motored slowly back by the same route, driving as gently as possible over the many bumps and wheel ruts to avoid giving too much pain to Hughes. No Germans were encountered, although we could see the dust from their vehicles on the main road towards Reggio.

At Vignola I was surprised to meet Jock Eyston with the ox-carts, who had made the journey from the mountains in record time by marching day and night, flogging on the weary peasants who were anxious to get back to their homesteads. The doctor took Hughes up to the Convent of Santa Maria, in Baiso, where I was assured that he would be properly cared for by trained sisters.

We rested for a day in the Vignola area, while the stores were being unloaded into a farm I had chosen as my headquarters. Lying under the olive trees, we looked up at the swarms of Allied aircraft overhead. Away to the south, we could hear the rumble of artillery from the front. There was no longer any doubt as to whether the Allied offensive had really started. My only worry was how best to help. I contemplated moving north to seize a crossing over the Po, but rejected the plan as too ambitious for my small force.

There were several false alarms during the afternoon. Excited partisans came in with information about a horse-drawn column, which was supposed to be approaching from the direction of Castellerano. I was so sceptical of Italian rumours by this time that I always held the so-called eye-witness until one of my patrols had proved the truth of his information. If his report proved to be false, he was given fatigues in the camp for the rest of the day. This had the effect of considerably reducing the spate of ill-founded rumour with which we had been swamped for the past two months.

On this occasion, my patrols could not confirm the story. The next morning persistent reports came in about this mythical German column, and I am afraid that I allowed myself to be panicked. I moved the whole column up on to the high ground covering the road, where we waited in ambush for hours with no sign of the enemy. Finally, when it seemed that nothing had appeared or would appear, I sent a jeep down into Castellerano to make absolutely certain of the German locations.

This jeep returned sometime later with the exciting news that the Germans were withdrawing headlong through Sassuolo in the direction of the Po. It appeared that the Americans had broken through near Bologna, and that the whole German Army was in full retreat. The roads, they said, were packed with German transport.

Now was the time to strike. I detached a section under Lieutenant Eld with orders to mortar Scandiano, the nearest important town on the plain. The remainder of the column moved up under my command to the last foothills overlooking the valley of the Po. As our main position, I chose a hill which commanded both the crossings over the River Secchia—one a ford and the other the bridge at Sassuolo. I sited both our Vickers guns on the forward slope and placed the 75-millimetre howitzer just behind the hill. An abandoned slit-trench on the forward slope provided a perfect observation position. Through my glasses I could see a continuous stream of trucks, guns and carts, toiling through the ford. Further round to the east an endless column of vehicles was crossing the Sassuolo Bridge and motoring along our front, barely five hundred yards away. It was a wonderful sight—the sort of target the gunners dream about at Larkhill. But still I hesitated to give the order to fire.

An infantry battalion appeared to be resting under the trees in a farmyard at the foot of the hill. They seemed to have no sentries and to be utterly exhausted, but if I opened fire would they attack our position ? If so, I doubted if we had enough strength to resist them. For half an hour I sat there, staring through my binoculars, at one moment half-inclined to say yes, and then changing my mind against the thought of the possible results. We were not used to plunging ourselves, wittingly, into a pitched battle. As guerrillas, our policy was to tip and run, only attacking when surprise was on our side. My men looked at me with doubtful, pleading eyes. They could not believe that I would miss such an opportunity, and looked at me as much as to say: "Please, sir, if we miss this, we will never be able to hold up our heads again."

I grabbed the walkie-talkie. "Are you aligned on the ford?"

"Yessir."

"1,500 yards, one round H.E.—fire!"

There was an enormous "woof" from behind the hill. A shell whistled overhead and, through the glasses, I saw a white puff of smoke appear in the river bank, just north of the enemy column.

"Down one hundred. Fire!"

Crash!

"Up fifty. Fire!"

Crash!

I saw a shell score a direct hit on a large lorry, towing a gun, which capsized in the middle of the ford.

"Five rounds rapid. Fire. . . . Fire, I said!"

"I am firing. Why don't you use the proper fire orders?"

"Go on, don't argue. You cannot miss anywhere around there."

Our gunnery was always a little unorthodox, and quite a lot of back chat went on over the walkie-talkie. Eyston was a proper artilleryman and disapproved of my casual, Armoured Corps way of giving fire orders.

I sent a runner round to tell the Vickers to engage any opportunity targets they saw on the road in front. Soon they were rattling away on the right, and thick columns of black smoke came up from the lorries they had set on fire. Odd, single shot "phuts" told me that either the enemy was firing back or our Garibaldini were lending support to the Vickers. Shells were bursting all round the ford and the confusion was indescribable. Altogether we set about twelve trucks on fire in the river, and perhaps five more on the road. Horses and carts bolted or over-turned in the water. The most pathetic sight in all this carnage was a party of about ten ambulances, which withdrew from the main column to form a circle. They lit fires—a signal, I think, of distress to let us know that they were bearing the Red Cross. At this moment, a flight of Spitfires (I believe they were Brazilian) was attracted by the smoke. Spotting the dense jammed column in the ford, they dived down through the thick pall to add their contribution to the chaos.

A few bursts of spandau were coming back at us from the farmhouse, so ill directed that they were more of a nuisance than a menace. I told Rex, the leader of our Garibaldini, to put a stop to it with our American 60-millimetre mortar. The excitement was greater than anything I had experienced since the Battle of Crete.

We now switched the gun to the Sassuolo Bridge and within a few minutes had straddled it with three well-placed shells. Five enemy lorries were destroyed, but somehow they still managed to sneak across in penny packets between our shells.

A lucky shell scored a hit on some sort of car park in a factory yard, which caused black smoke to obscure the target. This one-sided battle went on all day with very little retaliation from the enemy. Towards evening, after we had fired over a hundred and fifty shells, I withdrew back into the foothills.

Early next morning, we received reports that Scandiano was jammed tight with fleeing Germans. Shooting off the map, we put down our last twenty-five shells in a final hate on the town.

I moved the remainder of the column up to cover the main road with machine-gun fire, while I myself went off on a reconnaissance in a jeep. During the day, Eyston destroyed and captured a large number of horses and carts. Rex and his Garibaldini did particularly well, their blood now being well and truly roused. They asked as a final treat to be allowed to take their men into Reggio on one of the captured carts, wishing to have the honour of being the first partisans into their home city. Eyston, in his usual kindly way, realised that the war was almost over, and allowed them to go.

I by-passed a pocket of Germans south of Sassuolo and crossed the River Secchia by the ford at Castellerano. The streets were full of Italians in gay colours, who mobbed my jeep and thrust presents into my hands. To avoid Sassuolo, I had to go back quite a long way into the mountains. Coming back down the Montegibbio road towards the plains, I passed huge bands of partisans marching on Modena. They were carrying enormous Italian flags and singing songs as they straggled along on their way back home. It was truly the end of the war for them. Some of them would be seeing their mothers and sweethearts for the first time for two years. As I passed them, they turned their happy faces towards me and screamed, "Viva McGinty." Tears came to my eyes, I was so happy. These were my people. Maybe I had cursed them, had kicked them, had despised them, had driven them into danger, but they bore no resentment. After I had left the Reggio Commando Unico, the Germans had crossed at Gatta and had burned Villa Minozzo to the ground. Smaller men would have blamed me for the disaster which had fallen on them after I had left them to their fate. What were they, but good, honest peasants, who had been forced into a bitter struggle for which they had no liking. They were men of peace and to them I was McGinty, a partisan chief. "Viva McGinty." Now they could go back to their grapes and their cattle; now they could sleep with their wives and play with their children; in the evenings they could sing and drink the good vino ; on the steps of the church, after Mass on Sunday morning, they could tell each other how they won the great war; stretched out before them was a life of happiness—no more insecurity, no more Mussolini, no more Brigata Nera, for they were free; they, the common people, had won their freedom.

Then I came to my Russians, trudging along in step behind Modena on a horse. They drew off to the side of the road, and shouted: "Hurrah! Hurrah! Hurrah!" The same cry I had heard in the charge on Easter Sunday. Modena dismounted and pumped my hand. He had taken Lama Mocogno after a hard fight and was feeling keenly the loss of his lieutenant, Nicholai. I detected a certain sadness in the whole band, and think I understood. To them this was the end of a phase in their lives. Now they were faced with the prospect of their return to Russia. What would happen to them? Some of them had fought in the Wehrmacht and were liable to be shot as traitors. They had all consorted with the British capitalists. Their future was uncertain.

Just short of Montegibbio I met up with Eyton-Jones and his Italians. There was a new jauntiness in their step as they marched along singing songs about the "Battaglione Alleato." Eyton-Jones' eyes were glistening as he told me of their successes on the road. The Italians had done well, and Tito was justified in being proud of them. I congratulated them all, and told them to make all speed for Modena. It was unnecessary advice.

On the main Sassuolo road through the plains, I came

across a tiny band of dusty figures lying in the ditch. Their red berets had faded to a shade of light pink; their bearded faces were tanned into the colour of old leather by the sun ; not one was dressed like another, but there was a gay twinkle in their eyes.

"Yes, we've seen the Yanks. All in bloody great tanks, but they haven't taken Sassuolo yet. Have a bit of chewing gum? Didn't seem a bit surprised to see us."

And then another:

"I bet that was you apooping off with old ' Molto Stanco ' yesterday, wasn't it, sir? Recognised the old one-two."

And Harvey, beaming all over his face:

"We had a good old party two days ago. With the Battalion Stop. Those boys are good. We took on a Jerry column at nil range from a cornfield. It was like butchery. We set five trucks on fire and captured a lot of prisoners. You know the one in the bowler hat. He got a bullet through it and could not be more pleased."

And Ramos:

"It is too-bad-a, sir. My brother Bruce, who was with-a-me in Spanish war is killed, sir. I wanta leave to bury him, sir. He was shot in the head, when Mista Tysoe taka the jeeps from Torre Maino to attacka jerry, sir. You knowa he my brother from a long time, sir, although we make it better to have a different name, sir!"

And another:

"Makes you laugh to see all these Iti farts, don't it, sir? You'd think they won the bloody war."

"How's Dusty?"

"How's Jock?"

"Old Taffy Hughes stopped one. Cor strike a light! Hear that, Jordy. Old Taffy pulled anuvver fast one to get 'imself 'ome before us. Can you beat these sergeants?"

And another:

"What about the wounded up at Febbio, sir? Can I go up to get them? You know Noris is up there, sir, and she shouldn't be left alone too long with Corporal Layburn and Mulvey about. Why, they might even be able to walk by now!"

By the next day we were all together in Modena. The Americans had passed on, leaving the small amount of mopping up in the town to the partisans. We helped in the street fighting a little, but I soon realised that the Italians were best left alone.

Some of the partisans had developed a cunning technique for looting. They shouted, "Sniper," and fired a fusillade of shots at the upper storey of a house. They would then rush the back door and, within a matter of minutes, would emerge overladen with valuable things.

A wireless message came through, ordering us back to Florence and telling me to disarm the Russians immediately. I am afraid to say that I had not the moral courage for what seemed to us at the time to be such a cruel, unfair and premature act. I knew that there would be arguments and bitterness. Those clever people in remote Florence could never understand the mutual trust between comrades-in-arms. We had fought together, some had died together, and now, in the hour of victory, we were asked to take away their arms. The partisans were parading the streets, armed to the teeth, firing rounds into the air to show the pretty girls how they had dealt with the Germans. Nobody would dare to attempt to disarm them for some weeks to come. Imagine the feelings of the Russians if they were to be herded, unarmed like prisoners, amongst such a victory drunk crowd.

I left orders with a rear party to disarm them in Reggio, after the victory parade in four days' time. This party was also to move our dead to a central graveyard, with Ricky and Guscott near the scene of our big attack on the headquarters at Albinea. When the Allied Government officials arrived, they were to give them a nominal roll of the whole battalion. Quietly, I slipped off with the remainder of the British towards Florence. Noris was the only Italian to accompany us, refusing firmly to leave the wounded.

I was miserable at having to leave in such a hole-in-the-corner fashion, but it was better than facing Barba Nera and Modena with orders which they would take as a breach of faith.

The troops were in high spirits as we drove along the road. They had draped a swastika flag over the gun and two of them travelled on the carriage. Witty remarks were shouted at the big, lumbering American convoys, and every pretty girl was greeted by a chorus of whistles.

It was a brave little convoy: four jeeps, two civilian cars, two captured lorries, a German ambulance and the gun. We were all covered with the grime of months in the mountains, and our shabbiness was in sharp contrast to the huge armoured columns we passed on the road. They must have wondered who on earth we could be.

We were the "Battaglione Alleato" (S.A.S.), otherwise known as the "Battaglione McGinty," whose motto was "Chi osera ci vincera," which being translated means "Who dares wins."